BILLION

HOW I BECAME KING OF THE THRILL PILL CULT

SHAAHIN CHEYENE

COVER: © David LaChapelle with Permission of David LaChapelle

Accelerated Intelligence Publishing

Library of Congress Cataloging-in-Publication Data Cheyene, Shaahin.

Billion How I Became King Of The Thrill Pill Cult /Shaahin Cheyene.

1. Cheyene, Shaahin. 2. Adventure & Business—New York (State)—New York—Biography. 3. Wall Street (New York, N.Y.) 4. Securities industry—New York (State)—New York. I. Title.

www.shaahincheyene.com

www.thrillpillcult.com

ISBN: 978-1-7365015-0-4

Book Design by HMDpublishing

Cover Design by Fernanda Jiménez Design

Edited by Brittany Storniolo; Copyedited by Sasha Rerrie

Foreword by Chris Voss, *Never Split The Difference: Negotiating As If Your Life Depended On It*

To my boy Soma and wife Mahdis. May we live an extraordinary life and make a dent in the universe together.

Author's Note

Stuff we write hoping that people don't actually get offended and sue us.

This is a true story, based on my best abilities to recall various events in my life (which are certainly flawed). Some names and identifying characteristics of certain people mentioned in the book have been changed to protect their privacy. In some instances, I rearranged and/or compressed events and time periods in service of the narrative, and I recreated dialogue to match my best recollection of those exchanges.

In my opinion everything here is true, but it may not be entirely factual. In some cases I have compressed events; in others I may have made two people into one. I may have occasionally embroidered. I learned early that the most important thing in life is a good story.

Names, characters, places, and incidents may be the product of the author's faltering memory or imagination or may be used fictitiously. Any resemblance to actual persons, living or dead, events, or locales is entirely coincidental.

Table of Contents

Foreword:

As an FBI hostage negotiator, I persuaded terrorists, bank robbers and kidnappers to see things my way. Similarly, on the other side of the tracks, Shaahin started from less than 0 and used persuasion and influence to create over a billion dollars in revenue.

I created and used field-tested strategies, not only in my work, but in everyday negotiations. Through the help of mentors, grit and simple trial and error, Shaahin learned some of these tactics by default.

With that said, it is almost endless what he could have done if he had had the right training and guidance in these techniques early in life.

So many of the tools that you will find within these pages align with what I know to be true. Strong communication skills will help you to get more of what you want out of life.

Everything in life is a negotiation. From your morning coffee order to a job interview to getting your kids to do their homework, your life could be in a completely different place just by improving how you negotiate.

Prepare yourself ahead of time, and be willing to authentically connect with the other person. Hear what they have to say and see things from their point of view—it can make all the difference in the world. The person across the table from you is your partner; someone to be worked *with* in pursuing a mutually beneficial outcome.

Negotiation does not have to be adversarial. If both parties feel heard, both can walk away satisfied through collaboration. Compromise is not a "win-win," as neither side feels that they got what they wanted. Never split the difference, as that creates a bad outcome for both sides.

When the stakes are high, every step matters. You have to access all the negotiation tools you have at your disposal, including strong problem-solving skills, improvisation and emotional intelligence. A critical part of our negotiation strategy involves "black swans." A black swan is a piece of information that can dramatically change the trajectory of the negotiation in your favor. When discovered during the fact-finding stage, they can assist in structuring your approach. This includes deciding which techniques to use based on personal and business background research. Mapping out your strategic plan allows you to determine the best time to reveal the black swan in order to garner a competitive edge. Asking targeted questions during the interactions may also lead to a black swan being revealed. To use the information to gain the upper hand requires you to pay attention and be able to pivot and adjust your plan.

Remember that the other side will also be looking for black swans to help them. Be aware of the hidden things that, if discovered, would weigh the negotiations in their favor. Incorporate defense strategies into your game plan, and be prepared to deploy them as needed. During discussions, any changes in body language or tone could be a sign that something is being concealed. A sudden change around a particular subject should be noted and the issue investigated to see if there is anything that could be exploited. Black swans should not be laid out for all to see. Having one in your back pocket may provide you with the edge you need at a pivotal moment and give you the advantage you need to bring the negotiations to a close. You will see in the book how Shaahin used a black swan to strategize a new approach in a make-or-break situation. Combined with innovative and creative thinking, the knowledge he gained from a surprise source enabled him to catapult his business forward, even while being challenged by a larger adversary.

Learn from previous interactions, but don't let them blind you to what is being communicated in the current moment. Never assume you know what the other side wants. Look at each exchange as an opportunity to uncover as much information as possible.

There is power in deference. Asking questions, especially "what" or "how," allows the other person to feel powerful, even though it gives you the upper hand. Questions allow them to feel heard, and also provide you with clarity on their true intentions and motives. This makes the negotiations "we-centered," as opposed to "me-centred." Shaahin has mastered the skill of encouraging others to open up and expose what they really want.

Mirroring is my Jedi mind trick. Repeating the last 3 critical words of what someone else has said makes them feel heard. People love to be mirrored; they love to be encouraged to go on. Mirroring focuses attention and makes people more receptive to what you have to say. Their responses, in turn, indicate the actual strength of their position. You can also mirror their attitudes, beliefs, ideas and even modes of dress as people trust those who are like them.

Finding agreement establishes a bond. Enabling the other person to say, "That's right" confirms their belief in something as a fact, not an opinion. This helps you find what drives them.

Remember that words are only a small part of communication. What I call Tactical Empathy—recognizing and vocalizing the situation from the other person's perspective; being aware of their emotions; paying attention to their words, tone and body language to help decipher their motivations—Shaahin embodies, and he demonstrates it in his approach to life. This ability to show empathy and display a sincere desire to better understand the other's circumstances allows both sides to experience a true win-win, a technique shown throughout several examples in the book. It requires that you take emotions into consideration—both positive and negative. You can then work to defuse the negative feelings and magnify the positive ones. If you can draw out their aspirations, hopes and dreams for the future, you can demonstrate how you can affect that.

Learning these skills changes the way you respond to events in your life—big and small—and gives you more confidence in each interaction. If you prepare ahead and approach each interaction with a willingness to listen and connect as well a sense of deference, curiosity, positivity and empathy, you will build trust and emerge with the best deal possible.

We all need people in our lives, and to be able to influence those people using tactical empathy is an essential tool in every entrepreneur's toolkit. Whether you're aiming to improve your income, salary, the service you receive or your relationships, developing stronger communication skills allows you to achieve game-changing insights into human nature, and get more of what you want out of life. In the pages that follow, you will share Shaahin's wild ride through the 90s and beyond. I hope you enjoy this as much as I did.

Chris Voss
Never Split The Difference: Negotiating As If Your Life Depended On It
CEO, The Black Swan Group Ltd.

Introduction:

I had a hundred grand in a nearly collapsed In-N-Out bag. Ten stacks of ten thousand dollars each, five inches high when stacked on top of one another. Shorter than you'd think, but heavier, too. I wondered how long the greasy take-out bag would hold before the bottom gave out.

Borris had chased me down in the hallway a few minutes earlier with it. "Here's the cash for the Japanese order, boss," he said hurriedly as he tried to shove it into my arms. He carried the stack of bills in front of him like he was balancing a cake on a tray.

You could sense his urgency, his desire to rid himself of the money. He wasn't very comfortable with cash, but he knew that I was. In those days, I literally had piles of it lying everywhere. One of the perks—or hazards, maybe—of being a pill pusher.

"Fuckin' hell, Borris," I said, shaking my head. "You're just going to walk around like that?"

Borris was my right hand, my zookeeper. Think Wags from the Showtime series *Billions*. He was a good guy and meant well but was not, generally speaking, the cleverest man in the room. He blinked down at the conspicuous stacks of cash in his hands.

"At least put it in a bag," I said with a soft chuckle.

So Borris found a trash bin, pulled out an empty In-N-Out bag from inside, and dumped the cash in there.

"Sorry, boss. Wasn't thinking," he mumbled quickly as he handed me the bag. "Just didn't want to leave it lying around here—you know, with all that's been going on lately... ." He didn't need to tell me what he meant by that. Every three-letter agency in the country was after us, and leeches were lurking around within the company itself, threatening to bleed all our success dry. He was damn right to be cautious.

So I smiled and thanked him as I took the bag, tucking it under my arm before heading out to the gathering I was en route to that night. I could have left it there and had Accounting deal with it later—unless someone decided to steal it or throw the bag back into the trash while I was gone. Both were equally plausible. Borris was great at acting as a buffer between my staff and me, which made him invaluable to me in those days, but even he couldn't keep all of our employees in check. Not with all that money lying around the office all the time. Like I said—a hazard of the job.

"A billion in sales, boss," our lead sales guy, Kirby, wheezed out from behind his desk as I passed by. He was the company's resident madman, with a chronic habit for waking and baking. I wondered if maybe being perpetually high had finally made an impact on his ability to count correctly.

I spun back around, all thoughts of the party erased. "What was that?" I asked incredulously.

Kirby coughed and ran a hand over his unkempt hair. "Uh... I think we just passed a billion in sales?" He said it more like a question than a statement of fact.

"Oh, and also, CNN wants an interview today, and some guy from Tokyo wants you to send a car to meet him," my secretary, Julie, chimed in (yes, we still had secretaries back then).

I was confused. "How can that be possible?"

"Well, I don't think the guy has anyone to pick him up, so—"

I waved a hand impatiently to silence her. "No, no—how could we have done a *billion* in sales?"

The look in Kirby's slightly glazed eyes was as surprised as mine. "After *Montel Williams* and *Nightline* aired, retail and international sales went through the roof," he shrugged, scrolling through the numbers on his computer screen. "We sold out in most markets."

Fuck, I thought. The number seemed unfathomable to me. How could we have done a billion in sales without someone mentioning it earlier? How much is a billion dollars, anyways? Was it a thousand thousand or a thousand million? Would they ask me that on CNN? *No, they're not going to ask you that, you moron*, I told myself. Surely CNN knew how much a billion was without having to ask a teenage entrepreneur.

"I can't do the interview," I told Julie, ignoring Kirby and his outrageous claims for the moment. Maybe he really was just high.

"What? You have to," she said imploringly.

I checked my watch. "I've got a meditation ceremony I need to get to, and I think it's gonna run long tonight." She stared at me with her mouth hanging open slightly, unable to comprehend how I could turn down a spot on CNN for a spiritual gathering. Julie was still figuring out how to cope with all the crazy stuff happening in the company daily, and I certainly didn't make things any easier for her with my mercurial moments like these.

"But the interview's not until later," she whined, clearly hoping she could still convince me to change my mind. Kirby had zoned out again and didn't notice when Julie shot him a look, hoping to get some backup. She sighed in frustration when she saw none would be forthcoming.

"And I've got a party at my place tonight," I added, and Julie's shoulders slumped as she realized the battle was well and truly lost. "Which place?" She asked.

"Malibu," I said. "Some big Hollywood people are coming to the meditation ceremony, and I'm going to invite them all 'round to my place after. Why don't you stop by? I can finally introduce you to some of those American stars you've been dying to meet." I grinned at Julie, and she rolled her eyes in reply. She had moved here from England a year ago and was always complaining that she hadn't gotten to experience enough of the L.A. lifestyle, which was kind of insane, considering where she worked. I checked my watch and started toward the exit again. "Anyways, I've gotta go, sorry. Wish I could help!"

"That's completely within your power," Julie called after me, but I was already halfway to the door. "So wait, who'll do the interview?"

"Why don't you do it?" I said, flashing her one last grin around the doorframe on my way out.

I'm not sure if they all thought I was kidding or not. I wasn't sure myself. All I knew was that I was not about to miss my meditation event over a TV interview. In a business like ours, there was never any need to pander to the press. They'd be chasing us down for another interview in a few days, regardless of whether or not I went tonight.

With the greasy bag of cash in hand, I made my way toward the elevator but stopped suddenly. I'd almost forgotten, thanks to Kirby's ten-figure revelation still swirling around in my mind, but the In-N-Out bag reminded me that I had some important housekeeping to do. I turned back to the office and scanned the room, looking for two employees in particular.

"Chris? Emma? Stand up," I yelled.

They did.

"You're fired," I said simply.

Their jaws dropped.

"Don't act surprised. You know exactly what for," I said. "And don't worry about packing your stuff. It's already out back. Next to the dumpster." Their mouths fell open a little wider. They were lucky that was all I'd done. "Borris? Make sure they're gone by the end of the day. And that they don't take anything with them they shouldn't."

Borris nodded silently, and I turned on my heel and left. Those two had been stealing my pills and running their own side operation, selling them on the beach. I couldn't have that. I wouldn't.

Walking through the office door, I stepped out into the unadulterated California sunshine. Venice Beach was only a block and a half away, and the late afternoon breeze carried the faint smell of ocean air with it. It was 1996, the rave and party scene was huge, and Venice was the epicenter of it all. Two-and-a-half miles of coastline where every kind of subculture came together in a technicolor melting pot: stoners, ravers, hippies, goths, new-age gurus, street performers, and sideshows all lovingly called it home (and still do), and any night of the week you could find some underground party to go to that was pulsing with bass-heavy music and unbridled energy. This was the perfect place to set up a lucrative drug trade, catering to the ravegoers' never-ending appetite for designer highs, and that's exactly what we did.

Only, I was never too fond of the idea of going to prison. So, instead of selling ecstasy—the biggest drug in the world at that time—I found a way to win over ravers' hearts and minds with a 100% legal product instead. Now sales were off the charts and money was pouring in faster than we could count it. I looked down at the take-out bag clutched in my fist. We were at the top of our game, and it seemed like there was nowhere to go from here but up. What they never tell you, though, is how the altitude affects you when you're at the top. Less oxygen to breathe, your head starts spinning, then one misplaced step, and suddenly you find you're falling back down to earth. And the journey down is a lot faster than the way up.

As I walked over to my car, I bumped into a gorgeous young actress I'd met once before who lived in the area. She was even more stunning than I remembered, and she must have recognized me when she saw me because she immediately smiled and walked over.

She was wearing cut-off shorts that revealed her long, bronzed legs, and she gave off this breezy, carefree vibe that I used to find irresistible. And that smell, my God. It was something like patchouli and rose oil. Or was it peaches? Who cares. Whatever it was, she smelled amazing. I wasn't sure whether she was one of those types who simply gravitated toward anyone with money, or if she'd actually liked me from when we met before, but at that moment, I didn't really put too much thought into it.

"Where are you going in such a hurry?" she asked with a coy smile, then glanced down at the paper bag in my hand. "Lunch?"

"Actually, there's a hundred thousand dollars in here." She

laughed.

I wondered what she would say if she'd known I wasn't joking. "I was just on my way to my beach house, if you care to join me?" I asked instead. "We could go for a swim?"

"But I don't have my swimsuit!" she protested, with another one of those bashful grins.

"Guess we'll just have to make do," I chuckled. It looked like the meditation rendezvous would have to wait for another day. I've always believed in following my intuition—a philosophy that, more often than not, has managed to lead me to some of the greatest and most unexpected opportunities in my life. And right then, my intuition was telling me that this was going to be a much more productive way to spend my evening than going to the ceremony. Did I mention my intuition also sometimes got me into trouble?

The next thing I knew, I was blasting down the Pacific Coast Highway with my accidental companion in the passenger seat of my brand new, jet-black Acura NSX and the bag of cash stuffed in the footwell. I don't think it would qualify as a "sweet ride" nowadays (maybe more of a "classic supercar"), but back then, it was the epitome of cool—it even came complete with speakerphone functionality, a feature which I remember blew me away for its technological advancement. It was the 90s, okay?

As we snaked along the coastline toward Malibu though, even the company of a beautiful woman, her hand grazing suggestively over my knee and the smell of her enigmatic perfume blending with the ocean air, wasn't enough to keep my mind from the state of my fledgling business. She was talking to me—something about how she'd always loved the beach at sunset—but I didn't hear a word she said. I was having my first major life crisis, and I wasn't even 21 yet.

I had just started to get used to seeing the word "MILLIONS" on TV and in print articles talking about me and the business, but even that still made me slightly uncomfortable. My success was growing faster than I could keep up, and the more money we made, the more critical the media's narrative became. All I wanted to do was focus on running my company, not perform on air so that CNN or whoever could get the sound bite they needed to support their evening headline. That's why I always ended up pushing Rob, my frontman CEO, in front of the cameras on my behalf—that way, I could maintain some precious anonymity for myself. But now that we were making S, not millions, there was going to be even more pressure from the media for me to put my own face out there, and I didn't feel ready to be thrust into that limelight just yet.

Things moved so fast in those days. If I stopped to think about it for even a moment, it all seemed like just a blur of motion, circling around me too quickly to make any sense of it. *A fucking Billion? With a capital B! What the actual fuck?* I thought to myself. *Did I really make that much? Holy shit, I might need to actually get an accountant. Maybe I need a real lawyer now, too. Oh, this is going to get sticky.* I nearly went off the road at one point, my attention more on my own thoughts than the task at hand. *Okay, Shaahin, don't forget to breathe.*

Where was all this money, anyways? I mean, I didn't see it in my accounts. Was *everybody* stealing from me? Was it all a lie? Or was it real? How long could I keep this up before the whole house of cards came tumbling down?

A Billion dollars. And I had made it in just a few short years. Or had I? Where was the sense of satisfaction? Where was the relief, the feeling of security I had imagined? Was this what the pinnacle of success looked like? It sure didn't feel like it. The optics were all right—awesome car, stunning woman, stacks of cash—but I still felt like I didn't belong. I was certain that the press, my friends and my employees were all going to eventually find out that I was a fraud. Just a kid playing at being a millionaire. *Do I even deserve this?* I thought.

I pulled into the driveway of my beach house and pushed my existential worries aside for the moment. It was an epic structure that looked more like a national museum than a home, and it was right on Malibu's famed Celebrity Row. I had bought this place on a whim from the Beverly Hills Cop actor, Bronson Pinchot, who had spent millions designing it to be a replica of the quintessential Italian villa, overlooking arguably the finest stretch of white sand beach on earth. The waves were crashing rhythmically against the first-floor balcony, tinted crimson by the setting sun, and I heard a little gasp from my passenger as she stepped out of the car. "You live here?" she asked, looking between my T-shirted adolescent self and my incongruous home with obvious disbelief.

It was another piece of the perfect, billion-dollar-company-owner image that I presented to the world; another thing that barely felt real. She probably thought I was squatting in the place while the real owner was out of town, and sometimes I found myself thinking the same thing. I had lived there for nearly six months and, aside from my bed and a couple bean bags, I didn't have a single stick of furniture in the whole house.

As I headed inside with the In-N-Out bag, I remembered that my date from the previous night was still there. This was either going to play out very badly for me, or very well. I tossed the greasy bag to Adan, a vegan chef I'd hired to cater to my diet (which was still a pretty obscure lifestyle choice in those days). "Can you stick this in the fridge?" I said as he caught the package, arching a quizzical brow at the logo.

By the time I came back outside, my new arrival was already on the beach and had made fast friends with last night's conquest. The two of them were sipping drinks and nibbling on some vegan tapas in their sun loungers, making me think I'd definitely made the right choice in forgoing my meditation meet-up that night. I kicked off my shoes and was halfway to joining them when my hippie attorney came running out through the front door to intercept me. He seemed distressed, and more than just his usual, drug-addledand-in-over-his-head franticness. Something big was up.

Fame, drugs, beautiful women, fast cars, private jets, celebrities, millions in cash, and now a billion… fuck. As I looked down and from where I was standing, the fall seemed breathtakingly steep.
Better not fall, then, Shaahin.

CHAPTER 1:

AMBITION

"Success is not final; failure is not fatal: it is the courage to continue that counts."
Winston Churchill[1]

Every boy has some ambitions, right?

I had ambition in droves from a very early age. Especially coming from the third world and then growing up in a place where anything was possible (but where I also didn't feel like I truly ever fit in). I trusted in my hunger for success as the thing that would help *make* me belong. Mine was a lower-middle-class immigrant family living in one of the wealthiest postcodes in the United States, and I always looked around me and knew I wanted to be like all the rich people in our neighborhood one day. I knew nobody was going to hand it to me. I was going to have to fight for it myself.

Back in Iran, I'd led a completely different life. I had been surrounded by people who looked like me, thought like me, and spoke the same language. I didn't feel like an outsider, and I'd been free to explore the world in any way that I saw fit. My friends and I were largely left to our own devices. All of the neighborhood kids would get together and raise hell during the day, and I usually assumed the role of our de facto ringleader. Sources of amusement were few, so we had to be pretty creative when coming up with things to do to entertain ourselves.

---

[1]Although unconfirmed, this quote is commonly attributed to Winston Churchill.

Near my house, there was a dirt track that went down a steep hill, and one day my friends and I got the idea to turn it into our own downhill racing track. We took the shopping carts from the local supermarket and made helmets out of cardboard boxes stuffed with paper bags and sweaters (for safety), then took turns pushing each other down the slope. The cart almost never made it to the bottom unscathed. It would hit a stone or a rut in the road, flip over and catapult its occupant down the hillside; but our sprains and scrapes didn't deter us. I remember looking over the edge at the top of the hill, my face bloodied where the makeshift helmet had come flying off on my last ride and my arms wrapped in duct tape to staunch the bleeding from my various other wounds; heart pounding from the thrill of another death-defying launch. With one firm push from my accomplices, the cart was off, barrelling down the hill, and the only thing I could hear was the wind rushing past my ears and the sound of my own wild cries of victory.

In a way, I guess you could say my story is the perfect example of the great American Dream made reality. I was born in the 1970s, in what were pretty turbulent times in the history of Iran. A fundamentalist revolution was brewing in the country, and the circumstances surrounding this upheaval were totally unique. It lacked many of the customary elements generally associated with revolutions: defeat after a war, financial crisis, rebellion by the poor and disenfranchised, or a disgruntled military. In fact, a wholesale rejection of Western influence was at its core. It was an astonishingly profound change, which took place at lightning speed. Iran was on its way to becoming a theocracy under the guardianship of the Islamic Jurists that persists today. It was in these unorthodox circumstances in 1975 that I was born into a Jewish family on the outskirts of Tehran, the capital of the country. By 1979, the revolution had run its course, and my family—with me in tow—fled Iran for fear of persecution.

There were no long goodbyes and no time even to realize that I would never see any of my friends again. My parents simply said we were leaving, and I threw everything I owned into six suitcases in the middle of the night—just to be told that there was only space for me to bring one. My whole family snuck out of the house like furtive criminals, and we literally ran through the streets with our bags to get to the airport and board the plane that would take us to the West as refugees.

Overnight, everything changed. The week before I left, it had been my turn on the shopping cart with my duct tape bandages, hurtling down a dirt hill in Tehran. I didn't know that anything else existed aside from that state of perfect independence, or how suddenly I was about to be ripped away from it. One moment I was in the club, paying my dues, and then the next, I was out on my own in the world.

It's incredible how a person can be thrown into a completely different life just by a twist of fate. Ronald Reagan starts his book *An American Life* by reflecting on how luck played a similar role in shaping his life. "If I'd gotten the job I wanted at Montgomery Ward," he writes in his first chapter, "I suppose I would never have left Illinois." Similarly, if it weren't for the revolution, my family would never have moved to Germany and later, like so many other Iranian immigrants, to the United States. At the end of the day, I guess it all worked out for the best for my family and me. Who knows what kind of dreary work I would have pursued and the sort of colorless existence I would have lived, had I not come to the United States? From being destined for obscurity on the outskirts of Tehran to building a fortune worth millions of dollars, my life reads like an excerpt straight out of a rags-to-riches fantasy tale. Only, it really happened, and calling it a crazy journey is an understatement.

But my transition to life in a new country wasn't exactly smooth. It's always astonishing to me how unforgiving life can be to those who refuse to change it. As a little olive-skinned foreigner from the Middle East, I was bullied mercilessly as a kid by my Californian schoolmates—mostly for being a "towelhead," or some similar uninventive slur. I could have let them beat me down and ended up with all the ambition kicked out of me. But I didn't. I'd gone from being the head of my gang in Iran to a third-rate citizen in L.A. Now I had to adapt and figure out how to fight back.

When I was being bullied at school, I discovered the films of Bruce Lee, who I really believe was one of the ultimate life hackers. Lee was a thin Chinese man, a minority like me, who, despite all of that, managed to kick ass in the most badass of ways. I remember watching him thinking, *Oh my god, I want to learn from this guy*, just to discover he was already dead—he had passed away in 1973, two years before I was born.

When I was older, I bought *Tao of Jeet Kune Do,* his posthumously published collection of writings, which was a formative book for me, because it taught me about Eastern philosophy and Bruce Lee's personal philosophy of life—for instance, being like water, in the sense that water can move around other objects or take the shape of anything that it's in. That really spoke to me; that need to be agile and flexible and persevering in the way I approached the world. I later went on to read a lot of different self-improvement and business gurus' books (like *The Greatest Salesman in the World, Think and Grow Rich* and *The Trick to Money is Having Some*). The process of absorbing all of those ideas and incorporating them into the way I lived my life played a significant role in molding me into the person I am.

Reading all of this had a dramatic impact on me psychologically, mostly because I saw that there were people who, despite coming from a lower economic background, despite being bullied, despite being disabled—despite all that stuff—managed to make it. They had this real stick-to-it-iveness that gave them the ability to just not quit, to persevere no matter what. That spoke to me and inspired me, as a scrawny immigrant kid who was determined to carve out a path for himself in the world, even if it seemed like there were insurmountable barriers in the way of achieving that. I didn't want to be just another person who was marginalized or bullied—I wanted to be relentless and aggressive about going after what I wanted, but also fair. Reading those books taught me a lot about how to do that. And Bruce Lee was the start of that whole journey for me.

That all came about somewhat later, though. At first, the immediate problem I had to deal with was getting the stuffing kicked out of me regularly at school and on the playground, by guys who were usually five or six years older than me and quite a bit bigger than I was. I was a small kid, but so was Bruce Lee, and watching his movies had given me the idea to learn more about self-defense so that even when I was up against someone twice my size, I'd be able to hold my own. At first, I practiced martial arts by myself, just imitating the things I'd seen in movies and the techniques Lee had written about. Then I signed up for a weekly martial arts class in my neighborhood.

For me, it was the empowerment of having that skill set and of knowing that I could now defend myself physically, which added to my physical and mental well-being in general. As a child in school, it helped me immensely, giving me the confidence to stand up for myself and the know-how to back up my inborn fighting spirit.

Before learning martial arts, I'd been in a fair few fights, all waged in a graceless blur of flying fists and feet, and I had always ended up just as bloodied (if not more) than my opponents by the time the dust settled. That never stopped me, though. Oh no. When faced with the option of fight or flight, I always chose the former. I could never stand the idea of letting someone get away with injustice, or allowing myself to be the target of it. But once I knew how to handle myself a little better, it meant I wasn't risking my young life every time I decided to go toe-to-toe with a teenage bully who stood head and shoulders above me. And once the bullies figured out that I wasn't such easy prey, they quickly left me alone and went in search of richer pickings elsewhere, as is usually the case with bullies.

Learning how to control my body and mind was incredibly beneficial for me in other ways, too. Martial arts represented a practice of intense self-discipline that had an enormous impact on other aspects of my life, particularly when it came to pursuing my young dreams of success.

I may not have had many opportunities handed to me early on in life, but I did have grit. Growing up in the streets of Tehran, I'd learned to be independent, and the streets of California had given me a fascination with wealth and the various means of achieving it. Then martial arts gave me the self-discipline to pursue that goal relentlessly, no matter what it took.

"I'm going to have my own martial arts empire one day," I told my parents one morning over breakfast when I was about 12 or 13. "Just like Bruce Lee."

"You're only a yellow belt," my brother said tauntingly.

I shot him a defensive sneer and stuck out my tongue. "I'll get better, stupid!"

"Don't call your brother stupid," my mother automatically chimed in, her chiding an in-built response by now. "I don't think you should be dedicating your life to violence, Shaahin."

"I told you we shouldn't let him watch those fu-kung movies," Dad grumbled from behind his newspaper.

"*Kung fu*," I sighed exasperatedly. "It's called *kung fu*, not *fu-kung*. And it's not about violence. It's about discipline," I said, with a matter-of-fact nod.

My father snorted. "Discipline! That's something I doubt you'll get better at." I glared at the front page of his paper, but he was too absorbed in it to notice what was going on beyond the bifold.

Mine was a fairly traditional, nuclear, immigrant Jewish family, although relatively poor. Despite running a business for thirty years, my dad was always something of a failure financially. I also dreamed of having my own business—just not the kind he had. In fact, my number one goal was never to be anything like my father when I grew up. I guess you could say that he inspired me in all the wrong ways, and showed me exactly what I *didn't* want to do with my life.

My dad's formula for everything was simply to get by. Take two parts religion, one part culture, one part "I'll just go to work and hope that everything turns out okay"—that was the formula for how he led his life. Meanwhile, my mom was a dutiful mother. She took care of us; she cooked, she cleaned, she did her own version of the neurotic Jewish housewife thing. We were the typical immigrant family. The highest hopes that my parents could have had for me would be that I end up becoming a doctor, because they thought that the height of success was to be a doctor, or maybe a lawyer. But I had different plans.

We were a poor family in an affluent part of town, and even though I didn't know first-hand what it was like to be rich, I saw wealth and success all around me. People in the Pacific Palisades, where we lived, had money, and even some of our family members who had left Iran with money were doing quite well for themselves in America, but we weren't one of them. My mom had been a secretary for a big company in Iran before the revolution, and she became a stay-at-home mom after we emigrated. My dad had been an accountant in our previous lives and now worked at the dry cleaners he owned in town. Neither of them understood the wild ideas I had, like building a martial arts empire. It was all a little too bizarre for the now-safe world they lived in.

The life we lived was comfortable enough, but frugal.

I was never allowed to buy clothing new, from a store. Instead, the clothes that my little brother and I wore were always two or three sizes too big for us, because we would have to wait for a customer to leave their clothes behind at my dad's dry cleaners and forget to pick them up, at which point they became viable hand-me-downs for us. We used to pray that a kid would come in, like a cool surfer guy with great style, and forget to pay his bill or come collect his stuff, so that we could wear it ourselves.

I didn't even know what a real restaurant was until I was about 15. We ate at home—whatever my mother had decided to cook that day—and maybe occasionally went to a McDonald's or something as a treat, but the idea of sitting down at a restaurant and being able to order whatever you wanted was totally foreign to me.

Meanwhile, my friends in the Pacific Palisades were immersed in a totally different kind of lifestyle.

I would go over to their houses, and their parents would have fancy cars in the driveway of a big mansion, and they'd order takeout for dinner from anywhere they chose. I was awed at the idea of eating exotic Italian food when they ordered pizza. It wasn't just that I hadn't been used to eating stuff like that before, it was the sheer number of possibilities that they had to choose from—Chinese, Italian, burgers, whatever. All of the choices on offer simply amazed me.

This high-flying, pizza-eating life gave me a sense of looking at the world and wanting more than just oversized hand-me-downs and the defrosted burgers my mother slid onto our plates at dinnertime. But I also knew that I would have to get it for myself. Nobody was going to hand it to me. I was never naive about that reality. That was where my dedication to self-discipline and self-education would have to come into play.

So, with all of my hours spent reading, I set out at an early age to understand the kind of mindset and systems I'd need to develop if I wanted to have the level of wealth that I aspired to.

I think that drive to succeed is something that you have to find inside yourself, and I had an interest in doing that through entrepreneurship from the time I was young. As I got older, that desire just grew and grew. And it wasn't until I set off on this journey that I really learned how far I was willing to go to achieve it.

I was what you would call a "weirdo" in school. I had few friends and was always engrossed in thoughts far beyond my age: how to build a business, how to invest wisely, how to exercise self-discipline, and influence others—things which no other 11-year-old would ever contemplate. Other kids didn't understand me because I sounded too old to them, while adults simply thought I was strange for not acting my age. Nevertheless, I still wanted to fit in.

The only problem was that I was culturally clueless, so my attempts at assimilating into American society were frequently misguided. MTV was just getting popular at that time, and I soaked it all in, fascinated by the style and energy that these huge stars had. I loved the music of guys like Michael Jackson and George Michael, and I knew they had to be cool since they always appeared on this cool TV program. I figured if I could emulate people like them, I was bound to be popular, right?

Summer 1985.

My mission: to be like the cool kids. My toolkit: a doctor's prescription, two 2-liter bottles of the brand-new Cherry Coke, Twinkies, Kit Kats and 12 hours of uninterrupted TV time, spent studying MTV, VH1 and the hits.

12 hours turned to 24, and days turned into weeks. I had locked myself in my room in an absolutely obsessive fantasy world, soaking in all the coolness I could. Eventually, my long absence failed to go unnoticed. My friend, Sep, called.

"Dude, where have you been? You missed my soccer game."

"Come on, man. It's not exactly like we were going to get any chicks or glory at that game, anyways," I told him, crunching on a Kit Kat.

"Really, wise ass? Beth plays soccer!"

"She's a lesbian, you idiot! I mean viable girls. Like the ones the jocks are dating! Look, I have it all figured out."

Sep was not convinced. "Really? Do share, butthead." (Our teenage vocabulary was rather limited).

"No, really, hear me out—who is the one guy no female at the school can resist?" I asked him.

"Johnny Nazran?" Of course, Sep's mind jumped instantly to the school's future prom king and quarterback.

"No, dumb nut," I sighed, exasperated that I really had to spell it out for him like this. "Johnny's only popular because his dad is rich and has all that oil money from Iran. If he didn't pretend to be American, none of the cool kids would even hang with him. Anyways, he's small fries. Think bigger. Not in our school."

"No clue. But if this is another one of your wacky, bullshit ideas, I'm hanging up."

"No, dude, hear me out. Faith."

"What?" Sep snapped, clearly not following.

"You gotta have faith, a-faith, a-faith… ." I sang (somewhat) melodiously.

"George fucking Michael?"

I grinned when he finally got it. "Exactly."

"But he's a fag. Everyone knows it," he said flatly.

I scowled into the phone receiver. "Okay, first off, that's not true. And second, just watch his music videos. Dude gets pussy like it's no one's business!"

"So your big, ingenious plan is to… become George Michael?"

"Well, ish. I have the black leather jacket, torn jeans, and the earring. I just need the haircut and a really nice cologne, and I should be able to pull it off."

"Pull what off? Cologne? You have no idea what he smells like. You idiot. I'm going to ignore you if you show up at school looking like a fag. Just saying."

"No, it's going to be awesome! And when the females swoon, I'll be the one to say 'I told you so,' " I smirked, and I could almost hear Sep rolling his eyes at the other end of the line.

And so, my strategy began to take form. I was too scared to pierce my ear, so I got a fake clip-on earring (a cross, of course). I had to hide it from my folks, as they would surely have freaked. Not about the gay thing, but about the Christian symbol.

The appointed day arrived.

Leather jacket? Check.

Fake earring? Check.

Cologne? Check.

Lots of hair mousse? Check.

I squeezed on some fake designer, torn blue jeans I purloined from my dad's cleaners, and I was ready to go. I just had to make sure I had them back before the customer came to claim them next week. They were a couple sizes too small, so I could barely move when I put them on (a far cry from today's stretchy jeans).

I walked into homeroom, cocksure and arrogant, yet incredibly fragile at the same time. I sat down. I could swear I was dizzy. Maybe it was the tight jeans, maybe it was anxiety about my newly-gained identity and how it would be received. Nerves over how I'd deal with the hordes of women about to mob me.

To my surprise, though, it was very quiet. In fact, no one said a word.

I guess this is the new normal. Finally, I fit in. My plan worked, I thought hopefully.

That is, until someone threw a bag of spent sunflower seeds (spit and all) at my head, and the whole class broke down laughing.

"I told you, dumb fuck," Sep whispered at me before he hid his head in his book in embarrassment.

As I exited homeroom, a gang of jocks was waiting for me in the alleyway I had to pass through to get to my next class.

"Hey, faggot. What's going on? Halloween came early?" one of them jeered at me.

"Oh, no, I'm not gay," I assured them with an uneasy laugh.

"Who the fuck are you trying to be? George Michael?" Johnny Nazran himself broke in, looking at me like I was totally revolting to him.

"No. I mean… No, that would be crazy," I chuckled nervously again.

"Well, everyone knows he's a faggot. Just like you."

"Leave him alone, Johnny. He knows kung fu or some shit like that," one of the girls with them said, eyeing me suspiciously from over Johnny's shoulder.

I could take one or two of them perhaps, but these boys were much bigger and stronger, and my clothes were far too tight for me to be able to get any decent movement in. I never learned how to do martial arts while wearing skinny jeans. They must have seen the worry on my face and deduced I wasn't much of an actual threat, because the jocks just all exchanged a smirk and then looked back at me.

Shit!

The next thing I knew, my earring was being pulled off while one of the boys quickly jacked my leather jacket. Then, another jock pulled out a hot glue gun that had recently been plugged in during wood shop. The tip was still hot. Two of them held me down while Johnny pushed the gun into my bicep, causing a burn that looked like they'd put a cigarette out on my arm. The rest of them just watched and laughed.

Thoughts of Bruce Lee in *Fists of Fury* raged in my mind. I thought about fighting them all off with a kung fu scream, only to become the hero of the school and have my memory live on in glory forever. But all I could do was grab the hot glue gun and throw it somewhere where they couldn't get it, while not breaking character one bit. They might have hurt me physically, but they were not going to make me cry, scream or squirm. I wasn't going to give them the satisfaction.

"Is that all you got? All of you, against just me? Guess you guys are pretty tough, huh?" I taunted them, staggering to my feet. I knew they were going to beat the crap out of me, but I was still egging them on, regardless.

There was no way I was going to let them break me. I retreated into my most stoic thoughts and awaited the inevitable onslaught.

"I'm gonna kick your—" Johnny began.

But just then, a teacher appeared, and the boys dispersed quickly and quietly, all wearing guiltily innocent looks as they marched by under her beady stare. One or two of them paused to glance back at me on their way out of the tunnel, and I could see by the look in their eyes that something had changed in how they saw me.

I hadn't won this battle, but I hadn't lost.

So, Sep was right. Far from being touted as the new coolest guy in the 5th grade, I had nearly got the crap beat out of me by a group of boys, and the whole school started calling me "faggot" after that.

Nowadays, I probably would have been seen as brave for doing something like that, but in the 80s, people were a lot less accepting of little boys who imitated gay icons.[2]

After that, I came to the slightly melodramatic conclusion that I would never fit into "normal" society. When you've had your expectations dashed like that, it's easy to start thinking in absolutes. All I wanted was to fit in, and it sucked to think I was never going to succeed at that—that I would always be stuck at the fringes of regular society and would never truly belong in the way I had amongst my homogeneous friend group back in Tehran. But in time, I gradually came to realize that standing out from the crowd wasn't such a bad thing, after all. In fact, my weirdness was actually my greatest strength. While there were certainly complications that I faced as a child for being a weirdo, I found out there were some noticeable perks to my outsider status, as well.

For one, I had more time on my hands, meaning I could focus more on school and on developing my own knowledge in the library. I learned faster than most people, both when it came to books and life. Being different also meant I had the liberty to think outside the box. So, after several failed attempts to fit in with the school's "in" crowd, I quickly realized the error of my ways and decided to start my own group instead. I wasn't alone—there were other misfits, just like me, who were also lacking a place where they could belong.

This was my big chance at leadership.

I rounded up all the other weirdos, social misfits, and malcontents at my school and began sharing my ideas with them. There was Kal, a tiny Greek kid who was my closest ally in the group; Raj, a lanky Indian boy with the same hand-me-down clothes my own family made me wear; Marcos, a perpetual prankster from a Mexican immigrant family; and Mike, a soft-spoken African-American boy with an intense love of

---

[2] Although there were already rumors about his sexuality in the late 80s, George Michael didn't actually *officially* come out until his famous CNN appearance in 1998.

comic books. We were, without a doubt, the most culturally and ethnically diverse group in school.

We looked like an all-male United Colors of Benetton kids ad (except for our complete lack of fashion sense).

We became fast friends, united by our shared abnormality. We used to entertain ourselves with all the usual, rebellious activities that young nonconformists get up to: drinking, smoking, stealing, skipping class—anything that was a little dangerous or proved how edgy we were.

I was the informal leader of this rag-tag band, and alongside my role as mission commander for most of our disaffected plots, I also slowly started to influence them with all my talk about building wealth and being a self-starter. Eventually, I convinced the group that we should set up our own middle-school criminal enterprise, selling nudie magazines, candy and liquor from the boys' bathroom (all stolen, of course). Unglamorous as it was, this was my first foray into the business world, and I actually learned some interesting lessons about distribution and the importance of customer satisfaction from our little bathroom stall start-up.

My primary accomplice in this venture was Kal, who, at 4 feet tall, was just short enough to fit under the theft detection devices at the liquor store, making him an invaluable link in our supply chain. Moreover, he was too adorable for anyone to suspect him of doing anything nefarious, including stealing. Kal would sneak into the local liquor store (aptly named *The Blind Duck*), and on each visit he would purloin some fine literature, booze, and a pack or two of smokes to add to our stocks. It took about a month to accumulate a substantial enough cache of product to get our enterprise off the ground. It was like something out of a Hunter S. Thompson book, if all his main characters were pre-teens.

We had *Playboy*, *Penthouse*, and *Hustler* magazines; a vast stockpile of mini-bar-sized liqueurs; an enormous assortment of stolen candy; bags of whiteout, VCR head cleaner, paint thinner, and super glue (to be used as inhalants); a galaxy of over-the-counter meds pilfered from our parents' medicine cabinets; a quart of scotch and some beers. With this wide range of products on offer, we opened our doors for business and were an instant hit amongst the student body. Once the social rejects, now we were suddenly everyone's best friends. Apparently, if you can't become popular by socializing, you can always do it by controlling the supply of smokes.

Soon, we had made quite the name for ourselves at school, and our customers even branded our little business for us; they called us "The Retards," and we unofficially branded our business as "Project Retardo." It was silly, but to us it was about owning our weirdness. As I later discovered in life, that's how you win in the face of adversity. When your critics and competitors are trying to sabotage you by calling you names or shaming you for being different, you have to meet them head-on. You can't back down or stop doing the things that make you unique. You just have to own it. So that's what we did. We proudly called ourselves The Retards, and doing that took the sting out of other kids' attacks on us pretty quickly.

Now, we were officially hustlers. Our fame—or rather, notoriety—continued to spread around the school, and soon our little business wasn't so small anymore.

However, it didn't take long before a "business dispute" arose with a customer; the end result being that we got ratted out to our teachers. We managed to rush the evidence home before they had a chance to search our lockers, but Kal and I both got called into the principal's office the next day. We were put in separate rooms while they tried to sweat a confession out of us.

Now, normally, this kind of pressure would have brought two pre-teen boys to their knees, but I had been preparing for just this type of scenario. While the other Retards were busy partaking in our purloined collection of low-grade 80s porn magazines, I had been reading up on game theory and the prisoner's dilemma, and I shared this acquired knowledge with Kal. Somehow, I'd known it would come in handy one day.

Game theory is a field of study specifically concerned with how rational people strategically interact with one another. It looks at the decisions that we make, why we make them, and how the decision-making process can be impacted by the influence of other rational agents we come into contact with.

The prisoner's dilemma is one of the "games" commonly examined in game theory, and the scenario is exactly like the one that Kal and I found ourselves in that day: two prisoners, placed in different rooms and pressed for a confession, have to decide how much they're willing to trust one another not to rat out the other.

Incidentally, just a few weeks prior to this, Kal and I had been talking over this very problem.

"Imagine you and your partner get caught for stealing, but they have no evidence," I explained to him, sitting cross-legged behind the school gymnasium one afternoon, with a stack of books haphazardly spread out around us. "The only way you'll get caught is if one of you confesses. If you both say nothing, you both go free."

"Right—but how do you know whether the other person is going to turn on you?" Kal asked, giving me a somewhat suspicious sidelong glance.

"That's the kind of fascinating part. It's in both of their best interests not to say anything, right? But in practice, most people in the prisoner's dilemma crack. They turn on each other."

"I wouldn't do that," he declared confidently, still looking at me like he wondered if I'd really do the same.

"Neither would I," I assured him with a toothy grin, giving his thin shoulder a friendly shake. "We trust each other. But still, you never really know how you'll react until you're in that situation for real. If the cops were promising that you wouldn't get in trouble at all, as long as you rolled over on your partner, that could seem like a pretty attractive option."

"Especially if they say they're going to throw the book at you if you don't say something," Kal mused.

"Exactly! It becomes about self-interest and doubt. If you know the same offer is being given to your partner, then you might start to wonder: 'are they going to accept it? Will they turn on me to save themselves?' Even if your friend has zero intention of confessing, you don't know that because you're locked in another room, right? And usually, cops tell you the other person has already told them everything, even when they haven't," I said, rolling my eyes a little.

"So let's make a pact! I swear that I will never, ever turn you in, Shaahin," said Kal defiantly. Then he spat into his hand and held it out for me to shake on it.

Sitting in our separate interrogation rooms a few days later, I remembered that pact, and I knew that Kal did, too. We were loyal to one another, and we had the discipline not to crack under pressure. The principal and the vice-principal attempted to play on that inherent self-interest that the prisoner's dilemma highlights: they swore up and down that I wouldn't be punished as long as I told them what Kal and I had done. They thought I'd be selfish enough to throw my friend under the bus to escape a little detention, and I'm sure it would have worked on anybody else. But not us.

No matter how hard they tried, we both flat-out refused to turn on each other. We denied everything, although our peers knew damn well that we were the ringleaders of The Retards.

So, due to the fortunate lack of evidence and our loyalty to one another, the punishment we received was relatively mild. We were essentially given a summer of detention, and our principal made it clear that we were both on his "shit list," as he called it, from now on. For me, the part that stands out the most in my mind was when this middle school principal told me that, with my attitude, I was never going to amount to anything worthwhile. I had seen an opportunity, an untapped market that was crying out to be served, and had come up with the ideal distribution method for conveniently supplying them with profit-rich products. And this, to him, was a sign I wasn't going to make it in life? Clearly, he couldn't see the bigger picture like we 12-year-olds could.

Granted, we did get momentarily sideswiped in this case by our failure to provide excellent customer satisfaction, but we were quick to learn from our mistakes. Furthermore, with our indefinite detention sentence to serve out, we'd found an even better avenue for distribution than selling our clandestine wares from a stall in the boys' bathroom during break times.

Detention business was infinitely better.

We had a captive audience, composed of our perfect target market, and could be open for business for hours at a time, rather than a few stolen minutes. Word quickly got around that The Retards were still available for trading, and our sales continued to grow and grow. Kids would intentionally get themselves caught for some minor offense, just so they could visit their favorite underground store in the detention hall. We were still not "normal" kids, by any stretch of the imagination, but we outcasts had certainly gained a new level of respect on the playground. We stayed true to our misfit values, but we also managed to build a place for ourselves within normal, middle-school society by relying on our business instincts.

Seventh grade came and went, and we had plans to restart our enterprise—bigger and better than ever—once eighth grade rolled around again in the fall. We spent what felt like the shortest summer in history plotting strategies and restocking our supply of stolen goods; but before we had a chance to restart the business, it all came to a crashing halt. Kal and his family moved to some godforsaken, suburban hellhole on the outskirts of the San

Fernando Valley, and our partnership was officially ended. Now, once again, I was on my own.

Nevertheless, my time with The Retards had been a great learning curve for me. It had given me a taste of independent life and made me hungry for more. Most importantly, it also showed me that I had what it took to succeed (despite the principal's attempts to convince me otherwise), and gave me a newfound belief in my own abilities to build a better life for myself.

So I moved on through junior high and, like any self-respecting nerd, found new, weirder friends to associate with. I dedicated my free time mostly to practicing martial arts while listening to Pink Floyd and The Police and reading everything I could find in the science fiction and self-help sections of the school library, all the while planning my next big idea. When the first affordable Walkman came out, I took every last cent I had left over from my portion of The Retards' revenues and bought myself one. I had only enough money for one tape, and the one I chose was Michael Jackson's "Beat It," I can't even count how many times I listened to that tape, but it helped me shut out the outside world while I gorged my curious mind on information for the next stage in my journey.

Like most kids at that age, I was feeling the very teenage need to fit in with my peers. I desperately wanted to be cool, but no matter how hard I tried, I never seemed able to fit the mold. It felt like I was doomed to forever be the Project Retardo faggot.

Situated in the eclectic, affluent Los Angeles Westside, my school was a well-known incubator for aspiring drug addicts. In the late 80s, the social requirements for being considered "cool" included ingesting copious amounts of narcotics (purchased with lunch money) and having unprotected sex in strange places while on said drugs.

Although I had no profound moral objections to the idea of doing drugs, and would have loved to have come within 2 feet of a female without being hit, I simply did not have the money or the time to enjoy either. So, finding myself automatically precluded from most of the typical social activities that were taking place around me, I focused instead on the mission at hand. All my hours in the library had instilled in me a hunger—a passion to achieve greatness—and The Retards had served as an enticing teaser of what that greatness might look like. I had decided that I was going to make something of my life, even though at the time I still had no firm idea how to go about it or what that something would be, even.

How ironic that it would turn out to be drugs.

Journal Entry: Reality Distortion Field			
	Game Theory	Ambition	Weirdness
What is it?	Game theory is (in short) the study of human psychology when it comes to decision-making in an economic society.	Ambition is what gets you out of bed in the morning, and keeps you striving toward the fulfillment of your goals, even when everything is against you.	Weirdness is what makes you unique. Accepting and owning your inner weirdo makes you invincible.
Why is it important?	Whether it be for making sales or building strategic partnerships, understanding human psychology is critical in business. You have to know how to predict and influence people's behaviors to dominate in your niche.	Ambition is what drives us. The ultimate secret to getting everything you want in life is that you have to be willing to do whatever it takes to get it. Ambition is key to desire.	Everyone wants to keep you in a tidy box that they can understand. Deviate and you may fall out of favor with their expectations. But embrace the true you, and you become infallible. There is only one person that ever needs to accept you. Look in the mirror.
How to win:	With discipline and loyalty. Think of the prisoner's dilemma: you need the rigor to stick to your guns, even when other people are trying to influence you. Follow your plan, not theirs. Then, you need trust and loyalty with the people in your organization if you want your plan to actually work.	If you don't have ambition, pretend like you do until you get it. If you do have ambition, follow it unerringly. Never give up on your ambitions. Keep them at the forefront of your mind, and always make them the center of every action you take in life.	Embrace your weirdness. Own it, and use it to succeed in your own way.

CHAPTER 2:

BURN BABY, BURN

By the time I reached my junior year, I was fed up with everything. I wasn't learning any of the things I wanted to learn in school. On the other hand, my personal books on business and self-empowerment provided me with infinitely more useful information than what was getting meted out to me daily in my government-issued textbooks and by my underpaid high school teachers. So I dedicated my time to completing my self-assigned curriculum while listening to George Michael, rather than bothering with the pointless homework I needed to do to pass my classes. Parents and teachers both started noticing, and neither group was very pleased.

But while I may not have been learning the things they thought I should be, I was actually getting a great education. I was teaching myself the skills and mindsets that would help me build a business one day, if not become a doctor or a lawyer as my parents had envisioned. As Elon Musk says, "you don't need college to learn stuff."

I'm not trying to say all public education is useless or anything. Except, I kind of am. For a kid like me, who was intensely interested in very specific things, the generic middle school and high school curriculum is more likely to snuff out their interest than ignite it. There are so few avenues to explore niche topics, or to get practical experience that prepares you for the real working world. Entrepreneurship training? How to develop a winning mindset? Forget about it.

I was a smart kid, I just didn't see the practical use in learning certain things, like how to dissect a frog, when I was planning on being a retail business mogul one day. So I never did very well in school, because I didn't care enough to apply myself. If they'd had a course on marketing or supply chain management, I would have sat front row in that class every day. But nothing that my school had to offer me actually catered to that interest—and I think that's a problem that still exists in schools now, even in an age where curriculums need to change quickly to stay relevant, they usually don't. Kids still aren't learning the things that are really useful for success in the modern world.

Anyways, the end result was that I always underperformed in school, and my parents hated it.

They were worried about me and fretted over me all the time. One particular bone of contention was the fact that I had basically no friends at that time. My mom and dad hadn't been over the moon about the pack of outcasts I'd befriended in my younger years, but now that most of the weirdos had moved on to other schools, they thought I was in danger of becoming a social recluse with no people skills at all. I tried to explain to them that I didn't fit in with the crowd of surfer/stoner kids who still dominated my high school's population, but that didn't do much to allay their concerns.

I found that strange, especially considering that, being immigrants with a pretty conservative background themselves, my parents were always scared of the idea that my brother and I would assimilate *too* well into American culture, and thus inevitably spiral out of control in a fit of Western excess. Between these two extremes, I felt like there was this narrow, little line they'd drawn for me: I had to make sure I wasn't too unique, or too much like everyone else around us.

But that life seemed far too repressive for me. I didn't know why my parents didn't understand me, or see why a cookie-cutter existence was not ever going to be in the cards for me, and that feeling just added to the frustration and isolation I was already feeling at school. Things at home began heating up even more when I announced that I was opting out of the Jewish religion altogether because I disagreed with the politics of religion. Needless to say, that did not go over very well.

I'd recently read Richard Dawkins' *The Selfish Gene* for the first time and started immersing myself in the writings of a broad range of authors and scientists alike. I loved Alan Watts for philosophy and eastern wisdom and was totally blown away by so many of his revelations. The work of Richard Dawkins was mind-blowing as well. Dawkins' work is one of the principal modern works about evolution, and as someone who'd grown up in a religiously conservative family, the idea that the universe could be guided by something other than a divine being was nothing short of incredible to me. I felt like I had discovered a major truth that had previously been hidden from me, from my family, and from everyone I'd
known back in Iran. I thought, *If only they could all read this book, they'd be blown away, too.*

I had to share this information with them immediately. My expectations for how that conversation would go were a little out of touch with reality, to put it mildly. I assumed that once they heard that atheism was a viable alternative to living our lives shackled by guilt and religious duty, my parents would be just as excited as I was to leave it all behind.

I walked into the living room and proudly announced something like: "Guess what? We don't have to believe in God anymore! Turns out, he doesn't exist." I was holding Dawkins' book in my hand, ready to start showing them the passages that had made this revelation so compelling and clear to me, but I never got the chance to go into much detail. Far from thinking that rejecting God was a great idea, my parents were utterly dismayed. My dad started lecturing me about the corrupting influence of blasphemous Western literature and immediately confiscated *The Selfish Gene*. My mom burst into tears.

Their reaction was completely bewildering to me. I couldn't understand why they didn't see how great of an opportunity this was for us as a family. Of course, most people don't just abandon an entire lifetime of beliefs, all because their 13-year-old son told them they should. That was just my youthful, unrealistic optimism talking. Still, I was pretty disappointed that they hadn't been more receptive to the idea, and the chasm that I felt existed between me and my parents seemed to yawn even wider.

As the situation got more unbearable, I decided that my only option was to move out. Even though I was only 15, I felt ready to take on the world, come what may. There were no real choices open to me, and I didn't know how I was going to make it work, living on my own—the only thing I knew was that anything was better than what I was going through at school and with my family. I could have easily just stayed and lived a relatively comfortable existence, eating the food my parents gave me for free and trying my best to please them, but I didn't want an ordinary life. It just wasn't for me, and I couldn't betray who I knew I was.

I had this greater ambition to do some amazing stuff in life, but I just hadn't been able to bring myself to act on it because I felt very brought down by my environment at home, and I was tired of being middle-class or poor. So the freedom to do what I want, when I want, with whom I want, was something that was very important to me at that time. I needed to find that freedom to pursue my goals, and that's still the ultimate definition of freedom for me. Being able to have that kind of freedom, without having to worry about money, is what having a fulfilling life is all about, in my opinion. I then maybe went a little overboard, and got carried away when I was exploring the full depths of that freedom later on, but that's a different matter entirely.

I had nothing—no money, no friends' couches I could crash on—but something inside me pushed me to make that decision. I knew that if I wanted to achieve great things, I had to leave everything behind and be free to make my own way in the world.

The Journey of a Thousand Miles Begins with a Single Step

With my mind made up, I decided to leave high school and home by enrolling at the local community college, where I would further hone my business knowledge gained in the library and hatch my plan for starting my first real company. So, with an elaborate and well-researched presentation in hand, I somehow convinced my parents that a GED was better than a diploma, and they agreed to fund the tuition. Now I'd just have to figure out a place to stay.

Despite the uncertainty over what I'd do for money or where I would sleep, I was really looking forward to having the opportunity to study what I wanted. Unfortunately, the more I looked into it, the more I realized that community college was really just an extension of high school. They basically dished out the same useless information—only I would have to pay for it. Nevertheless, it was one of my parents' conditions for allowing me to drop out, so I went ahead and signed up for classes—none of which were about the psychology or business topics that I'd been looking forward to taking. This was my chance at freedom, and I was going to seize it, no matter what.

I took all my leftover cash from my days with The Retards and got a car, the cheapest I could find. It was a 1965 Lincoln Continental. I had no money, no friends, and no skills, but at least I now had a place to sleep, and I still had this drive to be successful. That would never leave me.

I slept in the back of my car, but it was always parked somewhere because I never had enough money for gas to go anywhere. I bought junk food or maneuvered bags of chips out of vending machines for free; basically just surviving eating the least expensive stuff I could find. I slept in the back of the Lincoln, every single night telling myself, *This is not gonna last forever. I'm going to get out of this rut.*

All I owned in the world was a single backpack and the clothes inside it, which I'd taken with me when I left home, and I lived out of that

45

backpack for the next few years. Even once I started my company, I always had that backpack with me, sitting under my desk. I still had it until recently.

I remember the last time seeing it under my desk, with its frayed edges and broken zipper, thinking to myself, *Maybe I should get rid of it.* But it was with me through so many things, and it reminds me of the fact that I made it from nothing on my own, with no help from anybody else. That backpack, to me, represents my own inner strength, which I discovered by going through that whole experience of moving out on my own. Whenever I looked at it, I knew that if I ever went back to a life where I had nothing—no home, no money, no friends— it'd be okay. Because it wasn't so bad. The worst isn't so bad. And that's a pretty liberating thought, you know?

It also represents the detachment that I had to cultivate at that time in my life, to disconnect from the need for material things and forsake it all in search of a higher purpose. I think that detaching from everything like that gave me the strength to do what I needed to do to build the life I wanted for myself. And, because of that, it only made sense that I should detach from the backpack itself one day, too. I let it go because, after all, it was just another material thing that I was attached to.

I'm a student of GTD—*Getting Things Done*, David Allen's great cannon on productivity. At the end of the day, I think having that drive to accomplish things is something that you need to find inside yourself if you really want to be successful. I had that interest from a young age, but when I got older, that desire just grew and grew. And it took this journey, leaving home at an early age, for me to truly understand how far I was willing to go to get things done. It meant giving up all comfort and security and being forced to make it on your own. That's why, when I left home, I stopped communicating with my family for a while. I think they were pretty distressed about that, but I needed to have a clean break from them at that moment, in order to find my own path in life.

I remember reading once about how Napoleon Bonaparte would burn his ships when he landed in a new place. The second the men made landfall, they would suddenly look back and see their lifeboats in flames in the harbor, and probably think to themselves, *Holy crap. There goes our ride back.*

In that situation, there's no choice but to fight. You fight and win, or you lose and get slaughtered. And Napoleon's men didn't lose—they conquered basically everything in their path.

So, for me, severing all ties with my former life was my way of burning the fleet. I guess I was trying to force myself to succeed by creating that kind of fight-or-die circumstance. I mean, I wasn't really going to *die.* I could usually find somewhere to steal a few hours of sleep, and if not, I wasn't going to freeze to death sleeping on the beach in California. I was almost always able to find free food to keep me going, even if it was just condiments and empty hot dog buns from the local burger place. Life, in general, had a way of working out, even if I had no money.

But it still was far from comfortable, and that constant discomfort gave me the hunger to fight and win. I told myself there was no safety net, no ships to go back to, and I was brutally determined to conquer wherever I landed. I had that hunger, because the alternative was to keep living without food, without a home, without income, and I knew that was not going to be my future. I knew I was going to kind of get out of it. I just had to put myself in that situation of discomfort until I could break out of it financially.

That's exactly what happened for me, and I never went back.

Journal Entry: Reality Distortion Field

	Detachment	Determination	Misaligned Expectations
What is it?	Detachment is not letting the desire for material things, or the fear of not having them, impact the way you pursue your goals.	Determination goes hand-in-hand with ambition, but it also involves having grit, drive, and the willingness to do whatever it takes to win.	Misaligned expectations are when you expect people, life, or the world to be one way, and they turn out to be another. This is the source of all anger, in my opinion.
Why is it important?	Because attachments are our safety net. Only without a fallback plan do you really go all-out to achieve your goals and figure out what's truly important to you (and what's not).	Ambition gives you the desire to succeed, and determination gives you the will to see that success through to the end. Without both, you won't make it to the peak of your climb.	Misaligned expectations inevitably set you up for disappointment, because you're trying to bend the world to your will. This disappointment can end up being a roadblock in your journey, if you let it.
How to win:	By knowing what really matters. Truly committing to something is uncomfortable. You have to make sacrifices. You have to struggle. If you're not prepared to do that, because you're too attached to creature comforts, you'll never step outside your safe zone and achieve something extraordinary.	If you don't have determination, cultivate it. If you do have it, let it guide you. Along the way, people will try to discount your ideas and circumstances will make winning seem impossible, but trust in your determination to succeed and you'll keep striving toward your goals.	If you want to avoid disappointment in life and in business, be unrealistic about the expectations you set (but be detached from outcomes)— particularly what you expect from other people.

CHAPTER 3:

THE CALIFORNIA WALKMAN

"Our chief want in life is somebody who will make us do what we can."
Ralph Waldo Emerson

Steve Jobs had a way about him.

It wasn't just his charisma, which was seriously lacking at times. It was his uncanny ability to assert his unshakeable beliefs upon those he served and those who served him. This unshakable self-belief, coupled with a strong will, put a "dent in the universe" and led to the creation of some of the most revolutionary products and companies we know today.

In the definitive biography of Jobs, Walter Isaacson writes about the "reality distortion field" which Jobs was able to cultivate and use to his advantage in order to make these impossible things possible. "The reality distortion field was a confounding mélange of a charismatic rhetorical style, indomitable will and eagerness to bend any fact to fit the purpose at hand."

Be careful when you enter into the reality distortion field of someone powerful. It may change you forever.

In the end, community college wasn't really for me. As it turned out, I spent most of my time doing exactly what I'd done in high school: independent research. The only difference was that the college had a computer lab as well as a library, so I split most of my time between the two. The internet still wouldn't become available to the public for another year, but the lab was the perfect place to study in peace. I'd been going there for over a week and had never encountered another person, aside from the stuffy lady who manned the front desk, when suddenly I heard a booming voice resonate through the room.

I whipped my head around to see where this incredible baritone had come from and saw a man walking in through the door. Judging by his attire, he seemed homeless. He wore an outdated tracksuit, with a large ballpoint pen in the pocket of his tattered shirt and scruffy flip-flops that exposed his massive feet. Feet which showed signs of age and character. *Those are the feet of a man who had traveled far*, I remember thinking.

I wondered what on earth had brought him to this forgotten corner of the college. Forgetting for the moment about the article I was reading, I started to watch him as he moved through the room and chose a seat. He removed several old books and other research materials from his bag, spread them out on the desk around him, and began typing intently on the keyboard. Everything he did seemed to me filled with purpose and grace. He was somehow otherworldly; larger than life. Each time one of his huge fingers hit a key, I heard the table shake. Each time he laughed at something he had just written, I thought the paint on the walls would start to crack and crumble away from the power of it. This was no ordinary man. I had never seen anyone like him.

I soon realized that the enigmatic seemingly homeless man had a routine. He came to the lab every day at exactly 4 PM, and left forty minutes later. He always sat at the same desk, always had a different set of books that he flipped through, and always laughed that thunderous laugh as he typed away on the computer. I was fiendishly intrigued to find out what the hell he was writing, and see what could possibly be so funny about it.

Giving in to my curiosity, I took the seat right next to the one where he always sat, and tried to act natural about it. As expected, right at 4 PM, I heard the booming voice announce his arrival, and the mysterious man walked up to his usual desk and sat down right next to me. Just being in such close proximity to him made me a bit nervous. I could feel a kind of power emanating from him that both scared me and drew me to him in a way that I couldn't describe—I just knew I had to find out more, to solve the mystery that this strange character presented.

As I watched the large man work, I tried desperately not to stare. And the more I tried not to stare, the more I found myself staring. I couldn't help it. I don't know exactly what it was about him, but I was captivated by his presence. He was a tall, African American man, with long, dark dreadlocks that fell to his shoulders and intense, wise eyes. From this distance, I could tell that he was surprisingly clean, despite his shabby appearance, and that he smelled like an earthy mix of exotic herbs I'd never encountered before. He seemed like a giant to me—a giant from another world. I must have looked ridiculous, just gawking at him like that, but I couldn't make myself look away.

The computer lab lady stepped out for a moment, leaving the two of us alone together in the room. Suddenly I felt exposed and vulnerable. What would I say to this colossus if he spoke to me? How could I explain my stalkerish behavior? I didn't even understand it myself. 'Oh, sorry sir, you just really fascinate me' sounded like a pretty lame explanation to me.

Then it happened. The mystery man finally acknowledged his weird new admirer and looked down at me, lips quirked into a bemused smile. I felt pinned into my seat by his gaze. I'm sure I must have looked like a deer caught in headlights while I started mentally fumbling for a justification to tell him. To my surprise, though, he didn't call me out on the strange way I was acting, he just pointed at something over my shoulder and said, "That there, young man, will kill you!"

I quickly spun around to see what the offensive item was, and saw the candy bar sticking out of my bag. "But I love those things!" I said indignantly. I'd been invading his personal space for the past 15 minutes, and all he'd noticed were my sugary eating habits? Now I was even more intrigued.

"You'll pay for it later," he assured me with a chuckle. I was just about to fire back another grumbling retort, but then I noticed a Mason jar in his hand. It was filled with a strange, transparent liquid that appeared to have fresh herbs suspended in it.

Giving in to my curiosity again, I asked him what it was.

He reached into his bag and removed a second jar, which he offered to me. I thought for a moment that it might be a bad idea to accept a homemade beverage from a complete stranger, but my intuition told me to try it, so I did. It was the first of many times in my life where my intuition would lead me to something incredible and totally unexpected. Pushing my misgivings aside, I unscrewed the top and took a small swig of the unnamed drink. It was strong and strangely herbal. It tasted like nothing I had ever had before, but I found it delicious, in a weird way. I didn't know it then, but I had just taken the red pill.

So I sat there with this living giant, talking and sipping on his herbal concoction, all the while falling even more under his spell. He let me read a little of what he was working on, which was a kind of manifesto about the brewing tensions between the public and the police at that time in

Southern California, and I could see why it had made him laugh. His writing was insightful, witty, and relentlessly entertaining, just like his commanding presence was in real life. When he smiled, his massive teeth nearly split his strong features in two, and when he laughed, the room shook, the lab lady visibly flinching at her desk every time. When he spoke, you would think he was an English professor. His vocabulary was so meticulous, and the concepts that he was grappling with were so deep, that he would say things and I would feel like I needed a dictionary to even begin to understand them. But most of all, he had this incredibly endearing mix of a total lack of vanity and a diabolical sense of humor that made me instantly admire and respect him. I think a lot of people must have felt that way when they first met him.

Eventually, he told me that his name was Ed, but that people called him the Walkman. I told him about my plans to build a business, and how the pursuit of that goal had recently led me to become quasi-homeless. At the time, I was sleeping on the floor in a friend of a friend's bedroom to avoid the freezing cold nights in my car, but I'd have to find somewhere else to go before the end of the week. Yet what I said to Ed in that moment was, "One day, I'm going to be rich."

He laughed, and imparted the first of many lessons that I would learn from him. Within 25 minutes of meeting him, he'd given me some of the best business advice anyone's ever given me to this day.

"Do you see all these things around us?" He asked, gesturing around the lab. I nodded.

"You know, you're struggling now. But every single thing around you was sold from one person to another at some point. So, as long as you can learn how to sell, you'll always find a way to thrive in life. It's all about mastering one thing. There is only one tool you need, and that is influence."

That was one of the most powerful things someone could have said to me at that moment. Here I was, struggling just to find something to eat, and this guy was telling me that I could make it in life if only I went about things the right way. It was exactly what I needed to hear. I kept probing him for more insights on how to start a successful business, and he talked about the importance of having great distribution, a great network of people to work with, and the ability to influence customers to buy what you're selling. I just sucked up everything he said like a sponge, feeling like I'd met some enlightened being who was showing me the path to take to rise above my current situation. I couldn't get enough.

The forty minutes were up far too quickly, and just like clockwork, Ed stood to leave. On his way out the door, he turned back and said to me, "You know, kid, you're gonna do great things one day." And with that, he was gone.

In life, there are always those moments that create such a deep impression that you know you will never forget them. There are certain people who can never be erased from your memory. Somehow, like a carefully woven fabric, they are pressed irreversibly into your long-term memory, and you can feel it happening the moment you meet them.

Meeting Ed was the most impactful moment in my life up until that point. I felt as though I'd just met someone from a completely different world—it was like coming into contact with an alien.

I used to go to the computer lab religiously every day to talk to him, but soon, he stopped coming to the lab, and, in a time before mobile phones, email, and the internet in general, my choice of ways to stay in touch with him was pretty limited. But I was hooked. I needed to keep talking with him, to keep learning from him, so over the next few months, I spent many days waiting for Ed to call and leave a message on the free voicemail service that the community college gave me. He would tell me where and when to meet him, and I would drop everything and make sure I was there.

Needless to say, I didn't actually learn much from my college teachers during that time, but I did learn a lot from Ed. Some of it had to do with becoming a successful person and building a business, but a lot of it was just about how to cultivate a winning mindset and have respect for your body and for yourself.

I remember, when he first told me about vegetarianism, I thought it was the weirdest concept I'd ever heard of.

"What is that? Like, what, do you mean you eat only vegetables?" I quizzed him, unable to fathom such a restrictive diet. "Well, no. You know, we eat veggies, fruits, nuts and grains—" "What about eggs? Or fish? Do you eat fish?" I interrupted.

I had no concept of any of that stuff, but his form of influence, his charisma convinced me. By the end of the conversation, I'd become a vegetarian myself, and within a few months, I turned completely vegan.

But switching from a mostly McDonald's-centered diet to a strict vegan one was just the beginning. Along the way, I would learn many lessons from this strange and captivating man.

My friend and mentor Wayne Boss (an old-school CEO, who built himself up from nothing to make millions through resurrecting troubled companies) attributes his success to three pillars or steps to getting something done: Knowledge, Courage, and Action. Only once you develop knowledge, Wayne says, will you have the courage needed to make your endeavors a success. Only once you have that courage will you be able to act decisively.

KCA

Knowledge-Courage-Action

K -Knowledge
Knowledge gives you
the courage
to make the right move.

A - Action
The one step
with which
nothing else is possible.

C- Courage
Courage is the confidence
you need to take
the next step.

© 2021 Wayne Boss

I'm a firm believer in these three steps. In my life, the start of that knowledge-building process began with Ed. I'd already learned a lot from the books I'd read, but he taught me to examine things and approach problems in a totally new way. After just a few weeks of talking with him, I started to realize that I knew nothing—but I was going to change that.

Settling into my wayward lifestyle, I took to sleeping on the beach, in abandoned buildings and my car, and on the occasional couch of people I met along the way. I had no money and almost no possessions, but I had some very precious gifts: I had all the time in the world, and I was free. I ate very little, but never seemed to go hungry. And it didn't really matter, even if I did. I could sustain myself on Ed's teachings alone.

After a while, I ended up dropping out of community college altogether, and just focusing on the lessons I was learning from the Walkman. At each meeting, he revealed a new lesson to me. Each lesson involved one important element of how to be a "Man of Power," as he liked to call it.

> *"The world is a process of our thinking. It cannot be changed without changing our thinking."* **Jay Samit, Disrupt You!**

One of the most important of those was how to influence people. Sales and influence are one and the same. If you want to sell, you have to be able to influence people to buy whatever it is you're selling. I began to understand that money, as we were taught, had no real value; it was the emotion behind it that was the real currency. If you could manipulate the emotion, it was every bit as effective as using the physical (or now digital) currency itself.

That kind of ability is what's needed to disrupt entire industries— and disruption suited me well.

In his book, *Disrupt You!*, my friend and author Jay Samit calls disruption the intense introspective process of questioning your assumptions about yourself and your goals. He says that being a disrupter is a state of mind.

With self-disruption, Jay realized he could accomplish what he before thought impossible. As it turns out:

- If he can express problems as a series of challenges, he can build a team to meet those challenges.

- Businesses don't sell products—they sell solutions.

Jay Samit shares that the mentality of disrupters is that of seeing obstacles as opportunities. Every closed door leads to an open window. Like the phoenix rising out of its own ashes, disrupters persistently reinvent themselves and their careers and are never afraid of losing their jobs, because they are the source that creates jobs.

To become a disrupter, you don't need an MBA or a fancy degree. You just need to think like a disrupter.

As an immigrant forced to find a hack to success, I was a disrupter, so disruption in business automatically resonated with me. Ed used to say, "How do you think outside of the box? Sometimes, you don't need to think outside of the box—you need to *crush* the box." And that's what he did. He was such a next-level thinker, such a next-level strategist, that one meeting with him would leave me sitting there having epiphany after epiphany, and just seeing everything come together, and the path I was going to take in life began to make complete sense.

He had a deep understanding of all these important concepts for building personal success and a successful business, and that was exactly what I needed to hear at that moment in my life. Time went by so fast that I barely even realized I had nowhere to live, was underage, and had no idea what the future would hold. For the first time in my life, I was free, and I was learning what really mattered to me. It was the greatest year of my life.

Have you ever looked at a cult leader and wondered, 'How can people follow this guy?' If you ever come across a dude like Ed, you'll understand. Physically, he was incredibly imposing, because he was a huge, powerful man. But once he walked into the room, he didn't make you feel intimidated at all. It was like everybody in the room disappeared except for you, and when he looked at you, it felt like there was this big spotlight pointing right at you, making you the center of everything. He gave you his intense, unflagging attention, and when he told you something, you were like, "Yes, sir. That sounds good. I'll follow you, no problem." Because he was a guy with a plan.

Leaders who have that kind of vision and are deeply committed to believing in it are really attractive to people, especially to people who have no plan themselves. That kind of belief in oneself, coupled with charisma, magnetism, and the ability to be oneself and still have people attracted to you for who you are is so rare, but that's exactly who the Walkman was.

Wherever he went, the same thing always happened: a lot of people got scared or confused by all that he represented and stayed away, and the people that remained wouldn't leave the guy alone— myself included. All of us were absolutely fascinated by him.

He really was an exceptional human being, with deep capacity for insight and introspection not only into himself, but into every person he came across.

Ed was also a true urban shaman. He was strange, mysterious, and cryptic, to put it mildly. He seemed to know everyone, and everyone knew him, at least on a cursory level. But when you delved deeper, no one really knew anything about him. They assumed he was a local madman or an eccentric homeless person, just like I had when I first noticed him in the computer lab. But really, he was so much more than that, even though I still find it hard to explain who he really was.

One of the reasons Ed was so hard to pin down was that you could never get a straight answer from him. His age, place of residence (if any), personal life and employment history were all a complete mystery.

I remember the first time I went to his house. I'd only met him a couple of times at that point, and was fairly sketched out by this stranger inviting me over to his place, especially considering he was quite a bit older than me. Maybe all of his enigmatic philosophizing—his whole mysterious demeanor that had kept me hanging out by payphones all week, waiting for his call—maybe it was all part of some nefarious plan to draw me in, get me hooked, and then lure me back to his house to induct me into a cult or something. Maybe it was a very elaborate plot to rob me, despite the fact I didn't have a dime to my name and was currently sleeping in the back of my car.

But, regardless, I went. I had my keys clenched in my fist like some kind of impromptu brass knuckles as I walked up to his door, ready to fight to the death if need be, but I still went.

Normally, we would meet in random locations. Sometimes, I wouldn't hear from Ed for weeks at a time, only to get a voicemail message telling me to meet him at a local twenty-four-hour café at 3:30 in the morning for that day's lesson. But I'll never forget my first visit to the place he called "HQ."

It was a three-story townhouse in Venice Beach, right by the boardwalk, and it was almost completely empty. There was hardly any furniture, just a table and a few mismatched chairs, and when I walked in, there was this powerful opera music playing through a speaker somewhere I couldn't see, but you could hear it filtering through the walls in every room. I definitely did not expect that— you wouldn't, from a dreadlocked black dude in L.A., but that was just one of many ways in which the Walkman defied any attempts at categorizing him.

I could smell the smoke from the electric grill on the back patio, where some veggie burgers were slowly sizzling away, but there were no other signs of life when I came in. I walked around the eerily-empty rooms, the whole place filled with the echoing of this tragically emotive soprano singing, and started calling out for Ed. I was still fairly nervous about being there—even more so now that I saw the place was fucking deserted and looked suspiciously like it may have recently been scrubbed clean to eliminate traces of a crime—and I was still clutching my keys in my hand defensively.

I went all throughout his house looking for him and the source of this music, until the only place I hadn't checked yet was the bathroom. Finally, I peeked my head in the door, and there he was—in the bathtub, bubbles and all, and he didn't have any music playing at all. It was him singing opera in the tub, just as casual as could be.

He didn't even seem surprised when I disturbed him, he just broke off singing for a moment to say something deeply profound, like, "You know, when you're done being scared, you can put down your weapon."

Then he told me that our meal was nearly ready and he'd be out in a moment, and went right back to belting out his epic song.

I felt a bit stupid then. Pocketing my makeshift blade and retreating to the living room, I realized he'd done it again—managed to catch me off guard, then destroy my defenses completely. I was no longer afraid; I was enthralled. We ended up spending the whole evening talking over veggie burgers and Ed's homemade lemon juice detox drinks. He laid out his comprehensive vision for the future and challenged me to think about building my own vision of what success would look like for me. That was probably the moment when I realized that everything was going to be okay.

Up until that point, I'd been totally lost, thinking that I might have to give up on my bid for independence and return home to my family, wondering how I was going to find my next meal. But right then, I had a warm, home-cooked meal and this brilliant sage to guide me, and I thought to myself, *You know, I got this. Everything's gonna be alright.* There was a better way to live my life, and I could see that now, and see what I was going to have to do to get there.

I had a plan of attack formulating—the man with the plan had rubbed off on me.

"I am a firm believer in luck. The harder I work, the more of it I seem to have."
Thomas Jefferson

I know it sounds simple, but one of the greatest lessons Ed taught me is that in order to collect (the object that you desire), you have to show up. Simplistic as it may seem, showing up is half the game. Most people never show up. The world is full of people who over-commit and under-deliver. Make that meeting. Take that class. If you say you are going to be somewhere, be there. Keep your commitments. By showing up you give opportunities a chance to find you. You don't have to do much in life to be successful, but the one thing that is non-negotiable is that you have to show up.

It was the summer of 1990, and the rave scene in Los Angeles was starting to become huge. There were underground events cropping up in warehouses all over the place. They drew thousands of people who spent the entire night drinking, dancing, and taking drugs, until the party dispersed and everyone stumbled back to their homes at dawn, leaving hardly any trace that the rave had ever taken place. While sleeping on the beach and crashing on couches, I'd been invited along to a couple of these events, and while consuming fistfuls of designer drugs didn't appeal to my clean-living lifestyle at the time, I still thought the raves seemed like a great business opportunity. I calculated how much could be made from ticket sales at the door, and how cheap the costs would be for setting up the event, and quickly decided I was going to organize my own.

The only problem was, I was broke. I couldn't pay upfront for DJs or renting a space, but luckily, Ed was a master of getting things done for free. He taught me how to talk to people, to negotiate to get the things I needed. First off, my goal was to sell 10,000 tickets, so I needed a pretty large warehouse.

How was I going to get that for free?

Well, there was a commercial real estate broker from the local area. I cold called the guy, at which point I further discovered that he was head-over-heels for a particular young lady, who just so happened to be a friend of mine. So I struck a deal with the broker, whereby I would secure him a date with her, in exchange for him "lending" me the keys to an empty warehouse in downtown L.A. for the night (and turning a blind eye). Knowing that this young lady was fond of fancy dinners out on the town made this one particular sale easy.

Now, the next thing I needed to make it a success was great music and security to work the door. Ed told me that I could offer the DJs and bouncers deferred payment at the end of the night, so I wouldn't need to fork out any cash until I'd already sold all the tickets. Moreover, I just needed to look like I was good for the money. If I was convincing enough, then no one would question me. It worked, and within a few weeks, I had set a date and had everything in place to throw a nicely-profitable rave, all with zero upfront costs.

On the appointed night, I was buzzing. I couldn't wait to see all the people coming in the door and count the money I was making from this event, which I'd put together all off my own initiative. But, of course, everything went hilariously wrong. We got to the venue to set up before the rave started, and discovered the guy had given us the wrong keys, so we couldn't open the front door. I tried to break the lock to get us inside, and right then the broker showed up with his date and started freaking out when he saw me taking a brick to the padlock. He tried to make us leave and call the whole thing off, but my female friend laid into him and managed to convince him to let us stay.

Once we were finally inside and setting up, it was getting closer and closer to the time when the doors would open, and we started to worry that none of the DJs were going to show up. We scratched together a single, cheap speaker and audio system to play music, but in a 20,000-square-foot warehouse, the resulting sound quality was just pathetic. One DJ did eventually turn up, but when he went to plug in and start the music, we realized there was no electricity in the warehouse.

Things were going from bad to worse, but I wasn't about to give up. I went out on the street and found a homeless guy sitting on the corner, who, by sheer luck, said that he used to be an electrician. I offered him a few beers in exchange for him jerry-rigging the cables so we'd have enough power to run our one, warbly little speaker. When he plugged us in, a shower of sparks flew from the junction box, and I felt a surge of triumph as I heard some EDM immediately start echoing from inside the warehouse. The show would go on.

Then people started to show up, and it really became a disaster. They had paid a lot of money to get in, and were understandably dissatisfied with our crappy speaker and the absence of the other DJs who I'd promised would be there. We didn't even have drinks for people to buy. I quickly ran back out into the street and found the hobo electrician again, and told him if he went and bought us beers for the evening, I'd give him a few more to pay him for his troubles. Thankfully, he said yes, because I was only 16 at the time, so I never would have been able to get my hands on alcohol myself.

I had no idea what I was doing—I was just making it up as I went along. Despite my best efforts to salvage the evening, most of the ravegoers left, demanding their money back on their way out the door. I was mortified, and I had to navigate this complete train wreck of a situation all on my own.

While I was dealing with this immense failure, at least someone there was experiencing some success. The people who did stay for the evening were mostly there for one reason: ecstasy. Drug dealers are always drawn to raves like moths to a flame, and one E dealer had set up shop just inside the door to the warehouse, plying his wares to my otherwise-disappointed clientele. I kept watching him begrudgingly throughout the night, watching the fold of bills he kept in his pocket continue to grow as the hours passed by, while the big bag of pills he was selling kept getting smaller and smaller.

Curiosity piqued, I sought him out at the end of the evening. He was a chubby white dude in an oversized black hoodie—he seemed like the kind of guy that would be right at home playing Dungeons and Dragons in his mom's basement, and yet he was the most popular guy there, by the looks of things. How did he do it?

"Do you mind if I ask—how much did you make tonight?" I asked him, and even though he seemed a little sketched out by my question, he nevertheless revealed that he'd done over $10,000 in sales in the last few hours alone. He flashed his wad of cash to me quickly as proof of his claims, and I just gaped at him in disbelief. $10,000?! Maybe I was in the wrong business.

For my own part, after dealing with pissed-off ravers, soothing the frantic broker, and handing out hundreds of refunds, I actually managed to end the evening with a few hundred bucks in profit. That was nothing, compared with the thousands this guy had made from just standing there, but it was still a small victory in my eyes.

Then, the "security" I'd hired turned out to be thugs, whose plan all along had been to rob me, rather than settle for the meager wages I was offering. They cornered me in the back of the warehouse at the end of the night, and I just barely managed to escape out the back door and leg it to my friend's car. We drove off, and made it about a mile before we got pulled over by the police, who promptly searched me and confiscated the suspicious roll of cash in my pocket, saying they thought I'd stolen it. I think it's safe to say that fate did not want me to make any money that night, because it's almost comical how badly everything was aligned against me.

I may not have made any profits that night, but I had still spent $0 on the entire event, so I hadn't lost any money, either. It was pretty insane—a teenage kid orchestrating a massive rave on his own, with no capital or connections to speak of. At the time, though, I didn't exactly see it like that. I was freaking out.

All night, I kept running to the payphone to call Ed and find out where he was. He didn't answer, had never showed up at the warehouse, and I didn't see him for more than a week after that. I remember being absolutely furious with him. Half of this had been his idea, and now that shit was hitting the fan, he was nowhere in sight?

When I did finally see him, I was enraged at what I perceived to be this terrible betrayal—the fact that my mentor had abandoned me in my hour of need. I was ready to lay into him for leaving me to clean up that crazy mess by myself, but the moment I talked to him, all of that anger just melted away. That's just the way he was with people.

Ed actually laughed when I said I was pissed that I hadn't made any money. He simply told me that it had never been about the money in the first place. It was about learning. He also pointed out how impressive it was, what I'd managed to accomplish on my own: get a multimillion-dollar warehouse for the night for free, escape from several burly thieves, and prevent angry ravers from tearing me to shreds in a drug-fueled rage. I just wasn't looking at it from the right perspective.

I looked at that night as a total failure—my first big fuckup in the business world. But that's not how Ed saw it. He was proud of me. I was fucking livid with him for making me deal with everything on my own, but I think that was exactly what he'd intended all along. He knew I didn't need a white knight to ride to my rescue. I needed to figure this stuff out for myself. And he was right—that failed rave was an important lesson in problem-solving for me. It really opened my eyes to a lot of things about how to plan and execute the delivery of a product or service. Like the importance of distribution.

"Always seek the distribution first," he told me, once we were done laughing about my homeless bartenders making off with all the beer. "It doesn't matter how great your product or service is, without a way of getting it to customers effectively. So, when you're thinking about how to make a business that will succeed, you need to think about distribution first, and product second." That was perhaps the most sound piece of business advice I've ever received, and something that would later play a big part in the idea behind my master plan.

But he also told me about the importance of under-promising and over-delivering. For that first rave, I went about it in completely the wrong way: I had over-promised and under-delivered, and as a result, all my customers hated me. But by going all-out and really trying to do it, I learned more in that one night than I would have if I put on a thousand events in a half-assed way. So, rather than being mad with Ed, I actually became grateful for the way he'd dumped me in the deep end and refused to jump in and save me, even when I thought I was going to drown.

Then we sat down and started planning out the next rave. He made me think about how I was going to take what I learned and apply it to make this one a real success, and that's exactly what I did.

Just a few months later, there I was, sitting atop a DJ booth, looking down at a strobe-lit mass of revelers with their hands in the air, all of them entranced by the music, lights, and whatever drugs they'd taken to put them in this trance-like state. Fifteen thousand ravers having the time of their life, and every single one of them was there because of me.

As I looked out over the crowd, I thought about what Ed had told me, and begrudgingly admitted to myself that he'd been right. Had I given up after my first failed rave, I never would have had this incredible experience of success. I didn't know it at the time, but giving up on the rave scene would have been one of the worst mistakes of my life, because it was the drug-fuelled, fanatical freedom of these events that would inspire my next, and even greater, success in life.

Journal Entry: Reality Distortion Field

	Learn by Doing	Mentorship	Knowledge, Courage, Action (KCA)
What is it?	The famous 'experiment often and fail fast' Jeff Bezos' Amazon mentality.	Mentorship is having someone to guide you and help you grow in ways you may never have experienced on your own.	Knowledge, Courage and Action are the three building blocks for getting a venture off the ground.
Why is it important?	You can't learn how to surf from a book. Because iteration is the only way to really figure out the way something will actually work in the real world, and it's the best way to learn your trade.	We're all mirrors of the people we surround ourselves with. Find inspirational, successful, insightful people, and their energy will help spur you on to rise to their level.	Knowledge gives you the confidence in your ideas and abilities. That confidence gives you the courage needed to act, to create something new and strike out on your own. It all leads to action, without which nothing is possible.
How to win:	By acting, rather than overthinking. You can plan your perfect business model for years, only to discover it doesn't work a few months after launching it. Just get started, and worry about perfecting as you go. There are no armchair philosophers who are successful in business—it's the people who act that win. Be smart, seek counsel, but do trust your instincts over all else.	Mentors often tell you what you need to hear, rather than what you want to hear. Don't let your need to be right get in the way of seeing their advice for what it is: an intelligent perspective from a trusted source that should be mined for all possible insight. Ideally, find many quality mentors. The more quality perspectives, the better.	Do your research. Educate yourself. Know the playing field. The more quality knowledge you acquire, the firmer your self-belief becomes. That confidence is essential when you're faced with challenges and uncertainty—things which may stop you from acting. But with knowledge and courage, action becomes easy.

68

CHAPTER 4:

THE WALKMAN WALKS AWAY

O ver time, I started to understand Ed more and more. His moral compass, ideas, and mannerisms were so out of sync with the rest of society. You could tell from his demeanor: he had "been there and done that." He had the air of a powerful outcast who had been to the other side, and had come back to liberate anyone who cared to listen to the wisdom he had to share. His eyes were intense. In them, you could see determination, patience, disobedience, non-conformity and power, all at once. But pinning down any concrete information on him still proved almost impossible.

It was only years later that I deciphered from his many stories that he had been around the East Coast during the 60s, where he took massive doses of LSD and got involved in political activism. There, he began an informal apprenticeship with a medicine man, which he said was when he found his true self, and then became immersed in spreading his knowledge to others. He led a double life, traveling the country as both a teacher of metaphysics and a political activist.

I think that experience was a major influence in turning Ed into the peculiar success that he was. In his book, *Unreasonable Success and How to Achieve It*, Richard Koch (famed author of *The 80/20 Principle*) talks about how everyone who has had unreasonable success in life has had a transformative experience that played a crucial part in leading them to that point. He says:

> *Reasonable success can follow from a linear and ordered career plan— doing all the 'right' things. But following a conventional path won't lead to unreasonable success.*

On the other hand, unreasonable success can spring from one or more intense experiences which call forth unsuspected talents or latent character. The seeds of extraordinary personal achievement are watered and germinate during a time of extreme weather—a personal crisis or other learning and testing period which marks a profound discontinuity in your self-belief, expectations, rare knowledge, direction, certainty, focus and potential.

Some people have transformative experiences without ever intending it, while others seek them out on purpose. Ed was the latter. He intentionally went through life in pursuit of earth-shattering, perspective-altering situations to which he could expose himself in order to instigate massive personal change, and I realized that that's exactly what I was doing, too. By throwing myself into the world with no safety net, I was creating a transformative experience that would lead me to unreasonable success.

The difference was that, whereas I was aiming at a single transformation that would give me the tools I needed to accomplish my goals, the Walkman was always undergoing some catalytic change, forever evolving into something other than what he'd been before. That's part of the reason why he was always so impossible to pin down.

From his years of activism, Ed had developed just the right blend of cynicism and optimism. He often used to say, "You have to believe that you can make it—only then will you be able to accomplish what you set out to do." On the one hand, a very optimistic message. However, there was rarely any meeting in which he didn't warn me of the status quo and the need to disrupt it, so the cynical side of his nature always seemed to be in uneasy harmony with his positive outlook on the future.

Ed always had a strategy for everything he did—every move he made was very intentional, and he had a keen sense of justice. The issues he was tackling were incredibly targeted, and he always had a very strategic plan in place for how he was going to approach them. Once, he wanted to address structural racism within the police in New Jersey, or something like that, and detailed his whole plan as to how we were going to do that. So first, we were going to have to change the narrative in the media, and then we'd get the police on our side, and then we'd make policy recommendations—he had all of these tactics laid out. And then we actually put the plan into action.

Probably the most amazing thing he did, though, was take on the Supreme Court single-handedly and win. He'd been stopped by the police, just for being black and walking at night on a street in a well-to-do area, which was something that was common practice in L.A. at the time, and was actually within California police officers' rights to do. But it was also unconstitutional and Ed knew that—he knew the Bill of Rights better than most lawyers do. So he sued the police. On his own. No lawyer, nothing. He built his own case and presented it himself, and the trial ended up in front of the Supreme Court itself, where Ed, a black man with no formal legal training, succeeded in having the law overturned.

The trial made him somewhat famous—which, I'm sure, was precisely his intention—and he used that notoriety to find bigger platforms where he could draw attention to the issues that mattered to him. He ended up getting invited on Oprah several times to discuss issues like racism and free speech, and did the rounds on lots of other TV stations. That was another crucial lesson the Walkman taught me that would pay dividends in my later life—how to bend the media to your will, and get them to build the hype around whatever you're selling for you.

For one thing, the police stopped bothering him. I heard a rumor that, all throughout San Diego and Los Angeles, there were signs in police stations with pictures of Ed's face, warning cops: If you come across this man, do not try to arrest him. Because it was just too much paperwork and hassle for them to deal with, and they wouldn't be able to beat him in court. I'm not 100% sure if that's true, but I certainly wouldn't put it past him.

He definitely had a bone to pick with the system. But he also thought that people like him and me could revolutionize the system. That was a really empowering message for me to hear at that age, especially as someone who had always felt like I lived on the fringes of what was considered acceptable by society. I gradually came to the realization that

Ed saw something in me, and his teachings were aimed at preparing me to achieve the kinds of great things that he knew I was capable of. That was the reason he kept pushing me and encouraging me all the time.

As a 15-year-old on the street, I got homesick sometimes, as is only natural. I would often think about giving up on my crazy plan to pursue freedom and independence, and returning to my family. But Ed gave me someone to be accountable to, ensuring that I kept my focus and stayed committed to my dreams.

"The day you give up on your dreams is the day you die," he said one afternoon, when I told him I was having second thoughts about my plans. My teachers, my family—none of them had ever put too much stock in my dreams before. They'd just thought I should follow the same path that everyone else did to "succeed" in life. When I was screaming inside for a chance to pursue my goals and do something extraordinary, Ed was the only one who heard that, and echoed that message back to me. He was right—I couldn't go back. Not ever.

It wouldn't be an exaggeration to say that Ed kept me sane through those tumultuous times.

Although Ed was showing me how to trust in myself and in my own intuition, I still felt like I needed his guidance. I knew that he never stayed in one place very long—those road-worn feet were always carrying him off somewhere, in search of new ideas and new people to teach them to—and the idea of losing him terrified me. I had no home, no job, and wasn't speaking to my family, so the Walkman was the sole constant in my life at that time. I couldn't imagine my wild existence without him to explore it with. The world was cold and scary, and without him there to paint it twenty-seven shades of strange and fantastic, I wouldn't know what to do.

One day, I told him as much. "I know you won't be around forever, but maybe you could stay in California a few more years, right? We could get a place together, split the rent."

Recognising the pleading tone of my voice, Ed calmly replied, "In the pursuit of your dreams, the control of your destiny needs to be with you. You can't keep relying on others to show you the path. So follow your gut, and keep moving forward."

That was just about the last lesson that Ed imparted to me.

A few days later, he left. Just as mysteriously as he appeared, he vanished seemingly into the ether, without so much as a goodbye.

My first reaction was that I had done something to upset him, but I quickly remembered one of his greatest lessons: Control your emotions—do not be led by them. This was not a man who acted through his emotions. This was a man of action and intention; every action he took was deliberate. Still, I was confused. I knew I had lost him, just as he had lost his own medicine man.

Days and weeks passed, and I was still trying to figure out what to do with my life. I was still sleeping without a permanent roof above my head. Some days I was full of motivation, and other days I was staring into the abyss. In those moments of dejection and despair, it was Ed's words that gave me the strength to not give up.

At this point in my life, the streets of Los Angeles were wearing on me. It had been two months since I had heard from Ed, and I was finding it hard to come to terms with the reality that I was really on my own, now.

It was strange getting accustomed to living in a world without Ed's tutelage, but I still replayed his lessons in my mind all the time.

At first, though, I literally cried like a baby. Then, I pulled myself together and reflected on the previous year of my life. I came to realize that I now had the tools to make it on my own, and that the Walkman's parting gift to me was the greatest that anyone could give: the gift of freedom and independence. Ed did not want me to use him as a crutch. As his teacher before him, he had saved the greatest lesson for last: the lesson on how to be independent.

This was a lesson he could not teach in any other way. I remembered how Ed used to tell me, "We are born into this world alone, and we leave it alone. You must know how to stand on your own two feet, and be guided through the waves of life by your intuition. You might not see more than two feet in front of you, but when you are on the path of the heart, never be afraid to be alone. Why? Because you never really are alone."

Looking back, if I had to narrow down my time with Ed to one key takeaway, it would be discipline. Being around him taught me so much about the importance of discipline, and even though I sometimes failed to be truly disciplined in my early entrepreneurial life, I was still a hell of a lot more disciplined than most kids my age, thanks to the Walkman.

Being on time is a discipline. Being of service is a discipline. Keeping a journal is a discipline. Constantly upgrading your mental environment is a discipline. Taking care of your body and mind is a discipline.

Most people lack discipline. They have no "way," and no system. They lack a clear path, and thus become lost easily. Anytime that real discipline is required, their ego acts up and they go for the convenient path, the one of least resistance. Discipline is resistance. It's resistance to the things that hold you back. It's you exercising control over your life, spirit, and energy.

Discipline is a quality of all successful entrepreneurs; it's the pure essence of quieting the mind. If there was a single quality on the path to success that's needed to build strength and character, it would be discipline.

When you finally meet someone who has discipline, whatever it may be, you are drawn to that person.

Why? Because, as I learned from my time with Ed, having discipline tells the world that you have a plan. It tells the universe that you believe in yourself and are willing to do whatever it takes to manifest your intentions. People like Ed, people with discipline—be it in their business, personal or mystical lives—are always charismatic characters who are sought out by others. Human beings, even though they might not know it, seek the grounding, power, consistency, and reassurance that discipline offers. Develop unwavering discipline, and you become irresistible in life.

I learned a lot about discipline by watching Ed and the way he lived, and from the wisdom he imparted to me.

"Do what you say; say what you do."

"Be on time."

"Do whatever it takes."

"As you build your product and brand, remember that the most important product and brand is actually you. You build your own brand through discipline."

Ultimately, he taught me that the trick is to build the "discipline of you." The specific disciplines that you cultivate don't even matter that much, so long as you believe in them. Find effective disciplines that have worked for others, and modify them to suit your own personal beliefs. Just be consistent once you start to live by those methods.

So, even though Ed was nowhere to be found, and I was still broke, virtually homeless, and lacking inspiration, I knew I had to remain true to my discipline. I knew I would need to pull myself up by my bootstraps or perish. I chose the bootstraps. That's what Ed would have wanted me to do.

Disappointed by my progress in L.A. and seemingly out of options to make money, I decided to move to New York.

I was so excited that I was finally going to find fame and fortune in my new life. I was going to make it New York, I thought, like I hadn't been able to do in L.A. So I spent the last of my money on a full tank of gas, and headed east. Those old cars use a lot of gas—I have no idea what I was planning on doing once that tank was empty, but, as it happens, I never got the chance to find out. I made it only a few miles from Santa Monica Beach before the car broke down.

As my car sputtered to a halt on the side of the freeway, I kept thinking, *This can't be happening, this can't be happening.* I couldn't believe how incredibly bad my luck was. This was meant to be my big break, and it was turning out to be just as big of a disaster as everything else had been since I left home. I sat behind the wheel, trying to coax the Lincoln back to life, but the noises it was making just kept getting louder and angrier. Before long, the carburetor was on fire.

I got out and poured some water over the engine to put out the fire, and then pushed the car under a freeway overpass. It was getting dark, and all kinds of strange characters were coming out to play for the evening. I didn't know the area at all, and felt kind of vulnerable out there on my own, so I climbed into the back seat and locked the doors. With no money, nowhere to go, and no one to call, I realized this is where I was going to live for a period of time—under the overpass, in the back of my "classic" car.

After resigning myself to the reality of my present situation, I was suddenly okay with that. I folded down the broken seats to turn the trunk and the back of the car into one long cabin to sleep in, and set about decorating my new temporary home. I took my favorite book, *Think and Grow Rich*, cut out the pages, and taped them to the roof of the trunk, so I could try to absorb that wisdom during this low moment in my life, and use it to rise above my current predicament.

I laid in the back with a flashlight, reading *Think and Grow Rich* night after night, repeating the same phrases out loud over and over again until they were indelibly imprinted on my brain.

I didn't think of myself as poor, or broke—I just thought that there was something waiting for me to claim it in the future. I think everybody has had that thought at some point in their life. Many people feel that they have some potential that's untapped, or some destiny that they're going to fulfill one day. Even when I was sleeping in the back of my car, with a tank of gas I couldn't use and not even a dollar to buy food, I still felt that way. The fleet was in ashes, and my first offensive had ended in abject failure, but all it did was make me more determined to win the next battle. I was going to make it, because there was no other option. Ed had shown me how to act on those feelings, and taught me to never stop fighting if I really believed in something. So that's exactly what I planned to do.

There was a hippie-dippie hotdog stand nearby that served veggie dogs, and I quickly realized that the ketchup, mustard, and relish were free. I survived for a while just eating that, plus the occasional "forgotten leftover," when a customer left in a rush.

Finally, though, I decided I needed to get a job to earn some money, if I ever wanted to get out from under the overpass. There was a photocopying shop a few blocks away that was hiring, so I applied and got a job there. It was definitely not the ideal role for me—it consisted mainly of doing brain-numbing tasks all day, like printing 500 copies of the same flyer—but it did give me a decent place to sleep. Summer was over, and my car was like sleeping in a refrigerator, so after I closed up for the night, I used to crash in a corner of the store, huddled up against one of the copy machines for warmth and letting the hum of the machinery lull me to sleep.

This arrangement worked for about a week, until I was rudely awoken one night by a sharp kick to my side. I quickly realized I had fallen asleep behind the copy machine again, and was now staring up at my cartoon-villain boss. He was this little, evil-looking demon of a man, with a mustache and a cane, which he was now using to jab me in the ribs, furious that I was squatting in his store. He knew I had no money and nowhere to live—I'd told him as much on my first day—but he didn't care.

The ghoulishly wicked example of a human actually proceeded to beat me with his cane and kicked me out, without paying me my wages for the week. I grabbed my backpack and ran out, my head throbbing from the cane-sized lump forming on the side of it and dismayed by the knowledge that I was right back where I'd started again.

As I walked back toward the overpass, I thought of Ed, and how he had taught me that perception and reality are two separate things and to soldier on when faced with adversity. I had a few bucks left in my pocket, and the first thought that came to my mind—believe it or not—was to get a sandwich. I didn't have enough money to buy food for next week, but right now, I just wanted to eat something real. So I went to a deli, bought a sandwich, and cursed all the times I had contented myself with the bare minimum necessary for survival. All of a sudden, I felt great. It's like I needed a good, swift kick in the butt to think clearly, and now, filled with this great fuel, I was ready to take on anything the world could throw my way.

Belly full and with a skip in my step, despite my bruises, I made my way back to the freeway overpass. I thought, *All right, I'm just going to get a good night's sleep. Then I'll figure out my next move tomorrow.* Not to be.

When I got there, the Lincoln was gone. The spot where it had been parked was littered with unpaid tickets. I had ignored the many, many tickets accumulating on its windshield for illegal parking, but now it had evidently been towed in my absence. There was no way I would be able to pay those fines. I was never going to get my car back.

Staring at that vacant space on the side of the road, I knew I'd reached the end of the line for the current path I was on. Now I needed to go big, or go home. But I had nowhere to go—not anywhere that required money, at least. I went to the only place that was free at the time: the library. I had to find a new path to success, and what better place to do that than where I had gotten my first taste of ambition to start with? I remember thinking, *There are people out there who've made a fortune, and some of them started from nothing. I just need to find out how I'm going to get there, and then I'll start from nothing, too. It's a gift, not a punishment.*

I found myself in the business and finance section of the Santa Monica Public Library. Now, at the age of seventeen, I knew nothing about corporate business or finance, except what little I had learned on the streets and from Ed. I didn't know much about industry or starting a company, either, but what I did know was that I wanted to do something big and make a boatload of cash. I just needed to equip myself with the right knowledge, first.

As I looked through the bookshelves for anything remotely intriguing, I noticed a man with a small gathering around him. It wasn't a huge library, so I could clearly hear him talking to the group, lecturing them on something to do with business.

"When you make a product or service, always start with the distribution," he was saying. It was so similar to something Ed would say that I spun around to double-check it wasn't the Walkman himself. "Don't start with the product or service; start with the distribution."

It wasn't Ed, but it made my old mentor's teachings start replaying again in my mind. Distribution. Focus on the distribution first, then the product. The idea in itself made complete sense to me, but I still didn't know where to start. Where was the elixir? That golden ticket, that bright idea—where was it? Why hadn't I had it yet?

I walked through the aisles and pulled out every book I could find on business and making money in general. I pulled every copy of *Forbes*, *Fortune*, and *Success* magazines I could get my hands on. I got *Think and Grow Rich*, *The Greatest Salesman*, and a stack of other "get rich" self-help books like the ones I'd devoured as a kid in school.

About six hours later, I came to the realization that to make the ludicrous sums of money that I was envisioning, my choices in terms of business models were fairly limited. There was religion, politics, petrochemicals, arts and entertainment, real estate, and drugs. I had no interest in religion or politics, and besides, becoming Pope or a third-world dictator seemed like a far cry from my current situation. I knew nothing about oil, and Los Angeles may have been the perfect place to get involved in the arts, it was also the most oversaturated market there was (not to mention, I have zero artistic talents to speak of). Real estate required money, which I didn't have.

By process of elimination, I was left with drugs as my only option to become rich and wildly successful. But how? Which drugs would I even sell? Where would I get the startup capital? I didn't even have a home, and was desperate to make money, but I quite liked my life outside of jail, and wasn't willing to risk the freedom that I'd only recently won. Ed had, in the harshest of ways, made me realize the significance of that freedom, and I was not about to throw it all away. Ending up in prison would have defeated the entire purpose of becoming rich, anyways—which was to be able to do what I wanted.

But maybe there was another way.

I kept pulling books from the shelves, trying to find anything that would give me an inspirational idea while also keeping me out of jail. Then, as if on cue, a book fell off of the shelf and literally hit me in the head. It was Robert Johnson's *Ecstasy: Understanding the Psychology of Joy*. The fact that I never actually opened the book, and that it had nothing to do with drugs, mattered not. The curious synchronicity—that it had hit me in the head at exactly the right moment—made quite an impression.

All of a sudden, the past few years flashed before my eyes: Kal, Ed, his herbal homemade potions, raves, ecstasy. The two words that struck me the most were: Herbal and Ecstasy.

I didn't want to pursue drugs as a business, because I didn't want to get mixed up with something illegal. But what if I turned the whole underground trade of ecstasy into something legal, instead? Ecstasy was the biggest drug in the world at the time, and yet the global supply had dwindled because the authorities were going after it very heavily. A legal version would help fill that demand gap. So, I thought to myself, *What if there's a way to make a natural version of this? A supplement with no side effects, and completely legal?*

That book hitting me in the head had given me this lightbulb moment. And it wasn't even the product I was thinking of, but the distribution—just like Ed and the library lecturer had said. The idea of a herbal version of ecstasy, for me, wasn't as much about creating a natural alternative to a dangerous drug, as it was about tapping into the huge potential of the rave scene as a distribution network. That a safer, cleaner, legal version of ecstasy would be of huge interest to customers was a bonus, but it wasn't the first thing that came to my mind. The first thing I thought about was drug dealers, and how incredible it would be to replicate their incredibly successful distribution model, but with zero risk of going to jail.

The best way to go about dominating your niche is by having excellent distribution. Distribution should always come first. So instead of finding a product and plugging it in the distribution, you find the distribution and then you make the match with the right product for that distribution channel. That's what I did with Herbal Ecstacy.

I looked at the rave scene—particularly the drug scene—and I thought, *Hey, there's a gap in this market. They're taking drugs, they're partying, they're having a good time, but there's no legal product. So, if I make one, and feed it into the existing distribution, this could be a huge success.* It was a gamble, in that I had to bet that the existing distribution (i.e., drug dealers) would adopt it, but it was one that I was willing to take. Eventually, I had enough confidence in myself and had done enough research that I was able to go out, hustle, and convince these dealers to start selling my product, instead of illegal drugs. And it worked.

I created my own niche. Nobody had ever distributed a supplement the way that I did. Back then, if you wanted a supplement, you went into one of these musty old stores, which smelled like vitamins and sprouts, and some old lady with her handbag and her bifocals would come out of the back to totter around the place and serve you, and that's what you would get. What I was proposing was something completely new, and was infinitely sexier and better adapted to the times we were living in.

The idea seemed amazing to me, and I thought, *I'm going to do it.* I had this sudden, fierce sense of determination, and I knew I was 100% dedicated to making this work. I mean, I didn't have any other choice. But I could see it all unfolding—see how this idea was going to be the thing which finally got me off the streets and into the life I was really meant for. I saw the millions of dollars, the private jets, and the red Ferrari–no, correction, *Rosso Corsa* Ferrari—I'd have, all waiting for me in my head. All I had to do was make my idea a reality—but I couldn't yet see exactly how I was going to do that.

I started to research. I came to the library every day, and I went through all the books I could find on drugs and herbs, so I could start working on a formula for my product. Then I spent my nights at raves and underground clubs, where I made it my business to watch and learn everything I could about the illegal ecstasy trade. I watched all the people as they came and went. I watched the money and little baggies of pills changing hands. I watched the way the drug dealers moved, who they approached, how they conducted their business.

I remembered what Ed once taught me: *"Become a student of people. Humans will never fail to surprise you. Become* fascinated *by people and their behavior. If you can learn why people do what they do, your path to influence will seem effortless."*

I usually went to raves to enjoy, through osmosis, the pure, unadulterated freedom that was shared by everyone on the dancefloor, the complete loss of inhibitions as ten thousand people all give themselves over to the music, and the sense of unity that came from this mass of partiers all worshipping the same DJ. It's an atmosphere that makes you feel high, even without taking any drugs. But on these research trips, I remained totally removed from all that. I was just an observer, standing behind the glass and looking in on this aquarium world.

I can't stress how important it is to be observant like that, especially when you're just starting out. In business, that's one of the most valuable disciplines that you can master, and for me, it was a critical part of my learning experience. I looked around me and observed every single detail. I noticed the dealers and their customers, and asked: what was unusual or different about them? What made them tick? What were their wants, their problems, their needs? I looked at the rave scene itself—from the type of music being played and the times of night when the tempos changed, to the kinds of smells in the air and the way the makeshift venues were laid out and decorated. Where was the exit, should I need one? Where would be the best place for me to sit? Where will be my power spot?

Most people stumble in and out of environments, without ever truly observing their surroundings. This is a huge mistake to make when you're just starting a business, in my opinion, because that kind of hyper-awareness is a discipline that will sharpen your senses and strengthen your intuition. By showing up early and simply observing quietly, you can gain a leg up on the competition, because you'll know the market infinitely better than they do. I can guarantee that none of my rival drug dealers were paying half as much attention as I was—and look what happened to their businesses once I came on the scene.

It all felt surreal, staying up until 3 AM to watch the evening unfold in this detached way. But I did learn a lot about how ecstasy dealers worked. I noticed that the flow of pills moved in a very particular manner: slightly older dealers supplied the younger ones, while the older dealers were supplied by an anonymous source from the United Kingdom, which sometimes limited their ability to supply regularly. The police were also intimately involved in much of the distribution, and dealers who "took care" of the cops regularly would be busted far less than those who didn't. The police would shut down the clubs, by lucky coincidence, always exactly around the time that drug sales had dried up for the night, giving the dealers plenty of time to conduct their trade and head home safely.

While observing the movement of drugs at all the parties, I also discovered that a major shift was taking place. The supply and quality of ecstasy suddenly degraded quickly and dramatically. Multiple manufacturers came into the game to fill the now-unmet demand at raves, and their formulae were extremely low quality. Dealers—desperate and trying to find quick profits—naturally gravitated toward these substandard suppliers, especially since they sold their bathtub-produced pills at a significantly lower cost than the real stuff. This cheaper product, however, was dangerous, because it often contained very little actual MDMA, but was instead pumped full of nasty substitutes, like ephedrine hydrochloride speed tabs, speedballs, caffeine tabs, aspirin, and off-the-map variations of designer drugs—all of which can produce serious side effects. Moreover, their pills didn't even resemble pure MDMA ecstasy, so consumers knew right away that they were getting a low-grade product (not that that necessarily stopped them from tossing it down the hatch). The result was unsatisfied, and sometimes dangerously sick, customers. This was my window of opportunity.

I remembered the hoodie-wearing E dealer who I'd met the night of my first failed rave, back in 1990. His product had been the only thing that saved the day, keeping all of my disgruntled customers happy enough to stay and keep partying, and as a result, he had made a killing, while I limped home with empty pockets at the end of the night. Now, there were thousands more unhappy customers just waiting for someone to come save the day for them, and I smiled to myself as I realized that I was going to be that guy.

Once I completed all of my research of the drugs scene, I came to the conclusion that the big profits were really being made by two parties: the manufacturers and the law. The little guys in between were taking all the risk and, in return, were getting only the scraps that fell from the big boys' table.

At the same time, I was learning a lot more about herbal remedies and supplements. In addition to my trips to the library, I took a roll of quarters and a telephone directory, stationed myself at the nearest payphone, and called every herbalist in town, as well as anyone who would speak to me and was even remotely qualified. I consulted doctors, college professors, authors... you name it. I was hounding them for information on the best herbs to include in my recipe, even though many of them thought I was crazy. I even managed to get through to the great naturopathic doctor, Andrew Weil, M.D.—a personal hero of mine. Despite also probably thinking me insane, Dr. Weil referred me to a number of other great resources, which helped me a lot in refining my ideas surrounding the ingredients for Herbal Ecstacy.

But I realized that merely studying formulas wasn't enough—I needed some practical knowledge to turn all of this theory into a tangible product. So I would spend my nights collecting information at raves, my days sifting through the books at the library, and my evenings trying to produce my own product.

I then began to formulate my first batch of magic pills. There were countless sleepless nights, but the stimulus of being so close to my goal kept me going. I remember thinking to myself that one day, I would write a book about this.

Meanwhile, I still had no permanent place to sleep. One day, when I was walking around inspecting suitable spots that I could crash on for the night, I had a lightbulb moment that would solve my problem. There were tons of fancy condos being built around L.A. at the time, and they were all in different phases of construction. With a little bit of covert influence, I convinced a local real estate agent I'd met to give me the access codes to his vacant units. I would take my sleeping bag and go there at night, open the lockbox, and get a key to one of the units. Even half-built, the places were really nice (even if I was just sleeping on the floor), and I would make sure that I was really clean and tidy, so I left no trace behind when I left in the morning. I set my alarm for 5 AM each morning, so that I could be gone before the construction workers arrived, and this little arrangement worked out great for me for a few months. I got to take hot showers, and have this whole, big, elegant place to myself, and I could do whatever I wanted there—as long as I was out by 5. Looking around my temporary bachelor pad, I used to think,

Man, one day I could really live in an apartment like this.

Of course, eventually, I got busted. One morning, I overslept, and woke to find a shocked man in a suit staring down at me in my sleeping bag. It was another broker, who must have come in early to prep for a showing or something. I was scrambling to my feet and grabbing my stuff before he had a chance to say anything.

He wasn't even angry with me. He actually apologized—like he was the one who was sorry for disturbing my sleep. Then he noticed the way I was hastily preparing to flee and got suspicious. "Wait, do I know you? You can't be in here, you know—"

"I'll just go now!" I stammered in reply, and made my escape off the balcony. At some point while I was climbing down the trellis outside, I realized the broker probably would have just let me out through the front door, but I was too embarrassed to face him for another moment. I made my getaway, and could never bring myself to pick another lockbox again after that.

Later in life, when I was running my business, I used to worry that stories like this would come back to haunt me. What if someone found out that, just six months prior, I'd been sneaking into vacant apartments to crash for the night?

All first-time entrepreneurs struggle with "Imposter Syndrome," and I had it bad. I was just this little street kid from the streets of Tehran, and now I was making millions of dollars? Yeah, right. Everyone was going to think I was a fraud. I felt like I *was* a fraud.

Throughout the nearly ten years that I ran my first company, I was almost constantly battling thoughts like these. At the time that I was sleeping in my car or on the streets, I would have loved to have had this problem—because if you have Imposter Syndrome, it means you're succeeding. You just haven't figured out how to accept your own success yet.

Back then, I still hadn't achieved the kind of success that I was striving for, and if you'd told me that, once I did, I would struggle to come to terms with it, I don't think I would have believed you. "What's so hard to come to terms with?" I would have scoffed. "Millions of dollars? Hollywood parties? Private jets? Paparazzi stalking you? Sounds like exactly my kind of life."

Yet, while that *was* the life I envisioned for myself, once I was actually living it, it really was hard to accept. I believed in myself, but there's always a certain degree of self-doubt or worry that creeps into the mind of any sensible entrepreneur—which is why Imposter Syndrome is so widespread. The trick is to banish those doubts whenever possible, and focus on winning. When you do that, you can "fake it till you make it," or rather, until you start being confident in the fact that you are, really, deserving of success.

As someone who came from such an obscure background, with such humble beginnings, that wasn't an easy mindset for me to achieve. Even once I had unreasonable quantities of success showered on me, I still worried that all I'd ever really be was that scruffy, street kid, escaping out the window with his sleeping bag, because he'd been caught playing at being rich.

Journal Entry: Reality Distortion Field		
	Seek the Distribution	Transformative Experience	Being Observant
What is it?	Seek the distribution is about starting by looking at which distribution channels are out there and what the market demands, rather than creating a product and then hoping to find a market to fit.	A transformative experience isn't always gentle. In fact usually it's hard, complicated, messy, painful, or all of the above, but that's also why it forever changes you as a person.	Being observant is when you pay careful attention to the people and the landscape you're operating in.
Why is it important?	Because it doesn't matter how great your product is, or how many potential customers you have, if you can't get that product in front of them.	Because, in the words of Richard Koch, "following a conventional path won't lead to unreasonable success." But also because comfort leads to armchair mediocrity. It's through discomfort and unreasonable change that we find unreasonable results.	Behind every deal is a human. Behind every human is a motivation. Most people don't consider things in a truly nuanced way, so by being the one in the room who notices everything, you can quickly gain a leg up on the competition. By learning about people, you learn to master the deal.
How to win:	Look at the industry you're in. Mold the product to fit the marketplace and its specific demands. Find the vulnerabilities in the marketplace and exploit them. Feed the market what it needs. Do not create a product and then scurry to find a market. Ask: How are things bought and sold within that industry? How could it be improved? What about in other industries? Is there a totally different distribution model that could be applied from industry X to mine, to revolutionize this space? Once you know how to get your product out there, you can develop it and target your audience in a way that best fits that distribution channel.	There is one train of thought that says you cannot force an epiphany. It either happens or it doesn't. The hack to this is travel. Get on a plane and leave the country to somewhere you are unfamiliar with. Challenge yourself and be open. I don't know anyone who has done this and who hasn't had a transformative experience. If you've never had a transformative experience, don't sit around and wait for one to come to you.	See the things which no one else does. Pay attention to every detail, and then think about how those details impact and interact with one another. In business, it's all about products and services changing hands. By seeing where, how, and why these transactions are taking place, you'll be able to spot ways to hack the system to your advantage. Follow the emotion. Become a student of people. C ultivate fascination

CHAPTER 5:
ECSTACY

When we talk about the musical revolution of the 90s, most people immediately think of the hip hop revolution and the L.A. rap scene. "East Coast, West Coast" rivalry was a big thing at the time, and several different hip hop crews emerged, all vying for top position as the icons of this new scene. However, there was another side of that musical revolution that usually flies under the radar of most people: raves. If you weren't there, you likely wouldn't understand.

Like hip hop, commercially popular EDM simply hadn't existed prior to the 80s, and the rave movement fully crystallized in L.A. during the early 90s, and the impact which it had on local culture was seismic. With high-powered music systems, even more powerful drugs, and a host of quality DJs developing their own cult followings across the state, partying was taken to a new level of psychedelic highs and thunderous, fanatical energy. This incredible atmosphere of wild abandon that characterized the rave movement is captured brilliantly by photographer Michael Tullberg in his book, fittingly titled *Dancefloor Thunderstorm*. The name alone perfectly sums up the whole zeitgeist of that era, which really was a whirlwind of color, sweat-slicked bodies, and experimental sounds.

Raves were completely taking over the nightlife of L.A. , and the result was that, very soon, clubbing just wasn't the same anymore. The rave community had sprung up and taken over seemingly overnight—there were barely any vacant warehouses not hosting these crazy parties, and there was a never-ending supply of cult followers to fill them. What was really surprising, though, was that the entire rave scene managed to remain pretty much unregulated—it hadn't broken into the mainstream, despite the large and loyal audience that had developed around it. This meant that there was somewhere I could actually go and mix with people I found interesting, since I still wasn't legal to hang out in actual bars and clubs.

So, as a 16-year-old who called the backseat of his car home, raves became a de facto home for me. Not only were they a great place to crash (a sleeping bag laid out in a back room or behind the speakers usually made a fine place to lay my head, once the ravegoers were all danced out at the end of the night), but they were filled with fascinating people. Part of the beauty of that underground culture was that there were no cliques or hierarchies—anybody and everybody was welcome, regardless of social status or class. People from all walks of life showed up, and for the first time since my days with The Retards, I started to meet other people who shared my wayward, outsider's spirit and built a group of friends.

While I never tried again to organize my own rave, I did start working as a rave promoter, which let me spend even more time at events. It wasn't always an easy job, since most of these parties were illegal and took place in "borrowed" venues, much like my own rave had. Usually, we had no power or running water, so we had to bring in porta-potties for the bathrooms. Most of the time, out-ofwork electricians were hired to climb a power pole and illegally steal power to run the sound system for the night.

Then there were those who weren't magnanimous enough to let such loud music play in their neighborhood, so, of course, they'd call the police and report us. Between the noise complaints and the trespassing violations, we rarely went through a night without at least some kind of police trouble. But, as I said, this was a musical revolution, and revolutions are generally met with a lot of resistance.

Since I was a recurring presence at these parties, I was becoming rather well-known to the LAPD. However, the constant run-ins with the law aren't the things which stand out most in my memories of those days. In fact, throughout all my time as a promoter, I was unknowingly being exposed to something that would change my life forever.

When thousands of teenagers gather to forget about the outside world and give themselves over to the collective consciousness of a pulsating dancefloor, there's one business that's bound to thrive in that environment: drugs. I still couldn't "afford" to try them myself, but these kids were ingesting everything—from pills to powders, nothing was off-limits. There was no shortage of supply, and no cap on consumption. At each rave, it seemed like literally everybody, except for me, was high on something. But the drug that was selling out the fastest and turning the most heads was ecstasy.

I knew I had to get my natural, alternative product out there as soon as possible. But first, I had to get my first taste of rejection in the business world.

My original idea for the product had been based on selling a herbal version of ecstasy, but I also wanted the name to reflect the notion of what I was trying to sell: smarter drugs. So my original concept for the branding was to call it E, instead of ecstasy, but to base it all on Einstein. $E=mc^2$, and all that.

I actually managed to track down an attorney who allegedly handled Albert Einstein's estate at that time, who happened to have an office in L.A. I went in, with no appointment, and sat in his waiting room for hours, wearing a borrowed suit, with a backpack full of the pills my girlfriend and I had made in her kitchen. When he finally agreed to see me, I sat across from him at his big, solid desk, with this whole sales pitch prepared detailing why it was a great idea for the Einstein branding to be on my product, but I never got the chance to tell him it.

He was on a phone call, and only half paying attention to me. The lawyer looked down at me, in my ill-fitting suit, clearly feeling very superior in his stiff turtleneck at his fancy desk. "So, you have a company?" he asked me, sounding unimpressed already.

"No, but I can start one," I assured him quickly. "I just want to license the name. I'm doing a supplement—have you guys ever done a supplement before?"

The attorney sighed. He hung up his call, cleared away the papers in front of him, just so he'd have enough space to gesticulate at me, and then began his lecture. "Hey, how old are you? Where are you from? You speak good English. You should go back to school, you know. I mean, where are your parents? How do they feel about all this?" The hand gestures began, mapping out on his desk the course he thought I needed to take in life. "See, this is how things are done: you get a degree, then you get an MBA, then you work for a company, then after some more years, you can start a company. And then, once you start a company, you can go this route, if you want to. But we only license to companies. You shouldn't waste your time doing this stuff, kid—focus on getting your degree, because that's what's going to help you do this for real one day." Then he smiled at me in a patronizing way, like he'd just given me the best advice anyone was ever gonna give me, and I should feel grateful for receiving these incredible words of wisdom.

Walking out of his office, I felt so dejected. I'd put on a suit and everything, and had been so excited to at least get a fair shot at this opportunity, but the guy didn't even consider my proposal. The meeting was over the moment he saw who I was. That rejection—being turned down, not because of my product or my business model, but because of who I was—took me back to my days as a bullied immigrant kid on the playground. Older boys used to beat the hell out of me, and I got knocked down more times than I can count, until one day I decided I wasn't going to take it anymore. I was going to get up, stand my ground, and fight.

Just like the kids who used to terrorize me, this man had brought me down and tried to undermine my confidence in myself. And just like when I was a kid, I decided at that moment that I wouldn't let him. It lit that same fire in me, and made me more determined than ever to fight for what I believed in. I decided that I was going to show that guy, and I did. As a matter of fact, I found a picture of him in one of his law firm's brochures, and I used to stick it up on the ceiling above wherever I was sleeping that night, alongside all my business book cutouts and inspirational quotes. I did it so that I'd remember him, and use his disbelief in me as fuel for my motivation to succeed.

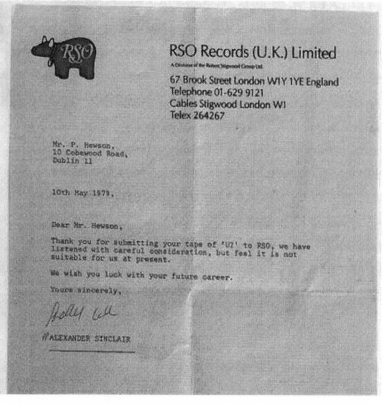

I don't have a copy of the rejection letter they sent me, but equally inspiring is
RSO Records' letter to Paul Hewson (a.k.a. Bono of U2) informing him
about the "bad news."

In the end, I forged ahead and went with the original idea I'd had for the branding. I named the product "Herbal Ecstacy." I made sure to misspell ecstasy with a C, to avoid any confusion with the illegal version—or to add more confusion, depending on how you look at things.

The first batch consisted of several baggies of black, herbal goo. I had managed to get a girlfriend, which was a big deal for me, and which kind of coincided with my place to stay, so I was motivated to make the relationship work. I went back to Santa Monica, to my girlfriend's house, to tell her bits and pieces of my plan. It wasn't difficult to convince her to get on board with the idea.

Her apartment became our makeshift lab. We made the first batch in her kitchen, and it came out as a thick, goopy mass, rather than actual, real pills. I somehow managed to piece together $1,000 in cash from various sources, and used it to buy all the raw materials we needed to try more variations, and start producing larger quantities. After a couple hundred batches and a number of failed attempts, I finally landed on one that seemed pretty effective.

I decided that selling my pills in little baggies, like the actual bags that drug dealers used to sell ecstasy, was a great idea. I printed up some butterflies on these little cards, stuck the cards in the baggies, and each one contained five or ten of these goopy, black spheres. It looked disgusting, and tasted even worse—but somehow, I knew it would work. I tried it on a friend I had at the time, who was a bald, middle-aged, 200-pound raver, with a body already so full of drugs that Keith Richards or Jerry Garcia would have stood in awe. He had the tolerance of an ox, so I knew if it worked on him, it would work on anyone.

He chugged down about twenty of the gooey black pills (the recommended dosage in those days) with a bottle of water. He almost gagged, but the promise of a free ecstasy high kept him hopeful.

It took about 45 minutes. "Wait a second, I think I feel it!" I heard him exclaim. "Yep, I'm rolling. Are you sure this is legal?" I nodded emphatically. Then he smiled. "Who cares? Can I have more?"

Of course, now, I didn't have more left. However, there was a mixing bowl in the corner with about the equivalent of ten more pills in mush form. He grabbed the bowl and downed the entire contents with a plastic spoon in a single bite. It was a sight to see. This man was a pro.

The most incredible part, though? The stuff worked! In fact, he mentioned the effects were strong enough to get a small horse high.

My next step was to sell the pills somehow. At the very beginning, I was looking at different avenues, in addition to going through drug dealers. The vitamin stores wouldn't even talk to me. Of course, I was packing the stuff literally in my garage and mixing it in my girlfriend's bathtub, or wherever else I could set up my home pressing machine for a few hours, so it makes sense they didn't want to carry my products in their stores. Even if they didn't know it was completely homemade, I think they could smell the greenness on me. What I had to do was prove myself first, and then, sure enough, all of the same stores who once refused to take my call would be pounding down my door to order stock.

Instead, I put the pills in my backpack, and went to the club. As I waited by the door with my long hair, Ray Ban sunglasses, microwave-sized pager, and raver Nikes, the club began filling up with revelers seeking the next big high. My bulging backpack was sold out in about fifteen minutes. After about an hour, the customers who were blissfully intoxicated by the gooey substance were sending other customers my way. The club owner demanded a cut of the sales, and I gladly obliged. I made several runs to my car, filling up my backpack with more gooey pills and returning to the club.

It was incredible. I couldn't believe how easy it was. By the end of the night, I'd made back the $1,000 I borrowed from my friends, plus enough to buy new materials to produce the next batch, and still had another $1,000 left over in pure profit. I'd gone from having the car I was living in towed, to being a high-efficiency "drug dealer"-slash-successful-entrepreneur, in just a few weeks, and it's hard to describe how that moment of realization actually felt.

My whole life, I'd been fighting for my breakthrough, searching for the thing that would lift me up out of the struggle mentality that I hated so much. I kept getting beaten down, but I never lost the fierce determination, the single-minded drive to build a better life for myself. Now, it was actually starting to happen. The visions of beachfront mansions and international holidays that I'd seen back in the Santa Monica Library were getting even clearer now. I'd validated my idea, and could see exactly how this niche I'd found was going to get me to that future vision of success.

> ## *"People, Process, Product. This is what matters."*
> **Marcus Lemonis**

According to serial entrepreneur and star of one of my favorite shows, "The Profit," Marcus Lemonis, a successful business is built on three pillars: People, Process, and Product.

My rise lacked none of these pillars.

I had found a drug-dealing utopia and was excited by the possibility of exploiting this new Shangri La to the fullest. Just then, an image of Tony Montana in Scarface appeared in my mind, and I couldn't help but grin.

As if summoned by my thoughts, a young man suddenly approached me. He was the "big dealer" in the club. I thought he was unhappy that I was infringing on his territory. "Hey, you the guy selling that herbal shit?" he asked.

In fact, he was out of MDMA (real ecstasy). His supply had dried up, but he had "some VIPs that needed to be serviced ASAP," so he asked desperately if he could sell my product to them instead. I said yes, of course. His clients were overjoyed with the results, and the guy returned to me three more times throughout the night to re-up his stash. Then, his smaller rivals saw what was happening, and suddenly they were approaching me to buy a few baggies for themselves. Like the first dealer, they too, kept coming back all night, buying more and more product each time.

Hundreds of other dealers followed in the months to come. Needless to say, they liked the idea of a seemingly unlimited supply, with no possibility of getting busted.

The speed of Herbal Ecstacy's marketing penetration was astounding. At one stage, it felt like every former ecstasy dealer in town was working for me. My product was everywhere and the "buzz" grew exponentially. I really was quickly becoming the Tony Montana of legal drugs.

And thus started my illustrious career as an herbal pill pusher.

From then on, I just kept traveling around to different parties, meeting with drug dealers and getting them to convert to my legal business, instead.

I used to say, "Hey guys, you know that the supply of ecstasy is running out, right?" I knew that it was running out, and I knew that *they* knew it, too. "You guys are going to be out of product. Plus, even if you have product, people could always get hurt. You can go to jail. There's all kinds of problems. Why don't you just try my pills? Let me front it to you. Let me forward you my product, give people a choice. You'll make just as much—if not more—with mine than you do selling the illegal stuff. No risk, and let me know how it goes."

I did that in one club in L.A. , and the guy came back totally floored. He sold it all in one night. Everything that I had in a backpack—I think it was $10,000 worth of merchandise—gone.

He got my pager number, and I started supplying him regularly. He introduced me to other drug dealers in the L.A. area, Miami, and New York.

We started out with a bunch of goo-filled bags that were literally made in a bathtub, and you had to eat all this goo, and it made you a little bit nauseous, just because of the sheer volume of it, but it did work—it made you a little bit high and excited. But it wasn't strong enough yet.

And then we concentrated it into twenty pills, which were like horse-sized pills, and people still got nauseous, but it was a far sight better than eating huge bags of gluey paste. And then we got it down to ten of these huge pills, and then managed to reduce it to fifteen capsules that were very tiny, so much easier to swallow. And then finally, we refined it even further, until we got it down to five beautiful pills, printed with butterflies on the front and the letter E in blue on the back. That was the final iteration of Herbal Ecstacy, and it worked great, because people could take one, or they could take five, depending on what they needed.

Finally, we got a Chinese herbalist in Chinatown to start producing them for us, and he had a hodgepodge of handmade machinery that he used to do it. And once we ramped up sales, we finally went to major manufacturing at one of the big supplement private label facilities.

I spent a good portion of several months traveling around in my little Nissan 300 ZX that I had purchased with the money that I had made, and meeting people with bags or briefcases full of drugs—not real drugs or anything, I mean Herbal Ecstacy—and giving them these pills in exchange for cash. I could have bought the Ferrari many times over with cash, but I waited. I wanted to make sure this whole thing was sustainable first.

I was printing money in those days. It cost me less than 25 cents to produce a five-pill baggie and they would retail for $20. I would sell them wholesale to the dealers for $10, and still make a killing, while the dealers also got to enjoy a very healthy profit margin, which kept them happy and always coming back for larger and larger orders.

But it all started with the distribution. It all started with finding this avenue that nobody else had, where it was completely blue ocean. This is an idea that was popularized by W. Chan Kim's book, *Blue Ocean Strategy*, which talks about how you want to always try to be in the blue ocean, somewhere where you are creating a niche or finding a niche and then dominating that niche, before all the sharks get in, and the water turns red from the feeding frenzy. "Companies make their own rules when they create a blue ocean," as Kim says.

And that's how it was with Herbal Ecstacy in the beginning— nobody else was doing it. Nobody else was selling stuff like that through the clubs, and I made millions selling it through the clubs, before it got the attention of stores, and stores started coming to me.

These people, who had been drug dealers selling illegal drugs, became legitimate retailers, and they got real-life distributorships and formalized territories. They started supplying retail smoke shops and sex shops, vitamin stores, record stores, novelty stores, and anywhere else where we could possibly sell our product. My estimate at that time was that we had penetrated over thirty thousand stores worldwide, and counting.

Herbal Ecstacy broke barriers, because it was *rock and roll*, or *rave and roll*, or whatever. It wasn't just a vitamin. If you had a vitamin and you tried to sell it in Tower Records or something in those days, the big record stores would laugh at you. But they bought our product. If you had a vitamin and you tried to sell it to Urban Outfitters, which was where all the cool kids would go to buy their clothes in those days, they would laugh at you. But they bought our product. They carried our product in thousands of 7-Elevens, and they sold it in GNC. They sold it everywhere. Before long, we were in forty countries around the world.

And it all started with distribution. It all started with me and a backpack, going into these clubs with hand-packaged product, and convincing the drug dealers to change their ways and sell a legal product.

It sounds incredible, but I took that initial $1,000 and turned it into $100,000 in less than a month. With that, I was able to stop living like a homeless person, and pay to perfect the product. I remember going from eating plain tortillas and leftover relish-covered hot dog buns to shopping for whatever I wanted in the grocery store. Now that I had cash, I was like, you know what, I'm gonna get an apartment. I found one right near the beach in Venice, and it was beautiful—a brand-new condo, just like the ones I used to sneak into, with jacuzzi tubs, three bedrooms, views, everything. I think it was around $1,000 a month, which was a lot in those days, and I paid the first year's rent in cash. I ended up staying there for about a year and a half, and I loved it. It made me feel like I was really starting to make it.

However, I still didn't quite have my stuff together. For starters, I had zero pieces of furniture. I bought a futon that I dropped in the bedroom, I had a few candles for lighting, and that was really it. The apartment looked just like Ed's townhouse—a transient home for someone who wasn't planning to stay put very long. The only personal item I had was my backpack, with all of my belongings inside, and one nice pair of shoes (my other splurge purchase at the time).

Even so, I thought that Ed, wherever he was, would have been proud of me. I felt accomplished and vindicated, but as I sat in my car one day, I looked at my reflection in the rearview mirror and told myself, "This is just the beginning."

Journal Entry: Reality Distortion Field

	Blue Ocean	Perfect the Product
What is it?	Blue ocean is W. Chan Kim's term for value innovation—being in a space where what you have is new, and there are no rules except the ones you make.	Perfecting the product is going through multiple iterations and user testing (once you've found the right distribution). I like to do this live, by letting the customer be the tester rather than testing before going to market.
Why is it important?	Because the best way to stand out from your competitors is to build your own arena to operate in, where there are no competitors (yet).	Without listening to customer feedback and constantly improving your product to fit their needs, your business will stagnate or get swallowed by the competition.
How to win:	Don't just incrementally improve on products and business models that already exist. Reinvent the system, and then dominate it, before any sharks move into your blue ocean. When they do, be prepared to pivot to stay competitive.	Your first product iteration is almost never perfect. But getting an MVP out there as fast as possible, is essential for figuring out what to do better or differently next time. This process never stops —you should always be perfecting your product and your process.

CHAPTER 6:

A SPIRAL UPWARDS

"You don't have to be a 'person of influence' to be influential. In fact, the most influential people in my life are probably not even aware of the things they've taught me."
Scott Adams

Before long, Herbal Ecstacy was taking the nightclubs by storm. Even those who didn't normally have any interest in drugs were wooed by the idea of a totally herbal product that gives you a buzzy high.

While this translated into a lot of sales, it also meant a lot more work to be done. For that, I needed accomplices. Fortunately for me, as stories circulated throughout the town, I was contacted by many hustlers who were interested in distributing my product. I spent several months with a pager and a backpack full of pills, and the pager would ring in and I would show up somewhere, and I'd give some dealer the pills.

Attracting small-time drug peddlers was the easy part. The hard part was making sure that the distribution was smooth and that nobody was trying to double-cross me. To make sure of that, I visited the raves personally and monitored the distribution. I remember thinking to myself, *Well, this isn't so bad. I'm making thousands every night, and all I have to do is keep tabs on people.* And while keeping an eye on the dealers-turned-distributors, I got to listen to my favorite DJs' sets, and surround myself with the crazy crowd of outcasts that were slowly becoming my new crew. I'd always had friends in the rave scene, but now, everyone suddenly loved me. I was the one making them feel good, and the one keeping them out of handcuffs at the end of the night.

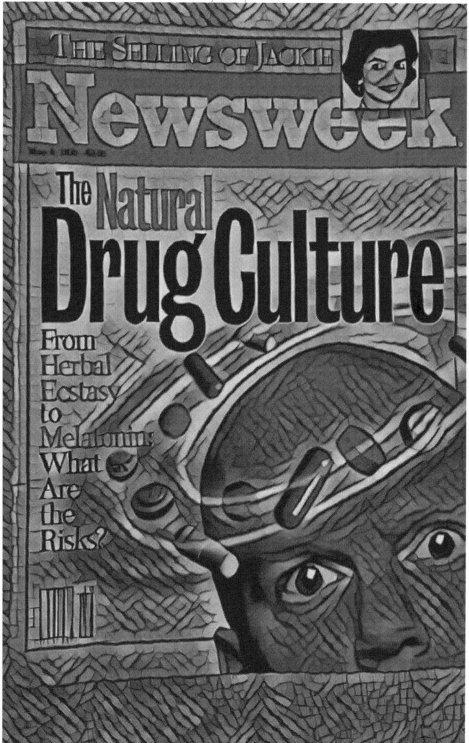

Even though I had money now, I still never partook in drugs myself—why would I, when I knew all about the stuff these guys were putting in their dirty MDMA pills? Besides, I had work to do. I really enjoyed the job, and the feeling like I was sitting at the center of this great, big, money-making network, with all the other worker bees just funneling cash to me.

I was no longer counting the money that was coming in. I just didn't have enough time. I kept stashing it at my temporary apartment. Soon, the drawers were filled, and I was running out of space to put the cash.

Often there were times when I thought I had enough. I wanted to take the money and run. I thought about quitting while I was ahead.

Whenever I needed to clear my head, I went back into my memory and asked myself, "What would Ed do?"

The answer was always: to keep moving and strive for more. So that's exactly what I did.

It all seemed to be going unbelievably well. Until one night, when it looked like my fledgling empire might just wind up getting me killed.

I was going about my business as usual. I was heading back to my apartment after a night at the raves, collecting feedback on the sensation of Ecstacy. The dark was just about to give way to morning, and in the soft blue light of pre-dawn, the streets were completely still and empty. I walked out of a pedestrian tunnel and into the chill morning air, but before I'd taken two steps, I heard a sound and turned my head just in time to see three guys rushing at me. One of them slammed me up against the wall, while the other two scanned the area for any signs of witnesses. There were none. *Great*, I thought dryly. *My murder probably won't even get solved.*

The guy closest to me wielded a knife at me and told me to listen carefully. I don't know if it was the soothing effect of that calm twilight, or the fact that I had been subconsciously preparing for this moment ever since I first disrupted the drug world, but I remained completely calm and focused in that moment. Even when the man pinning me to the wall produced a knife and waved it threateningly in front of my face, I didn't flinch. Inside, a part of me was afraid—I had thousands of dollars in cash in my bag, and despite my martial arts training, I didn't fancy my chances of victory against all three of these dudes at once—but it was like a tiny voice, buried somewhere in the back of my mind. I was aware of the fear, but I didn't really feel it.

"Listen very carefully to what I tell you," the ringleader growled, seeming a little unnerved by the way I was coolly meeting his menacing stare. He had two eyes tattooed on his muscled arm and spoke in a heavy accent that I couldn't place, but his glowing blue eyes told me that he was high on something a lot stronger than your average ravers' psychedelics. He glared wildly down at me, pressing harder against my chest as he leaned in closer. "You're in a big pond now, little fish," he said, and held the tip of his knife right under my jaw.

I didn't move an inch. I didn't say anything. I just kept staring back at him, letting him know that I wasn't intimidated by him, knife-wielding junkie or no. He didn't seem to know what to do, then. They were clearly expecting me to piss myself or beg for my life or something, but when they didn't get the reaction they were accustomed to, the three attackers appeared not to have a Plan B.

With one last, threatening snarl, the tattooed man roughly released me and stepped back. "Run fucker!" he said.

I stuck my hands in my pockets and walked away. I could feel the fury of his gaze boring into my back, but none of them tried to follow me. I guess they weren't really prepared to kill someone that day.

Oddly, I wasn't even shaken afterwards. I walked home, half considering whether or not I should put some added security measures in place, half musing over the circumstances of the obviously-premeditated assault. They had known who I was, where I'd be coming from, and clearly they wanted to scare me. But, rather than freaking out over the fact that these dudes might know where I live, I found myself intrigued by the whole situation. If someone had gone through the effort to follow me and threaten me like that, it must mean I was ruffling some serious feathers in the drug world— and that meant that Herbal Ecstacy was even more of a success than I thought.

So I started calling through my contacts, asking everybody about the blue-eyed man. One of my distributors identified him as Zed, a major figure in the supply of ecstasy throughout the rave scene in Los Angeles. Well, that made sense.

What I had seen in his eyes wasn't anger—it was insecurity, and fear of losing his distribution. But I saw that there was a solution that would work for both of us—eliminating Zed's fear, and removing him as a potentially dangerous enemy. I asked my guys to set up a meeting with him, and I sent a simple message to accompany the invitation: "Do you want to make legal money, or do you want to lose it all?"

He accepted, and we set a time to meet a few days later.

The meeting place he picked was the dusty interior of a disused warehouse that stored old Harley Davidson parts—his operational HQ. When I arrived, my plan was to remain silent and mostly let Zed do the talking. I've found this is usually the best way to begin any negotiation—by giving your adversary the chance to detail everything they want, while giving yourself the chance to listen and observe. You can figure out a lot about a person by the types of things they say, the way they say them, and even by the things which they *don't* say. All of that becomes ammunition stocked in your arsenal when it's time to launch your counter-attack, so I make a point of never going into a negotiation unarmed with this knowledge. It's something that Ed taught me, and also a tactic used by some of the world's best negotiators.

As was to be expected, Zed proceeded to enumerate a long list of demands. He wanted me to move my operation to Northern California. I was not to sell in any L.A. nightclubs. I had to find new dealers to distribute my product. Oh, and I had to give him 30% of everything I made. He went on and on, the demands growing increasingly bold the longer he spoke. The whole time, he paced back and forth across the warehouse floor in front of me, stabbing a finger in the air now and then to punctuate his points, while his henchmen nodded their vehement agreement to every word Zed said.

I stayed quiet as he told me all of the conditions in his absurd proposition, and when my turn came to speak, I didn't even bother dealing with the points he'd made. It was a waste of time to even discuss this fantasy of his. Instead, I just laid out the bare facts of the situation, as they appeared to me.

"I know the police are on your payroll. I also know you have a lot of pending cases against you right now, and that once your bribe money dries up, the police *will* arrest you," I explained, watching as Zed's expression gradually started to change. He knew the truth of what I was saying, just as surely as I did. I calmly continued, "I know Herbal Ecstacy is more attractive to your customers than your own product is, so even if I left, people would still seek out me and my pills. With or without me, you're out of the game, Zed." I shrugged simply. I didn't say it to be an asshole, or to antagonize him, it was just the pure truth of the matter. The writing was on the wall for Zed and his E-pushing brethren, and the sooner I could help them see that, the sooner we could all start making money together in a legal way.

Zed, however, was still resistant to accepting this uncomfortable fact. His ice-blue eyes were less crazed than they'd been the last time I saw him, but he was still definitely on something—maybe the drugs were inhibiting his ability to see reason in what I was telling him. At any rate, his response was to get angry. As he flew at me, the guys with me all took a step closer, ready to brawl if it came to that. Luckily, it didn't. Zed stopped a few feet from me, his arm shaking as he stabbed a finger in the air right in front of my face and yelled, "You think I'm scared of a little boy like you? Listen prick, I've run fuckers out of business who are ten times worse than you. Who the fuck do you think you are, talking to me like that?"

He was shouting so violently that I had to wipe some spittle from my face. Still, I wouldn't let his reaction faze me. I'd been anticipating a scenario exactly like this before I came in, and I knew exactly what I needed to say to reach the kind of resolution I was after. Always have a plan—another of Ed's lessons.

"I'm the guy who's putting *you* out of business," I said, matter-of-factly. "And I don't intend for that to scare you. I'm smart, and I have knowledge of this industry. I'm not running a gang, I'm running a business. Being scary is of no use in business. Being smart, on the other hand, takes you places." I could see his expression changing again, a mix of confusion and fading rage. Once again, I was responding in a way he hadn't expected, and now he wasn't quite sure what to make of it all. "Look, the reality is, you're desperate, and you need me more than I need you. You don't want to be put out of business, and spending a few years in jail isn't an appealing prospect, either, I'm sure. But none of that needs to happen. There's a much smarter solution."

I saw the remaining traces of Zed's aggression melt away, and he dropped his hand from in front of my face, crossing his arms over his chest as he stepped back a few paces. He eyed me up and down, taking in the slight teenager standing in front of him like he was suddenly seeing me with new eyes. I had to stop myself from smiling. He'd taken the bait—clearly, he was intrigued by what I was going to propose to solve these problems for him.

So, throwing his wannabe-kingpin act and his list of fanciful demands out the window, Zed asked, "What is it you want, kid?" There was more curiosity than anger in his voice now, but it was still laced with a touch of suspicion, too.

"What if there was a way that you and I could both stay in business, and keep the police from ever bothering you again?" I began, and even Zed's henchmen pricked their ears to listen to what I had to say next. "In fact, what if you could make twice as much money as you're making now?"

"You came here to ask me to sell *more* drugs?" He asked disbelievingly.

"No, I'm proposing that you stop selling drugs entirely, and sell my 100% legal product, instead," I corrected him. "I'll have my guys draw up a proposal and send it to you to review. We can iron out the details later."

With that, I turned to go, motioning to my distributors to follow. I wished I had a briefcase that I could have snapped shut decisively, just to seal the negotiation in true cinematic fashion.

"Wait!" Zed called after me. "How do I know you're telling the truth, and won't just rat me out as soon as you leave?"

So, Zed wasn't ready to fully believe me just yet. I stopped and walked back over to the tattooed man, taking a bag from one of my guys as I approached. Inside was a folder, containing a contract for distribution to several key territories. It showed how he could multiply his revenue by tenfold and zero out his risk. I have to admit, it was very convincing.

Then I played my final and most convincing card: money. I opened up another bag and dropped it on the table next to Zed, so that he could clearly see the packs of pills it contained. It was thousands in untraceable inventory, and while I knew there was a definite risk that I would never see Zed—or this money—again after today, I also calculated that he was likely to want more where that came from.

"Consider this your first paycheck, in advance. Don't worry, I trust you," I smiled.

Money makes the world go 'round, and for a struggling dealer like Zed, ten grand's worth of product was certainly enough to turn his head. His cold eyes lit up, and he immediately snatched the bag up off the table to do a cursory count of the money inside.

Then he reached out and shook my hand. "I owe you for this," he murmured, leaning in closer so his henchman couldn't overhear.

Zed cleared his throat in a pretty non-subtle way that said he was about to ask for something else, and glanced over his shoulder to make sure the others were out of earshot. "Actually, there was something else I was thinking about, too," he ventured.

"Oh yeah?" I asked wryly.

"I kinda promised my girl I'd take her to Hawaii for her birthday this year, and... ."

"Let me guess—you want me to throw in a week's vacation with your employment package?" I cut him off. I felt like a baller, being able to hand out free trips to formerly "formidable" drug dealers like I was the Godfather or something.

"I think that would go a long way toward convincing me to join your company, yeah," Zed nodded, puffing out his chest a bit as he regained his confidence.

I laughed and resisted the urge to roll my eyes. "Consider it done," I said, and walked out, feeling sorry for his girlfriend. Without my generosity, I doubt she ever would have gotten near those sandy beaches. Zed didn't strike me as the "grand, romantic gesture" type.

Nevertheless, I was happy to have Zed on board. He wasn't the brightest guy on the block and had a criminal background, as well, but he knew how to sell the product. Also, it gave me a lot more time to focus on the production side of things.

Rather than letting my fear rule me, and possibly losing everything I was building by reacting out of that flight instinct, I had turned my early-morning assault into another business opportunity.

Zed, like many others, had found himself pushed out by a rival boss, so he moved his now-legal operation to Miami, where he thrived to the end. Gradually, a lot more drug dealers turned out to be legitimate distributors of mine, too. They started opening up offices of their own, and I decided that it was time to set up a brick-and-mortar operation for myself. I rented a place in Venice Beach, and, eventually, as things grew bigger and bigger, I realized I had to start expanding my team, and that Zed and his buddies weren't going to cut it. Being the lone spider at the center of the web was becoming increasingly unfeasible. We were shipping to cities around the country, using industrial-scale manufacturers, and recruiting more distributors every day, and I was the single bottleneck through which every decision had to travel.

I needed a real team.

One of the first actual employees I hired was Borris. I met Borris on the streets of L.A. , outside a warehouse just as people were beginning to arrive for the party that night, and recruited him to join the company as head of HR. I had dozens of distributors in several cities around the country, and was hiring more employees to help with the production and marketing side of things, as well, so I needed someone to help manage everyone for me.

Borris was Eastern European, and while I believe he had a college degree of some sort, he wasn't what you'd call an intellectual. He was, however, extremely loyal, and for some reason—maybe because of his Eastern Bloc roots—he never seemed fazed by my bluntness or occasional harsh comments in the same way that the other employees were. I didn't mean to snap at people or be an unreasonable boss, but I was still a social outcast teenager who had never really learned how to play well with others, so sometimes I found it hard to relate to the people around me. At the same time, I was feeling the pressure of the entire company's success resting on my shoulders. We were rapidly expanding, attracting negative media attention, and dealing with new occupational threats, like our distributors getting jumped and robbed at the parties they attended. So I wanted things done a certain way, and when they weren't, I got pissed. People rarely lived up to my expectations, and I was constantly offending them when I informed them that they were a disappointment.

The solution to keep me sane and my employees happy was to install a buffer between us, and that buffer's name was Borris. I never offended him, and he could translate my shouted demands into a smiling list of deliverables for the team, so pretty much everyone loved Borris.

He was also excited to be a part of the company and the whirlwind of activity and growth that was going on within Herbal Ecstacy at the time. But Borris was never greedy. He handled large sums of cash every day, but he never stole from me, and never wanted more than the healthy salary I paid him. He was just proud of Ecstacy and what we were doing, and that's something I always loved about him. I felt like the two of us really shared an understanding about how special that moment was in our lives, and how much potential there was for this product to keep getting bigger and bigger.

He was in charge of hiring, firing, office managing, payroll, team meetings—like an HR manager and a project manager, rolled into one.

I hired a secretary, Julie, around the same time. She was a smart, relatively conservative woman from the U.K. with a knack for business operations, which meant she was kind of the odd one out at the office. Almost everyone else in the company was a former drug dealer, connoisseur or raver at that time. Julie, on the other hand, wanted a serious job and a serious career, and the poor woman somehow ended up working for Herbal Ecstacy.

Julie was great—there was always a lot of craziness going around, and despite that, she was very loyal and forgiving. She worked hard and was amazing at what she did, even when the things we asked her to do were often completely batshit, like sending a letter to the President of the United States speaking out against ephedra regulations, or ordering strippers and ten piñatas filled with $20 bills for an office party. She took it all in stride, in a way that very few people could have handled.

She was with me throughout most of the years of the company. I got lucky with her, but, you know, at the time, I really knew nothing about how to build a team. I thought I just needed somewhat capable people to help take over some of my mounting responsibilities, but I didn't fully appreciate how important it was to find people who were truly experts at what they did.

The result was a company full of loveable weirdos, just like the people I'd always gravitated toward, but almost none of whom had experience growing or running an international enterprise.

In *Think and Grow Rich,* Napoleon Hill lays out 13 principles for generating wealth, and number four is the importance of accumulating "Specialized Knowledge." That's exactly what I had set out to do when I started the company—researching in the library and at parties, tracking down industry experts, and experimenting with my own homemade formula. I knew that *I* had to be a specialist, but I didn't realize yet that it would serve me best if everyone else around me was a specialist, too.

In business, probably the single biggest mistake you can make is to be too generalist. Hill distinguishes between two kinds of knowledge in his book: general knowledge and specialized knowledge. He says that general knowledge is definitely the more popular of the two—university professors and academics, for example, have it in spades. Yet it's not very useful for the accumulation of wealth, which is why professors and academics, in most cases, are not particularly rich.

'We're Squeaky Clean'

And so say All: Herbal Ecstacy there's more in store

'We'd like to thank the FDA': The Herbal Ecstacy CEO says sales are up 20% since the agency threatened action

Hill also said that there's no such thing as "knowledge is power." That's a misnomer. Rather, he calls knowledge "potential power," and says that it becomes power only when it's intelligently directed through plans of specific action, and with a well-defined purpose.

In those early days of Herbal Ecstacy, there was so much to do. I was a kid, so how to establish a corporate entity, calculate financial forecasts, optimize supply chains—I didn't know how to do any of this stuff. But one of the things Ed taught me is the art of influence, which, in my view, is like "the one ring that rules them all" (from *The Lord Of The Rings*). The ability to hire people, the ability to influence people, to get them to help you with their specialized knowledge is incredible, because with it, you can do anything. You can do heart surgery, if you can get the right people together to perform the operation. If you can get an excellent surgeon, an anesthesiologist, and all the right people in the room, that heart surgery can actually happen.

It doesn't happen because of one person. It happens because of a group of people with the right specialized knowledge. Now, I don't mean that you could do heart surgery yourself if you do enough independent research—please do not do that (far too many skillsets are required). But it's possible that somebody with the knowledge of which people to target, and how to get those people to work together, can suddenly be able to accomplish the most complicated task known to mankind.

That's how building a business should be done. The key influencer themselves needs to have a general knowledge of the field, and of the specific task they want to accomplish, but they wouldn't have to learn how to do every one of the necessary steps themselves.

Take Amazon, for example, which is the space I'm in now. There are so many different moving parts that are essential components in a successful e-commerce business, like graphic design. It's an art, and it takes a very talented person to do it well, yet nobody on earth is poorer than the lone graphic artist selling hours for dollars.

Despite having that specialized skill set, most designers are working with a limited number of hours in a day, and they can only earn by selling their hours for money. Their job is so time consuming, so meticulous, so perfection-oriented, but sorely underpaid. So the key to building wealth isn't actually just about having specialized knowledge, a well-defined purpose, and a thorough plan of action—it's about removing that time barrier which prevents you from scaling your success to really towering heights.

If I need an amazing design for an Amazon product listing, I'll get together two or three great graphic artists, give them examples, pay them by the hour, and then the job is done. There's no need for me to learn Photoshop, or any of that stuff. I know nothing about that. I know what looks good on the platform, because I've been doing it for so long now, but I don't need to know the specifics of design principles. Instead, I leave that to the graphic artists, because they're the experts with specialized knowledge in that field. If you don't have that kind of knowledge yourself, you either need to acquire it, or hire the right people who do have that skill set.

Specialized knowledge is what you want, and the more niche you are with that knowledge, the better off you are. I know that I am one of the top people in the world at a very narrow band of activities— winning at Amazon—which is how to get my products to rank and sell on the Amazon platform. That's it. Most other things I hire other people to do, and oftentimes the result comes out excellent. Why? Because I'm a good manager of people. I'm a great project manager and I am an amazing systems builder. There are a lot of things that I absolutely fail at, and that I am not a success at. Those are things that I am very successful at now—I just wasn't as skilled at them back in the early days of my business career.

Herbal Ecstacy developed in a crazy way, but with my next company, I decided to get the smartest people I knew, which were scientists building pulmonary technology, and I got their advice when building the product (an early version of a nicotine vaporizer). I got the advice of Silicon Valley investors and people who were smarter than me to advise me when building that company, so I started out with a much stronger specialist team than I did when piecing together my motley band at Herbal Ecstacy.

Back then, I would hire anyone and everyone I could, just to fill gaps in my organization. We employed half of the eccentric locals of Venice Beach.

I'd say, "Oh, we're missing a marketing-this or an HR-that, let's hire someone for that." And on the day they arrived to start the job, what I was basically doing was telling these new hires, "here's this problem we have—you're here to solve it for us." But I didn't have a clear end goal in mind, or a detailed strategy for reaching those objectives. I just saw a need that arose in the moment, and looked for someone to fill it.

Now, I take a very different approach to hiring. I don't hire to fill a gap. I have to credit my friend, Marx, who taught me this particular insight. Marx is a few years older than me, and he's an extremely successful businessman, who told me that when you hire, you hire to find people who can execute on systems. Marx teaches that the three things that you cannot outsource are strategy, sales, and team building. Those things you have to set up yourself. Everything else you can add to your GTD (*Getting Things Done* by David Allen) system and delegate.

I learned that I have to solve those problems. I have to think through those problems, and that's where the heavy lifting comes in, because the strategizing is the hardest and most crucial part. Then, after you've identified the objectives and the strategy, it's about creating the tactics for achieving the strategy. Once you have a system, then you can hire the best person possible, who's most qualified to execute on that system. That's what I do now.

But back then, I would hire people to solve problems, and those people would inevitably disappoint me. Every single person I hired would disappoint me, and it was an ongoing problem—but it wasn't a problem that started with them, it started with me. That was part of the problem of being such a young guy, who ended up at the helm of this company that was growing so much faster than anyone had ever expected.

~❖~

"What's the best way to climb to the top? Be a failure."
Scott Adams

How do you win consistently? The answer is really simple: you want to make sure that you have successes, but that you also have failures. The trick is to make sure that the size of your successes outweighs the cumulative size of your failures. You need to be able to weather twenty losses so you can have one success—this means that the size of that one win has to far outweigh the twenty losses.

You can have lots of little failures and just one big success, and still be winning. Or you can have lots of moderate-sized successes and a couple big failures, and still be doing pretty well. It's just making sure that the successes outweigh the failures. I know that sounds very simplistic and obvious.

One of my favorite books is by Scott Adams, the creator of Dilbert comics, and it's called *How to Fail at Almost Everything and Still Win Big*. It's an awesome, awesome book. In it, he talks about something that I hold very dear to my heart, which is that goals are really bullshit. They're largely unachievable. He talks about how the world pushes this concept of, "You just need to be passionate and have good goals, and you'll make it!"

It doesn't work. I know people who have made millions, and even billions, of dollars, and never had a goal in their life. I've never really had a goal in my life. What you want to have is systems and strategy.

This is something one of my friends and mentors nowadays, Wayne Boss, talks about often: objectives, strategy and tactics. One of the things that is super important for any business owner to put into place are systems for testing, failing, correcting, testing—maybe failing again—correcting, testing, getting it right, then scaling.

Only by going through that process will you arrive at the right formula. You don't know what is going to work until you try and you fail, and then tweak it and succeed (just like with my first attempt at organizing my own raves, and with developing the perfect formula for Herbal Ecstacy).

So if it's goals versus systems, forget about goals. Having a goal is not as important as having a system in place to achieve success in whatever you're doing. You could have a goal to make one hundred million dollars by this time next year, but if you don't have a system for doing that, then it's not going to happen.

Herbal Ecstacy, for example, did not happen as a goal. I had no goals for the company, I just had a general objective of being successful.

And then I created systems. Not just refining the formula, but building out the systems, like how are we going to sell it? Who are we going to sell it to? I had to find out what works and what doesn't, through trial and error. And then, following through on that feeling of success, and scaling that. That's how I won. That's how you win.

But systems will also change. Take e-commerce and the work that I do now on Amazon—with online marketplaces you can have a system that works great, gets your product ranked number 1, gets you the best reviews from real reviewers, and gets you selling tons. And then tomorrow, you wake up and it's not working anymore, because of an algorithm change or new trends or a global pandemic. So you have to be ready to pivot. You have to be ready to stop and turn on a dime to a different system, one that will work in this new environment.

So, if it's goals versus systems, forget about goals. Go with systems.

These were all lessons I learned from my first company that were invaluable to me later in life, but I had to earn that education by experiencing some pretty harsh learnings along the way. And one of those was Rob.

Journal Entry: Reality Distortion Field			
	Win Bigger than You Fail	Specialized Knowledge	Systems over Goals
What is it?	Make sure that the size of your cumulative successes is greater than the size of your cumulative failures. This can be one big win or (more likely) several good-sized ones.	Specialized knowledge is the opposite of general knowledge, and is one of Napoleon Hill's 13 principles for achieving wealth.	Systems over goals is a way of planning and operating your business that's process-oriented, rather than objective-oriented.
Why is it important?	Because failure isn't something to be afraid of—only failing too big or too often is. What's important is what you do in those moments of failure.	Deep understanding of a niche topic is what's needed to accomplish great things—like heart surgery. It takes a team of specialists, not a single general practitioner.	As Scott Adams points out, the endless pursuit of goals is meaningless if you don't have the proper systems in place to achieve real results.
How to win:	By learning and growing from your failures, rather than letting them discourage you. Often, the greatest successes in life come from a smaller failure that happened first, which gave you new strengths and insights. Every time you fail, use it as motivation to win even bigger next time.	Make sure that not only you, but everyone on your team, is a specialist in their field. If you have excellent systems in place and get niche experts to run them, even the most complex task becomes a relatively simple, routine one.	It's okay to have goals, but focus, first and foremost, on building the right systems to reach those goals. Design every standard operating procedure in a way that produces the maximum possible value for your business (and your customer), and you'll be setting yourself up to achieve success, regardless of what your goals are.

CHAPTER 7:

WINNING

During this time, I used to pay regular visits to the local Pick 'n Save store for supplies. Once, as I was walking through the aisles gathering plastic baggies and containers for manufacturing the pills, I bumped into a guy I knew from around the area. At first, I didn't notice the tall, muscular man coming toward me, as I was busy eyeing a scantily-clad, voluptuous woman, browsing the wares further down the aisle. But then a guy stepped in between the two of us, blocking my line of sight.

I instantly recognized him. With his clean-shaven head and a little gold Star of David earring in one earlobe, he looked exactly like Mr. Clean (if Mr. Clean was outspoken about being Jewish)— something I remember thinking the first time I met him at a party in Venice.

"Hey man, don't I know you?" he asked. "Shane, right?"

"It's Shaahin, actually. My friends call me Sean."

"Ah, right, yeah. You're the guy who sells those legal E pills! You still doing that?" he asked, and I finally turned my undivided attention on him, once the woman at the end of the aisle walked out of view.

Rob was a funky guy. A permanent fixture in the Los Angeles underground rave scene, he was always hanging around some party or another, usually messed up on actual ecstasy or some elaborate narcotic cocktail, which made him much more entertaining than he was when he was sober. He was incredibly popular amongst the ravers, due to his fun-loving demeanor and welcoming attitude, which made people instantly feel comfortable around him. As long as he was high, he had this positive, playful energy that drew others to him, which kind of clashed with his Jewish baldhead appearance. He may not have had any useful, existing network of his own which we could tap into, but he was a ham and the perfect candidate to field the media attention, while I dealt with the business side of things undisturbed.

I liked Rob, but I also knew that he wasn't very stable. In fact, he was an accident waiting to happen. In those days I would look at that and just ask, "Where do I sign?" But what he did have was a great potential. In addition to being well-loved amongst my target customers, he had some powerful potential connections around Los Angeles from his failed career as an actor in the 80s, and tapping into and cultivating that kind of network with my tutelage would have been a great asset to me at that stage in Herbal Ecstacy's growth. It was just a chance meeting in the dollar store, but suddenly, I saw an opportunity.

"I am, yeah, and it's been going really well. The company is growing so fast right now, and I'm always looking for new people to hire because of the rate at which we're scaling," I told him, and by the way his face lit up, I could already see he was interested. After what looked like a promising movie career fizzled out quickly, Rob had ended up doing a number of odd jobs and getting involved in wacky network marketing schemes that never seemed to pan out, or even last longer than a month or two. But all of that could change if he joined a company like Herbal Ecstacy.

"Really? I'm actually looking for a job at the moment—maybe I could help you guys out!" Rob suggested, and I smiled. If I could tap into his personality as a PR tool, we could expand even more rapidly than we were already. Maybe he could go in front of the public, and I could just be the wizard behind the curtain.

I offered to explain it to him over a cup of tea, and Rob was more than willing to oblige. Twenty minutes later, sitting in a café down the block and sipping our vegan chai lattes, I told Rob all about the

product and tried to whet his appetite for the job even more. "So, I've spent a long time formulating the pills to get them just right. It's almost exactly like ecstasy, in terms of effects, but without any of the downsides. You get the smooth, tingly feelings, the euphoria, the rush, and the excitement of ecstasy, minus the massive hangover or the other nasty side effects. On top of that, it's all-natural.
Nothing illegal, nothing the feds can bust you on."

Rob was listening very carefully, as if he was worried about missing out on key directions to locate a treasure chest. Seeing his interest was piqued, I continued. "It's about $20 for a dose, and it could last up to four or five hours, depending on the person. People in the clubs have been loving it. And the dealers have all become our distributors, because the markup is insane, and they finally can stop being paranoid about police raids all the time."

Rob's eyes lit up when I mentioned the high margins, and he instantly invited me over to his house in Venice Beach for dinner the next day to discuss the job opportunity further. He lived on a fairly quiet walking street in Venice Beach, and as I pulled up out front, I noticed two men leaving the house who then got into separate cars and drove away. Not thinking much of it, I walked inside and was greeted at the door by the same curvy blonde from the previous day. She was wearing lingerie, partially covered by a pair of loose fitting hot pants, and looked like she could have been cast as an Anna Nicole lookalike. She immediately introduced herself as Krissy, Rob's girlfriend-of-sorts. When she said that, I suddenly snapped my eyes away from her very much on-show, huge breasts, and hoped Rob hadn't noticed me eyeing her in the Pick 'n Save yesterday.

There were three other women in the house, all dressed in hot pants and bikini tops, and all equally attractive. Rob was sitting on the couch with them, listening to the latest techno music, looking extremely high on whatever drug cocktail he had mixed up for himself this time.

Over dinner, Krissy and Rob told me that they were running a quote-unquote, "Massage in Lingerie" parlor. The women gave men massages while wearing lingerie, and whatever else happened was between them and their "discrete" clientele. I didn't *think* they were actually prostitutes, but who knows—maybe that was just my slightly naive perception of the situation.

After we'd eaten, we retired to the living room to party for the evening, and things got even weirder. Rob turned up the speakers until the window panes all buzzed from the reverberations of the bass and started dancing around the room like a madman, all by himself. The rest of us just laughed, and Krissy seemed barely to notice at all—I guess she was used to his antics, and besides, she was too preoccupied with the half-naked girls that kept circling her like she was their madame. Every so often, she would pull one of them into her lap and start kissing her, then give them a curt smack on the bum to dismiss them when she got bored. Rob had one of the girls dressed in pink lace lingerie walking around carrying a silver tray with small glass containers balanced on it, each one filled to the brim with Herbal Ecstacy and some other pharmaceuticals mixed in, like a platter of mind-altering canapés. I had to politely decline several times when the little containers were offered to me, thinking, *Who needs drugs in a place this crazy, anyways?*

The whole thing looked so ludicrous to me. Rob dancing to EDM, his scantily-clad harem passing drugs around, Krissy making out with the girls from time to time—all while random men came and went up the stairs. These people were insane. This guy was going to be exactly what I was looking for. "I'm in. Where do I sign?" I asked jokingly.

Rob tried to pitch me on selling them Herbal Ecstacy so that the girls could offer it to their clients, but after speaking to me for about 5 minutes, he realized that my ambitions were far greater than that. I wanted to coach him to build contacts in the EDM scene and then to cultivate and access those contacts. I wanted to mold him to be the person I was not. I wanted him to be my alter-ego, of sorts.

However, I had one weakness back then, and it was that I did not want any publicity for myself. We were starting to get requests to do interviews with the media, but I had declined every one so far. I wasn't sure that I would be great on camera, nor did I think anybody wanted to see a kid fronting this company, or hear any of my wacky worldviews. I felt like my social outcast persona could end up damaging the company's image, and that was where Rob came in. He had acting training, he was older than me, and he looked like a super conservative guy when he was wearing a suit. So I thought, maybe it would be better to put this guy, wacky as he is, in front of the TV cameras, while I stayed in the background and collected all the cash. Also, I have to admit, the idea of hanging out with all of these scantily clad females at his place did appeal to me, even if it was a madhouse over there.

After explaining to him what a "CEO" did, I convinced Rob to take a job as our acting CEO. Although I retained sole decision-making authority as the president of Herbal Ecstacy, Rob was going to be the face of the brand and also help with sales and expanding the company to new markets. I came up with the grandest and most corporate-sounding name and logo I could muster with in those days. Thus, Global World Media Incorporated was born.

The next week, he started working for me, along with a couple of the girls from his "Venice Operation." I took a large office right on the beach in Venice, and started hiring anyone who needed a job. Most of them were put in positions that no self-respecting CEO would ever hire these people for, but that was all part of the learning experience that I had to go through in those early years. I was a kid, and I didn't know anything about hiring or organizational structures, so it was inevitable that I was going to make a few mistakes along the way. I just tried to make sure that they all made me wiser. Soon the massive sign went up on the inside of the Venice Beach office in all of its glory. Global World Media Incorporated was now official.

Suicide Squad

> *"When a certain event can be certain suicide to anyone wanting to compete with you, but you can survive it because of your unfair market advantage (i.e., unparalleled cost or value), then you likely have what I call suicide margins."*
> **Shaahin Cheyene**

I always operated on what I liked to call suicide margins. To me, this meant that I could practically commit suicide with the products and company, and not only survive, but still come out of it with a large profit.

To me, a suicide margin was a minimum of 10X cost. So if something cost me $1, then I would need to be able to sell it for at least an average of $10 to my customers. But the higher the margin, the better. This suicide margin allowed sufficient space for me to make all the mistakes I was inevitably going to make as a young, untested entrepreneur, and still be profitable enough to grow the company and live a very comfortable lifestyle.

During my Ecstacy days, mistakes were plentiful. I had millions of dollars of merchandise stolen by employees, cops and robbers alike. Product was regularly confiscated without explanation and never returned by all manners of authorities from around the world. Millions of dollars of merchandise was lost in a fire one year. Millions more were lost to dishonorable resale customers who never paid their bill. Tens of millions were paid in legal fees and court costs as we lobbied to keep our products legal and on the shelves. More money was simply given away during my fits of madness. All this would have been enough to drive any "normal" company under, but, due entirely to the suicide margins that we operated on, the products are still around today. I'm not really involved anymore in the business personally, but it does still exist.

Margins change with volume. Everything is a volume game. Although you may not have the volume when you first start, what matters is what the margin will be when you do have the volume.

Jeff Bezos is the perfect example of this. Amazon operated at a loss for a very long time, and look at them now. It's nice to have suicide margins from the start, but it's not, strictly speaking, necessary. However, you should be as close to a suicide margin as possible. If you don't have a profit margin of at least 3X-5X from the very start, you need to find another product. After 10,000 units are sold, you should be very near your suicide margin requirements.

This is not a technical business "how to" book, so I won't go into microscopic details about finance, margins, and volume, but what I will say is that the lower your profit margin, the less likely you are to succeed.

With Herbal Ecstacy our costs were $0.25 (with packaging), and we sold it wholesale for $10 and retail for $20, so we actually had a 40X profit margin. The best part of it all… we had NO COMPETITION. We were the only game in town. 100% pure, blue ocean!

But when I was younger, I would just move fast and create a lot of problems along the way, and those problems might never get solved. Now that I'm older and have learned from those mistakes, I come up with solutions further upstream from my problems; before they can occur. I find solutions to problems that don't exist yet, and implement proactively.

Dan Heath is one of my favorite authors. Along with his brother Chip, they write some seriously epic books. This is something that Dan Heath talks a lot about in his book, *Upstream: The Quest to Solve Problems Before They Happen*, which just came out earlier in 2020. He looks at how an upstream problem-solving methodology can help businesses predict and address problems before they ever have a chance to impact you. In Heath's words, "Downstream actions react to problems once they've occurred. Upstream efforts aim to prevent those problems from happening." In the early days of Herbal Ecstacy, that was a skill that would have benefited me greatly, but I hadn't developed the ability to think ahead like that just yet. I was always reacting to problems, rather than finding solutions to them ahead of time.

Hence, the need for suicide margins.

Despite all the mistakes I made, though, the company just kept getting bigger and bigger. We went from selling $100,000 every couple of months, to selling that almost every day. Then we started branching out into a bunch of different products. We weren't just making pills with ephedra, we were making drinks and herbal cigarettes, and entirely new legal highs that didn't contain ephedra at all.

Herbal Ecstacy was one part of the business, but we built it out into a multifaceted retail empire. We sold millions of dollars in T-shirts, and there are still people today walking around Venice Beach wearing our Ecstacy butterfly shirts. We printed them ourselves, using cheap factory cast-offs from American Apparel (an L.A. based T-shirt manufacturer), and figured out a way to line them with glow-in-the-dark fabric, so they sold like crazy at the raves.

We also started our own globally syndicated magazine and record label, and produced albums for talented local musicians, one of whom in particular was pretty good and ended up selling millions of copies. We branched out and developed our own shampoo, our own branded drug detection tests, and detox drinks which people in all walks of life could drink to pass a drug test (if they'd been buying our competitors' illegal products, instead of ours) and even sold a kit to test real ecstasy for purity. We had thousands of "franchise" Ecstacy stores and satellite stores that carried Herbal Ecstacy in a special section dedicated to our products.

One day, I was hanging out at Rob's place with him and Krissy, and it was the typical sort of gathering that he always had going on. A group of half-naked masseuses were draped over the sofas in his living room, drinking and sharing around a tray of cocaine while customers came and went up the stairs in the foyer. I had an herbal cocktail with some juice mixed in, but I politely declined every time the tray was passed around. Even though I had the money now to afford an expensive cocaine habit, developing one was pretty low on my to-do list at the time. I didn't mind if the others did it around me—nearly every one of my employees came to work high on some substance or other—but it just didn't seem particularly attractive to me, personally.

So I just sipped my drink, sitting back in one of Rob's leather chairs and smirking softly to myself. I was just approaching my 18th birthday, and already I had a fat bank account, a CEO managing all of our promotions, and was spending my Tuesday afternoon in a beachfront mansion, surrounded by hot women in lingerie. Life was pretty fucking good. I was living out every teenage boy's fantasy, and thinking back to where I'd been just a few short months earlier—sleeping in my broken-down Lincoln and reciting
Think and Grow Rich to myself to keep me going—I couldn't help but grin. I'd always known I was going to do it, but *damn* did it feel good, knowing that I actually had. And the only place to go from here was up.

As I was ruminating on how sweet my first taste of success was, another model-cum-masseuse came traipsing down the staircase in a bikini top and a pair of boyshorts. She padded barefoot into the living room, grabbed a drink, and once she'd done a sweep of the room and determined there were no free seats available, she walked over and plopped herself down in my lap without so much as a "hello."

I certainly wasn't complaining about being used as her recliner. She was stunning, and I could fully appreciate her gorgeous body from this up-close vantage point. When she leaned forward to help herself to a line of Rob's coke, the quality of my view increased substantially.

"What's your name, sweetie?" She asked, wiping her nose and pivoting around to smile down at me.

"Lisa's new," Rob explained quickly, as though apologizing for her ignorance. "This is Shaahin, babe. He's my boss, not a customer."

"Ohh, a *boss*, huh?" Lisa chuckled. She had a drawling East Coast accent that made her sound both tough and cute at the same time. "You look a little young to be a boss to me."

I arched an eyebrow up at her. She'd started toying with my long hair, which now hung past my shoulders. "I'm very good at what I do," I said, with a casual shrug. She was beautiful. Her petite frame seemed to fit perfectly against mine, and her dark eyes glittered when she looked at me, like she was challenging me to some kind of duel. I could tell Lisa was fiery, and the way she was dangling her limbs over me said she was probably a pretty free spirit, just like me. I was instantly intrigued.

"And what is it that do you do, Shaahin?" She asked, that coy spark shining in her eyes as she slid an arm around my neck.

"He's the king of the thrill pill cult," Rob declared, hoisting his drink dramatically in the air, and all the masseuses fell into a fit of giggling. But Lisa kept looking at me with that inquisitive look on her face, a small smirk playing at the corners of her full lips. I met her gaze calmly, although inside I was roiling. I wanted her, and she knew it. Judging by that smirk, she felt the same way.

It wasn't long before we left and went back to my place, and after that night, she ended up staying for a week. Not only was she gorgeous, with dark, wavy hair that had been kissed gold in places from hours spent laying out in the California sun, wide brown eyes and a body to die for, but she was fucking crazy, in all the right ways. Lisa was a party girl with unlimited amounts of energy, and when we went to raves, she could stay out dancing long after even my feet gave out—and she wasn't even used to parties like these in the way that I was. She'd recently moved to L.A. from Jersey and had the typical spitfire attitude that you'd expect from an Italian-American girl from the mafia capital of the United States. She took zero BS, from me or from anybody else, and when she got angry, she'd curse you out so hard, you thought she'd been possessed by a convict sailor. But she also had a softer side, which not many people got to see. She had come out here to make a name for herself, and was driven to succeed in her own sphere as a dancer, so she understood my own ambitions and my dedication to my business. She was easy to talk to, and I quickly found myself looking forward to getting back home at the end of a crazy day to tell her all about the weird stuff that had gone on with the company. She shared my excitement and supported me in what I was trying to achieve.

Lisa never gave me a hard time for going days or weeks without calling, because I was wrapped up in a new distribution deal or some marketing campaign that we were executing, and while she knew I was never going to be 100% faithful to her—not at that time in my life—when I was with her, I was with only her. She seemed to be okay with the fact that the first woman in my life was always going to be Herbal Ecstacy, and I loved her for that. No other girl at the time was ever so understanding about my dedication to my work.

I also was able to keep tabs on Rob and the goings on inside his Venice Beach operation, with Lisa acting as my spy, of sorts. She would report back to me on the crazy parties that happened and the things Rob said about Herbal Ecstacy, because I still didn't completely trust the guy with handling the PR aspect of the business.

By the end of that week, Lisa had become my unofficial girlfriend.

She still kept her own apartment in town, but soon she had basically moved in with me, spending most of her free time hanging around my apartment or accompanying me to raves. She decided to give up the lingerie massage job in order for her to take up a lucrative bikini modeling and stripping career. I was fine with it, as long as there was no <cough> "touching" involved—I even asked Rob for help with connecting her to the right people to book more jobs. Her career started picking up, and Lisa was out of the house most nights at the strip club or doing photoshoots, but I didn't mind too much. When she was away, I could invite as many women over as I wanted to—and there was no shortage of them lining up to go out with me in those days. We had an understanding, or so I had thought.

Within just a few months of starting the business, I was able to buy myself a house on Malibu's famed Celebrity Row, and I moved in next door to Hollywood's elite. As soon as I did, Rob and I started organizing these huge, blow-out parties at my place and using connections in the entertainment industry to ensure my gatherings were always full of the biggest names in town. Those sorts of people were perfect brand ambassadors for us, and once they'd tried Herbal Ecstacy, they always came back for more, and told their friends about it, too. Soon, I was getting calls on my pager regularly, asking me to come by some Hollywood party and drop off pills for the guests, and I quickly became a regular fixture at these events, striking up new friendships with my famous clientele. None of them knew who I was or where I'd come from, but they all loved me (naturally, since I was supplying them with drugs to keep their crazy escapades going all night long). But they also seemed intrigued—how had this young kid appeared seemingly from nowhere and now was popping up everywhere all over town?

It's like people could smell the success wafting off of me, even if I did still mostly walk around in jeans and T-shirts, with my long, straight hair hanging loose down my back. Models, celebrities, businessmen—all of them seemed to suddenly gravitate toward me, drawn in by the magnetic energy that the buzz around our product had created. Most days, I still couldn't believe how well I was doing—I was only 17, but I had a hot girlfriend, a beautiful home, and money pouring into my account from the sales of Herbal Ecstacy. I spent my nights at parties and raves, not just to keep an eye on my employees, but also to let loose and enjoy the freedom that I'd finally won for myself. Rob was helping me grow the business to new heights, and while we still weren't a mainstream brand yet, our domination of the underground party scene was basically complete.

And still, that was just the very beginning.

By the time I was 18 years old, I was earning well over $350 million dollars a year.

With that level of success comes exponentially more problems, and that was something I was only just figuring out for myself. One day, I opened a letter and found that it contained a bill from the IRS to the tune of $2 million. I suddenly realized I needed an attorney, fast.

Rick, my neighbor, who was a semi-popular musician at the time, recommended that I talk to a lawyer friend of his, named Tom, even though he warned me ahead of time that he was a bit of a crazy guy.

Tom was, indeed, a crazy guy. He was a good-looking dude in his thirties with a license to practice law, but also a bit of a vacant stoner— like a real-life Dr. Gonzo, Benicio del Toro's character from *Fear and Loathing in Las Vegas*. I'm pretty sure he had just barely passed law school by the skin of his teeth, but he did have an actual law degree, although I later found out that his license was suspended for non-payment of dues. He later got it reinstated, but that alone was enough to tell me that he was a little sketchy, to say the least.

He was also a bit of a ladies' man, and because of his blue-eyed, all-American look, he always seemed to attract beautiful women in droves. His house almost looked like he was running a saucy massage parlor operation like Rob and Krissy's, because he seemed to have about 12 different girlfriends living there all at once. Well, like Rob's place, if you let a bunch of animals and hippies loose in it.

Tom was a hippie and a vegan himself, but his girlfriend-in-chief, Becky, was a super-hippie. I was a strict vegan, and was in those days a pretty strong advocate for veganism as a lifestyle. When I went on dates, I'd tell girls that I would buy them anything they wanted, but that if they ordered meat, I wouldn't pay for it. It was just against my principles. But Becky was a whole different story. She was downright fanatical about veganism, to the point where she used to go out in the middle of the night before Yom Kippur to break into the homes of Hasidic Jewish families in the area, and rescue the chickens that they were planning on slaughtering the next day. Then she brought them home, and they all roamed around free in her and Tom's house, until she could find a new home for them or someone to adopt them.

Only, I don't think very many people wanted to adopt chickens, so they were just there, shitting all over the house and leaving eggs everywhere that nobody ate—because we were all fucking vegan. It was just insane. Everyone in Santa Monica knew her as the "Chicken Lady," and while she was smoking pot with her hippie friends downstairs and wrangling these dozens of free-range birds, Tom was literally living in the attic of his own home, just to have somewhere to work where he wasn't constantly distracted by clucking and Becky's long-winded vegan activist rants. They also had a sort of open relationship going on (mostly unbeknownst to Becky), so whenever Tom descended to the chaos below, he'd have his arm around some 20-something year old hippie chick, smoking a joint and looking like he had no idea what was going on, but didn't have a care in the world. Becky always seemed angry and jealous and turned on at the same time. You never knew what was going on with them.

The most insane part about it? Tom didn't mind in the slightest. He seemed perfectly delighted to live this weird, wacky, hippie lifestyle, with his hot, crazy girlfriend turning his house in Santa Monica into a barnyard, and all his possessions crammed into the attic. He didn't seem stressed out at all by it all—he just took all the absurdity smoothly in stride.

So of course, when I first met him, I thought to myself, *Yes, this is the perfect guy to be my attorney.* If he could handle Chicken Lady-levels of crazy, surely he could handle Herbal Ecstacy.

I asked him how much lawyers usually make in a year, and he told me $75,000, so I offered him double or triple (I forget which), and he accepted on the spot. I don't think poor Tom really knew what he was agreeing to at the beginning. I gave him an office of his own in our new company headquarters, which was still completely bare, without a single chair or table in sight (much like my mountain house getaway in Topanga), and handed him a huge stack of motions and legal notices on the first day he started. It was enough work to keep an entire law firm busy for months, but Tom was just one guy without so much as a secretary, and he knew fuck all about pharmaceuticals or international business law. We kept him extremely busy. And, bless him, he tried really hard, and was incredibly loyal, but also equally incompetent.

I remember I used to see him at the office, walking around looking all disheveled, like he just stumbled out of the Chicken Lady's den, and he'd reek of weed and the unmistakable scent of the chicken coop, but he'd be off on his way to do some deposition for a big federal case we were embroiled in. It was bizarre.

Tom was a fun-loving guy, and there was no shortage of fun when you were working for me in those days. As I said, Tom did enjoy partying, doing drugs, and anything else that went against convention—that, combined with the fact that he had no issue being on call 24/7 to handle all of our insane legal needs, made him kind of the perfect lawyer for me. He was completely in over his head, but, despite all his shortcomings, Tom knew how to get the job done.

We had a discussion about the fact that Herbal Ecstacy was very likely going to be facing a lot of FDA charges and multiple other lawsuits, on top of those we were already being slapped with, so he quickly fashioned himself as an FDA attorney. Before the internet, it wasn't much of a hassle to forge a new career identity and come up with fanciful stories about your past pedigree. So that's what Tom did. He didn't actually learn anything new about FDA case law, he just told people that he had.

Tom was somewhat of a master bullshitter in that way. I remember once, I found out that a wacky employee of mine—a warehouse employee who'd been an unpaid intern just a few weeks before—had somehow ended up representing us at court for some preliminary hearing. When I heard that Jared from logistics had been stuffed into a suit and sent with Tom's business cards to the courthouse to pose as our attorney, I (understandably) freaked out, and drove over to Tom's house to confront him about it. When I got there, he was lounging by the garden, with a sleepy, satisfied, super-stoned look on his face and a cute redhead on his arm, like he didn't have a care in the world. Becky was huffing about and giving them side eye as she tended to one of the chickens.

"Why are you not in court right now?!" I demanded, staring at the pair of them in disbelief as they both broke out in a fit of uncontrollable giggles.

"I'm too high! Oh, have you met Ruby? Isn't she lovely, Shaahin?" He sighed cynically, running his hands through her amber hair. "How could I leave her?" When he saw that I was only mildly amused by his ridiculously high state, he pouted at me imploringly. "I'm sooooorry! I'll never do it again, I swear. Besides, it was only a simple motion filing. A monkey could do it."

I sighed, too, and sat down to join them in the garden. I never could stay angry at Tom for very long, despite the crazy things he put me through sometimes.

Nevertheless, he did get the job done, like I said. Even if it was often in fairly unconventional ways.

For instance, one night, the girls from Tom and Rob's places were hanging out with us at a little cabin that I kept as a mountain retreat, and they were complaining about how bored they were all the way out there in the middle of the woods, with nothing to do. So we decided to call some people over for a party.

In typical fashion, as soon as the word got out that I was having a party, everybody in town showed up. The next thing I knew, there were hundreds of people at my humble little hunting cabin in the woods. So much for a peaceful escape. Soon, everybody was naked, drunk, high, or a combination of all three, and most of us were hanging out in the jacuzzi together. Loud music was blasting, despite the fact that it was now the middle of the night, and it probably reverberated through the canyons so that people miles away could hear us, but they were mostly too far gone to care. It looked more like a rave in downtown L.A. than a party in a quiet, woodsy neighborhood.

Sometime around 1 AM, we heard the sound of sirens approaching, and I immediately understood that somebody had called the police on us. I was, at that time, sitting in the jacuzzi, surrounded by several equally-naked females and two of my favorite pit bulls, who had jumped up on the sides of the hot tub to get in on some of the action. Everybody was having a great time, until the sheriffs showed up, pointing their flashlights around and demanding to know who was the owner of the house. Avoiding being in the public eye was still a pretty high priority for me at that time—especially with the mounting lawsuits and increased media attention, the last thing I wanted was for word to get out that I'd been getting into trouble with the police—so I needed someone else to deal with this for me. That, and I couldn't stand up out of the jacuzzi without some level of embarrassment.

That was when Tom rose to the occasion. I told the officer to talk to my attorney, and pointed toward Tom. He was on the other side of the yard, currently locked in what seemed to be a drinking match with a big-breasted stripper, while several other scantily-clad women cheered them on.

The policeman looked at my lawyer, then back at me, with a look of pure confusion on his face. He asked, "*He* is your attorney?" Clearly, he thought I was bullshitting him. But I just nodded, and so he shrugged and walked off to confront him, casting me a look that said he'd deal with me later.

But Tom didn't let that happen. He told the girls to take me inside, so that he could speak to the officers alone. I'm not sure what happened after that. But what I do know is that, whatever he did, it worked.

We had to turn down the music for a little while, but the cops never came back again. When I came back out in the morning, I noticed the sheriff was naked in the jacuzzi with one of the other partygoers, passed out with his head lolled back against the rim of the tub. The only thing he was wearing was a fluffy Hawaiian lei, floating around his neck in the water. He didn't seem at all like he'd minded too much about the party getting out of hand, after all.

And that was how it was in those days. We'd do something crazy, Tom would magically manage to clean up the mess, and then we'd do it all over again the next day, louder and wilder than the day before.

Tom was good at fixing potentially-awkward situations, but when it came to actual lawyering, he was grossly underprepared for the kinds of legal issues the company had to deal with. It was crazy, having this somewhat bedraggled and grossly ill-equipped stoner guy wandering around trying to defend us against IRS and FDA and FTC actions— every three-letter agency you can think of, they probably sent us at least a warning letter or two over the years. And Tom had no idea how to handle any of it, really, but somehow, despite his terrible organizational abilities and his wacky personal life, he did usually manage to pull it off in the nick of time, every time.

I remember one day, I was sitting with Lisa out on the balcony of my Malibu house, when I saw Tom pull into the driveway in his beat-up, old, auction-bought Police Interceptor. I walked over to the railing to see what had brought him to my house in the middle of the day, and he got out of the driver's seat wearing just his boxers, a few chicken feathers blowing out of the car door in his wake.

"She's fucking crazy!" Tom yelped up at me, his blonde curls all askew. It was obvious who he meant. "She's convinced I'm gonna leave her, and she's been chasing me around with a meat cleaver all morning, threatening to kill me or herself, or both! I didn't know what to do. I just grabbed my keys and ran," he finished breathlessly, leaning against the hood of his car for support.

"Tom, don't we have a deadline for submitting that counterclaim today?" I asked, wondering how he planned to finish the necessary paperwork when he was standing half-naked in my driveway.

"I know! I know! I had to leave my computer, though. That's why I'm here—do you have a spare I could use?"

I sighed and looked over at Lisa, who just laughed to herself and shook her head as she flipped through the magazine she was reading.

I ended up giving him some clothes to borrow and taking him to a store in town to buy him a laptop to use until he could regain access to his attic office to reclaim his own.

He crashed in my spare bedroom for a few nights, and then his fight with Becky ended as abruptly as it had begun, and he was back living in the chicken sanctuary, happy and oblivious as ever before.

Journal Entry: Reality Distortion Field

	See Opportunity Everywhere	Suicide Margins
What is it?	Seeing opportunity everywhere is the ability to look beyond fear, failure, and hardship to find new ways to win, in any environment.	Suicide margins give you enough profit from each sale (at least 10x costs) to make mistakes and have it not matter.
Why is it important?	Because having the agility and innovation to turn problems into solutions, and challenges into opportunities, is what being an entrepreneur is all about. If you can't see the opportunity, you better believe someone else will.	Early on in business, you're bound to make some mistakes. Some of them will be expensive. With suicide margins, you have a cushion to recover. Without them, you're in danger of failing before you even get going.
How to win:	Create your own path, rather than following the one which the world presents you with. Sometimes, we feel like life is giving us no choice, even if there's always a choice. But if all you do is react to circumstances as they happen to you, you'll never be able to take control of a situation and turn it to your advantage. Even when things seem insurmountable, focus on solutions and invent your own way of getting there.	Find a product or service that you can deliver on a mass scale with very low production costs, and a way of distributing it easily and cheaply. If you're looking into a business model that doesn't have 10x profit margins, look for one that does. Or keep some pretty large reserves handy to cover any emergency expenses.

CHAPTER 8:

SELL THE SIZZLE, NOT THE STEAK.

I guess there were always some red flags there with Lisa, but I just didn't register them at the time. I knew she probably did more drugs than could be reasonably considered healthy, and she had mentioned that she used to deal them a little herself back East, and, well, I'd met her at Rob and Krissy's place, so that in itself was also kind of a warning sign. But at the time, I didn't care. She was gorgeous, fun to be around, and most importantly, a good person at heart. Probably the best person in my life, back then, and the only one I could be sure really wanted me for me, because she'd been around since the beginning, before we were making the really insane amounts of money. So I ignored all the other stuff. None of that mattered to me.

Soon I learned that Lisa may have had some deeper issues than I had ever imagined. I'd always known that she was slightly unstable, and I had picked up on the fact that she had a slightly checkered past back in New Jersey, but I never realized how much baggage she was really dealing with until the day she almost got all of us arrested.

One weekend, Rob, Lisa and I drove up to San Francisco together for a small rave, where we had a stall selling Herbal Ecstacy. A few of our guys were coming with us to man the booth, and they took a van with all of our product and signage and headed straight to the convention center, but we decided we were going to stop off in Haight-Ashbury along the way to visit a few stores there that stocked our pills. In those early days, we were still a new company and had to build up our relationships with our clients, so we liked to maintain a personal rapport with them as much as we could. We had boxes and boxes of Ecstacy in our little pseudo-drug dealer baggies in the back of Rob's hatchback, ready to restock the head shops in Haight-Ashbury when we got there, and were planning on trying to secure some more long-term distribution agreements with the stores who usually sold the highest volumes. But for some reason, Rob—the ostensible CEO of our little empire—had decided to drop acid that morning, together with some actual E pills, a combination which I believe is called "candy flipping," for reasons which remain unknown to me.

All I know is, he was tripping the fuck out on the drive up there, and so was Lisa, who had joined him in his narcotic indulgence prior to us leaving. Just as I was pulling off the freeway, the two of them were peaking, their eyes as round as saucers and wearing these dumbstruck expressions, like they were both two steps closer to God. And that's when I saw the blue and red flashing lights behind us, and heard the unmistakable "woot-woot" of a police's siren signalling me to pull over.

Now, I was as sober as can be, but with these two idiots tripping faces in the seats next to me and a trunkload of pills in some pretty suspicious-looking baggies, I definitely had cause for concern being stopped by police right at that moment.

At this point, Rob couldn't even formulate sentences. He was talking all kinds of crazy mumbo jumbo, describing whatever he was seeing in the psychedelic alternate universe he currently inhabited, so for all intents and purposes, he was completely useless to me. I'm also pretty positive that he had more drugs on him, since he normally had a few different substances stashed about his person at any given moment, and I'm sure that Lisa had at least some weed on her, for sure.

I turned around, and saw that Lisa had gone totally white. In a shaky voice, she said, "Look, I gotta tell you, there's a warrant out for me in New Jersey. I can't be arrested by the police. They can't look at my ID or check my prints, otherwise we're gonna have serious problems."

That seemed pretty strange to me, but I didn't really have time to question her on it. The cop was already walking up to our car, and the last thing I needed was for him to overhear us talking about an outstanding arrest warrant.

So the cop walks up to the window, and I roll it down and give him my best, most upstanding-citizen smile, and he takes a look inside the car. He sees the two of them, just high as kites, their eyeballs popping out of their heads, and immediately tells us all to step out of the car.

I got out, and Lisa and Rob followed suit as quickly as their sorry mental states would allow.

"What seems to be the problem, officer?" I asked, totally innocently.

"What seems to be the officer, problem?" Rob blurted out, giggling to Lisa in a whisper.

The first thing the cop said was, "Have you kids got any drugs on you?"

"No, sir!" I replied, abashed. "Why would I have drugs on me?" Meanwhile, there were thousands of bags of unmarked pills, ready to burst out of the boxes in the trunk of the hatchback. A good look inside would show a sea of blue and red pills emblazoned with E on one side and a butterfly on the other. I remember thinking to myself, *Oh my god, this is it. It's all over. My young life has ended here and now.*

All of a sudden, though, Rob snapped out of it. It was like the word "drugs" hit him like a bucket of ice water, and he just straightened up, looked at the officer, and started speaking. Totally rational, logical, grammatically-correct sentences, when a moment before he'd been speaking in tongues. I think he may have even noted case law in Latin. Rob kind of reeked of white privilege—you know, an educated, good-looking guy from a well-to-do Jewish family—and he loved to take advantage of that fact at moments like this. "Officer, hey, you know, this is San Francisco," he broke in. "I grew up here. Did you grow up here?"

Of course, the officer *had* grown up in the area, and within seconds he and Rob were chatting about their respective childhood hometowns. Rob noticed he was wearing a Freemason's ring, so he started in on that next, talking about how his dad was a Mason also and what chapter did the officer belong to? Rob shook the man's hand with the "special handshake." *What the fuck is going on?* I thought to myself.

Immediately, you could see the cop start to soften a bit, because now he was fascinated by Rob. He didn't know whether Rob was a drug-addicted criminal, or if he was unknowingly friends with his dad. It was working really well, until a strange look slowly dawned on the cop's face.

Rob stopped talking.

The cop kind of fell out of his trance for a second, and said, "Wait… Wasn't there a third person with you?"

I looked behind me, and Lisa was gone. She was running off in a beeline toward the freeway underpass, quick as her tanned little legs could carry her. She was pretty far off already, and I guess the cop couldn't see her from where he was standing.

I was just about to start trying to smooth things over with the cop and find some way to explain away the totally sketchy optics of the situation, when Rob immediately jumps in and goes, "Oh, yeah, but we were just giving her a ride."

"What was her name?"

"Oh, Sara something, I think," I said quickly, before Rob had a chance to speak. He'd been too far gone to catch her warning in the car, and I didn't want him giving the cop her real name.

The cop was still a little suspicious, so he sent me to go sit on the curb while he and Rob talked it out. Even though he was still visibly tripping, he managed to hold a conversation with the guy for the better part of an hour, and I guess what he said was fairly convincing, because the officer walked over at the end of it and handed me the keys to the car. "Don't let him drive, okay? Just get him somewhere safely where he can cool off for the night."

"Of course, officer!" I assured him, and drove out of there as fast as we could without him pulling us over again for speeding. I couldn't believe our luck that he hadn't searched the car, and once we were out of sight, I leaned over and kissed Rob on his shiny, bald head. "That was amazing, man," I laughed. Rob dropped another tab of acid.

By the time it was all over, though, we couldn't find Lisa anywhere. I drove around by the overpass and the side roads nearby, but there was no sign of her. Now, mind you, this was before cell phones, or any of that stuff, so we didn't know how to call her. I was just hoping she'd show up at some point, or find a way to the hotel we'd booked for the night.

I drove around to our clients in Haight-Ashbury and got rid of all the pills from the back of the car, leaving Rob to trip out in the local psychedelic bookstore/headshop while I dealt with our customers, and then we made our way to the hotel. When we got there, Lisa had already arrived and was waiting for us in the lobby. Rob went off to his room to continue the journey into the depths of his own mind by himself, and Lisa and I checked into the suite I'd reserved for the two of us, with me already preparing what I was going to say to her about that afternoon's roadside debacle.

She rolled a joint once we got into the room, and drew her knees up to her chest in the center of the king size bed as she smoked it, looking smaller than I'd ever seen her before. She didn't even wait for me to ask before she started talking.

Lisa explained that she had gotten into trouble with the cops for dealing drugs back home, and been let out on bail before her arraignment. In that time, she went to visit a friend of hers who was dying in the hospital, a paraplegic girl that Lisa had grown up and went to high school with, and the two of them had struck a deal. Since they looked similar enough for it to be convincing, Lisa would take her ID and passport and skip out on her bail to start a new life in Southern California, using her friend's identity. That's when she'd met Rob and Krissy and started doing the massages.

Her name wasn't even Lisa—it was Janet!

Once I recovered from the initial shock of finding out that my girlfriend wasn't who she said she was, she hit me with another revelation: her ex-boyfriend, some relatively big-time drug dealer who had ties to the mob in Providence, was looking for her. She had sold drugs for him, and when she got caught by the police, she'd stolen some of his stash and a few thousand dollars from his apartment to fund her travels out west. Whether he wanted to kill her for her treachery or find her and take her back with him to Providence, she wasn't sure, but I could tell either option equally terrified her by the way she broke down toward the end of her story.

Pale, shaking and still wide-eyed from the last throes of her acid trip she started to cry; there was nothing I could do but hold her and tell her that it would all be okay. I was going to protect her. I wouldn't let anyone—not the cops, or her sketchy ex—do anything to her, not while I was there.

For the rest of the night, we stayed up, eating room service while I told her all the tricks Ed had taught me about what to say if the police stop you and ask for your ID. By the end of the night, everything was back to normal again between us. I joked about whether I should start calling her Janet now, and she teasingly smothered a pillow over my face, telling me she much preferred her life as Lisa, thank you very much.

And that was that. We never really talked about it again—that is, until the next time her past came back to catch up with her.

The Sizzle

"You never get a first chance to make a first impression."
Shaahin Cheyene

"A carbohydrate-rich, high in sugar, carbonated drink in an aluminum can." Sound appetizing? Or would you prefer: "Refreshing!"?

Every great salesman knows it's the sizzle and not the steak that sells. The steak, of course, is why the customer comes back, but the sizzle is what gets them there in the first place. They smell the savor of the meat cooking, hear the fat crackling as it hits the grill, and suddenly the only thing they want in the world is a steak. They can already taste it on their tongues, see themselves cutting into it while the juices seep out across their plate. It doesn't matter if, once it arrives, it's dry, well-done and tasteless—they've already ordered it. You hooked them. That's because the sizzle is the first impression you make on your customer, and the steak is the second.

This is why—as a wise man named Willy Wonka knew—the wrapper is always more important than the chocolate inside. Anyone can make chocolate, but it is only a few who have the vision to create a magic wrapper that will have the whole world beating down their door.

It's how you market your product that will make people find you, talk about you, and subsequently remember you, while the quality of your product is why customers will keep coming back for more, and recommend you to their friends.

With Herbal Ecstacy, we were so successful because we sold the sizzle. How did we do that?

Well, there are two ways to sell a product. The first is the oldschool way, which involves spending a lot of money on repetitive ads. Hit your customer over the head enough with the product, and they're bound to want it. This system does work, but you need to have piles of corporate cash and be ready to drive your message home with a sledgehammer over and over again.

The second way is to seduce your customer to fall in love with your product, to become unforgettable, and to create a state of being that your customer can't live without. This system requires little cash, and is truly the path of least resistance for the peaceful entrepreneur. Whereas the repetition system requires a sledgehammer to drive the nail home, this system requires 4 ounces of pressure, and the nail will happily insert itself into the wood.

One thing I learned from Ed about the importance of being able to influence people is that, if you do it really well, your marketing becomes automatic. And the key to that is eliminating your first impression. Slap a steak on a grill, and let the mouthwatering aroma bring the customers to you.

In business, as in life, people always say, "You never get a second chance at a first impression." But this is total BS. There is no such thing as a first impression. If you've done your job correctly, before your customer has ever seen your product or service for the first time, they should already have an impression. They're already dying to order it. In his book *Pre-suasion*, Professor Robert Cialdini (the author of the groundbreaking book *Influence*) breaks down this delicate art of making the sale before you even open your mouth.

So, in fact, the exact opposite is true. You never get a *first* chance to make a first impression.

As consumers we are emotionally motivated—it's not our logic that moves us to make the buying decision, it is our emotions. We buy things because of how they make us feel. If you can leverage the power of that emotional response, not just in how you create your marketing materials, but in your branding and the kind of associations that people automatically make with your product, then you've made a pre-first impression on your customer before they ever visit your store. And there's a whole discipline dedicated to doing this.

Neuro-Linguistic Programming, or NLP, is the science of conversational hypnosis. A methodology built on the principles of traditional hypnosis, NLP focuses on creating a walking, talking, hypnotic state and maintaining that state in yourself or another person throughout the course of your interactions with one another. In essence, what the savvy guerilla marketer does is tap into this system of pre-suasion to create a post-hypnotic state, meaning that we, the customers, are in their thrall long before we've ever held the product in our hands. We already have an emotional reaction pre-programed into us, because we've been primed by their marketing ahead of time.

Let me explain what I mean by that. Rather than creating a product name, you should instead "create a state." With Herbal Ecstacy, this was done with one word: Ecstacy. This said everything I needed to say, and instantaneously created a trance state in my customers. Your product name should always be provocative like this—that is to say, it should provoke a particular emotional state in the consciousness of your customer, while also being simple, straightforward, and to the point.

The same goes for your chocolate wrapper. Customers are bombarded with products and services on a daily basis, and most packaging looks the same. There may be a slight difference between each, but rarely is a product refreshingly or entirely new. So, in order to create a state, you have to make your product stand out from the crowd. No one wants to be ordinary; no one wants the exact same thing that everyone else has. Making your product stand out gives your customer the sense that they are unique, extraordinary, and smarter than the other people who didn't buy your product. This is creating a state. The name of your product is critical, since that's what forges the emotional connection between you and your customer, but it's your packaging and branding that firmly implants you in the mind of the customer.

In the pill business, everyone packaged pills in bottles. That was the industry standard at the time when I started the company. If you had a pill product, then it came in a white bottle, with a standard label. But who had decided that pills should come in bottles? Was there a committee somewhere that sat down and agreed that this is how pills were to be packaged and sold?

I decided to break this mold. With Herbal Ecstacy, first I sold it in plastic baggies like those used by drug dealers, further creating a state that linked my product to the emotional associations my customers already had when it came to designer drugs. That worked brilliantly, and people loved it. But as we started to be carried in more retail outlets and stores, we needed a new packaging design that still conveyed that state, but that could appeal to people when they were in a brightly-lit store, rather than in a strobe-lit warehouse rave.

So I created a small pyramid box to hold the pills, and printed them up in all types of crazy colors and sizes. We packaged the product exclusively in pyramids for years. It became our trademark in the marketplace. People knew that they could always buy a bottle from some other company, but if they wanted to stand out—if they wanted the true "feeling of Ecstacy"—they would buy the pyramid.

At one point, I went into a major vitamin chain that was carrying our product and noticed people coming into the store, not even looking on the shelf anymore. They simply grabbed a pyramid and checked out. It was so instantly recognizable that it stood out like a spotlight on the shelves, and people were instantly drawn to it.

The promise of a golden ticket inside the chocolate is what set Willy Wonka apart from the rest. So we made sure that our packaging promised a golden ticket inside, too. We used every tool available to achieve this end: impactful words, colors, shapes, sounds, smells—every sense we could play with, we did. It's not just about thinking outside of the box, it's about creating your own world that completely hypnotizes your customer.

Destroy the box. Then build your own reality.

The Steak

> *"Keep in mind that imagination is at the heart of all innovation. Crush or constrain it and the fun will vanish."*
> **Albert-László Barabási,**
> *Bursts: The Hidden Patterns Behind Everything We Do*

Now, Herbal Ecstacy was a good product, but it was also constantly being improved (mainly with the help of loyal, drug-addled rave addicts, who would take whatever we gave them under the guise of "free drugs"). We started off with fistfuls of goo-filled capsules, and ended up with five small, but powerful, tablets. In between, we had every incarnation imaginable. Was it a good product, and one that delivered on its promises? Yes. Were some incarnations better than others? Absolutely. But the fact is that it was the sizzle—the hype and propaganda—that brought the customers to our doorstep. The steak only kept them coming back. Once they were there, we had an opportunity to improve our product with their feedback, but we never would have even made it that far without the sizzle.

In retrospect, we could have been selling sugar tablets that were a complete placebo, and we still would have made millions. Although, I never really would have done this—the staying power of the products in the marketplace and the company's reputation would have been dismal, and, once word got out that they were just sugar tablets, we would have been done for. But there would have been a decent span of time to make a boatload of cash before that happened. The point is, not that I could have been selling sugar tablets, but rather that it's the sizzle that ultimately gave my product life and created a customer base. I learned that consumers ALWAYS judge a book by its cover. Always.

During the product development phase, I think the goal should therefore be to get your product to market first, and worry about improving and perfecting it later. It's almost always better to ship first, and have first-to-market advantage with an improvable product, than to wait and have a perfect product. The fact is, there is no "perfect product," and no matter what you do, you will never make it perfect. While you're nitpicking and guessing at what your customers might want, the competition will be busy taking their product to market, gaining market dominance, and eating up your potential customers. Better to create a niche, dominate it, and be first to market, then take your time and improve the product with the feedback of your customers.

As long as you've got a great sizzle, get the steak out the door and improve your recipe later. But don't spend years perfecting your marinade without ever firing up the grill and slapping it on there.

So, fast forward six months. We were selling hundreds of thousands of pills, all around the globe, and I was now a bona fide teenage millionaire.

Rob was fielding dozens of interviews a week, as the press started to wonder what this new product was and why it had garnered the attention of so many loyal customers in such a short period of time. We were signing new partnership deals in different countries every day, and constantly expanding our manufacturing capacity. I was getting checks for ridiculous sums of money dropped on my desk every hour.

Yet, incredible as it may seem, we had spent only a miniscule amount on advertising for Herbal Ecstacy. The reason for that is twofold. Firstly, the negative publicity we got echoed loudly in the global marketplace. The more they wrote about how dangerous we were, the more people believed that the product must work really well. Secondly, it was because we were so good at selling the sizzle that people just came to us, without us needing to devote a huge marketing budget to ads. We did buy ads, but those aren't the reason why we were so successful, so quickly.

Still, I figured that, with how well we'd done using organic growth alone, we could easily sell millions of units if we invested just a little in some targeted exposure opportunities.

While weighing up my options for the best channel to market our product, I came across a newspaper advertisement promoting the world's largest natural products trade show: The Natural Products Expo. I had heard of these trade shows previously, and since our product was, in essence, a natural herbal product, this seemed like a great opportunity to reach a new customer segment.

I made a few calls and booked us the largest booth they offered, right in the center of the convention hall, which is always the prime location to attract a lot of foot traffic at these events. I paid for a really extravagant booth to be made for us, decked out with all the technicolor, trippy trappings that Herbal Ecstacy was known for. Staying true to my vision of disrupting the status quo, I hired the most insanely beautiful women (dressed promiscuously, in boas and such) and several handsome men (to flirt with the vitamin buyer ladies) to run our booth at the event. We hired a live female DJ and dancers in cages. Well… they didn't say we couldn't do that stuff, right?

The day of the expo, our stall looked more like a turn-of-the-century opium den than a trade show booth. In a convention center that smelled like vitamins and tweed suits, our company oozed sex appeal and fun. Especially in the 90s, vitamin trade shows tended to be pretty drab, dull affairs, devoid of any glamour. The natural products space wasn't filled with luxurious vitamin brands and sexy energy drinks yet. It was very conservative and very boring. So Herbal Ecstacy was rather out of place, but that was exactly where we wanted to be.

It was around 1994, and the company was approaching the billion dollar threshold in terms of total revenues. Even though I wasn't fully aware of that fact yet myself, the rest of the world certainly seemed to be. A billion dollars is bound to generate interest from the media, so when we attended the show, the press, the attendees and even a majority of the businesses and vendors exhibiting at the show were all at our booth.

The reaction was insane. Imagine a sea of white plastic company banners and nondescript pill bottles, and then a huge party cruise liner rolling through, blasting music and setting off fireworks, while hot models toss armfuls of multicolored pyramid pill boxes to passersby. That was the kind of energy we had, and it blew every other exhibitor clear out of the water.

But, as it turns out, the sex and glamour we were selling did not align with the beliefs of the organizers. The show was run by a conservative religious group whose leader, albeit likely gay, was a devout Christian with a rather extremist, ultra conservative mindset. Clearly, there was some sensibility he had which we deeply offended.

Our booth was approached several times by the show's staff, and they tried everything they could think of to get us to leave. But we had paid for the booth and gone through great expense to be there, so I wasn't having any of it. Moreover, our pills were flying off the shelves.

Despite the antagonistic circumstances, the first day of the expo was a huge success. Thousands of people from all over the world came to our booth, and we were selling products by the bucketload. I think we must have made over a million dollars on that first day alone. So, naturally, I told Rob to flatly deny all their requests for us to quietly pack up and go, and things started to heat up from there.

The next morning, when the models were heading to the booth to set up for the second day, they were stopped by a dozen or so Tradeshow Union enforcers, who blocked them from reaching our stand. I showed up in time to see these big, burly guys sort of reticently leading the girls out, like the last thing they wanted to do was remove thirteen beautiful women from this otherwise-mind-numbingly-boring trade show. The girls tried to flirt with the union goons, which seemed to work for some time, but then their female union boss showed up, and all bets were off.

In addition to getting banned and booted from exhibiting at the event, they also made it clear that we were no longer welcome on the premises, and that we wouldn't be getting a refund of any kind. They couldn't even provide a rational reason for our expulsion—all they could muster was the weak excuse that we were immoral and "unchristian."

So we stood in the parking lot with our flat-packed booth, our staff looking glum, and a truckload of pills that were eager to be consumed. I decided that, given the success of our venture so far, it would be a waste to squander all the attention we'd garnered at the show. After a quick discussion, we decided to set up shop in the same town, and publicize it as our own alternative natural products expo. In fact, we agreed we were going to call it "The Other Natural Products Expo."

All we had to do was find somewhere to host it. Our little caravan set out down the road, and before long, we came across a restaurant called The Jolly Roger. As soon as I walked in, I could see it was the perfect place—it had a big dining hall, with enough room to set up the stage and comfortably fit hundreds of eager customers inside. I walked around for a few minutes, looking for the manager, and couldn't find anyone to talk to about booking the place for the week, but a few moments later, a middle-aged man arrived and introduced himself as the owner of the place.

"What can I do for you?" he asked, taking in our peculiar group with a quizzical expression. He didn't immediately curse us out for being sinners, so I took that as a positive sign.

I told him about the predicament we were in, explained that we wanted to rent out his restaurant for the whole week, and said that I was ready to pay any price he named.

I had been sure this plan would work, and would solve our problem of being stuck in this town with an insanely expensive booth and nowhere to set it up, but we were dealt another blow when the guy informed us that the banquet hall was booked until next month. Not willing to admit defeat, I pulled out $10,000 in cash from my briefcase and held it out to him. "I'm sure there's something you can do."

I could almost see the plump, balding man start to salivate as he looked down at the stack of bills. Before taking it, he glanced up at me once more, now looking even more confused than when we'd first walked in. I'd seen that look before—it was a face that said, 'Who the fuck is this long-haired little kid, and how does he have so much money in that briefcase?' But however strange he found the situation, especially with the circle of models and Venice Beach ravers behind me, and Mr. Clean standing in his suit with his thick arms crossed over his chest, the owner seemed prepared to let his curiosity lie.

After a few moments of silence, he smiled broadly and took the money. "Well, of course, there's something we can do," he said, shaking my hand energetically.

Just then, the stubby manager walked in, took one look at what was going on, and instantly his leathery face fell into a suspicious glare. "Jim, can I have a word?" He wasn't really asking. The manager grabbed Jim by the arm and hauled him over to the corner of the room, from where we could still clearly make out every word of their stage-whispered squabble.

"Why the hell not, Will?" Jim hissed, waving around the stack of $100s to emphasize his point.

"Jim! You know the lifestyle people have Saturday nights booked every week, and they've been about the only thing keeping us afloat. You wanna piss them off? For what? For some goons who we'll never see again past Sunday?"

The owner's fist tightened defensively around the money. There was no way he was going to give it back, not now. "Hell! I'm not losing this opportunity. I need the cash. Just have the kid talk to the lifestyle people and work it out!" He huffed, then stuffed the bills in his jacket pocket and marched off into the kitchens.

"Okay, kid," Will sighed, scrubbing a hand through his hair as he approached our group again. "We have a customer who's booked all the Saturday nights here indefinitely, but the thing is, they don't start their event until midnight. So, if you can work it out with them, we can give you the space. We just have to have you out of here at midnight, in any case." We agreed, and he told us to come back in an hour, so we could meet with their other customer and try to secure his blessing for the arrangement.

Still, I remember thinking it was all kind of strange. As we went out to find lunch somewhere more vegan-friendly than The Jolly Roger, I thought, *Why would they have to have us out at midnight? This is a banquet hall in a restaurant, attached to a convention center, in the middle of suburban America. What kind of event doesn't start until after midnight?*

I forgot to ask what the "lifestyle" group was, but a part of me wondered if they were maybe ravers or something, like us.

It wasn't a done deal yet, but in those days, I took every "maybe" as a "yes." So, over lunch, Rob made a call and got over 50,000 flyers printed that read: "Come join us at The Other Natural Products Expo." We designed the flyer like the front page of a newspaper, with black-and-white images of Rob, the models and I being kicked out of the show. Then, once we finished eating, we got the girls to sneak back into the event (by flirting with the union security goons again), and circulate the flyers around to all of the attendees. The word was out: our rogue show, which was to open later that night, was actually bigger and better than the original. People had been wondering where the fun booth had disappeared to, and now that they knew where to find us, it was pretty much guaranteed that The Jolly Roger was going to be at full capacity that evening. Now, all we had to do was make sure we had a venue for them to come to.

While the girls were generating a buzz around the event, Rob and I returned to the restaurant to meet the mysterious ringleader of the lifestyle people. When we got there, the banquet hall was equipped with disco rave lights, all ready to go, and I thought the riddle was pretty much solved at that point. Upon asking, we found out that the lights were for the group that came in after midnight, so it seemed like we'd be able to sell our products all night at our impromptu expo, and then carry on selling through till morning once the disco dancers arrived.

"What kind of group is this, again?" I asked Will while we waited for the other man to arrive, but he just shrugged and said he didn't know a thing about them, aside from the fact that they went by the name of "Alternative Lifestyles," or something like that.

A little while later, the guy we were waiting for showed up, and my first thought was that he looked like a lawyer or something. Everything about him was very clean and organized. He wore a conservative business suit, and nothing about him was peculiar or out of the ordinary in any way, except for the stud earring he wore in one ear. My gut told me that convincing him to split the place with us might not be so easy, after all.

I quickly went over and introduced myself, holding out a hand for him to shake.

"Hi, my name is—"

"Son, it's okay. They told me what you're after, and I don't think this is going to work out. They'll have to give you your money back," he said abruptly, not even waiting to hear who I was or what we wanted. Then he gestured the manager over, told him to have Jim give us back our money, and turned to walk out.

I dropped my still-unshaken hand down to my side. "Why is that?" I asked, taken aback by his rapid refusal.

"Well, we're a <cough> private membership organization, and our members value their privacy. We can't have just anyone here before we start." He spread his hands as if to say there was nothing he could do, and nothing more to be said on the matter.

Under the collar of his shirt, I suddenly spotted a small tattoo—a red circle with what looked almost like a "V" drawn inside—and it instantly triggered my memory. I'd seen that symbol before, and I knew what it meant.

"I understand," I said, nodding along to his concerns. "What kind of organization are you, if I may ask?"

"We're called Alternative Lifestyles, and we're a group for adults," was all he said.

Usually, I'm pretty controlled with my filters, but at that moment, I think my filters must have been broken.

"Holy crap… You're swingers!" I blurted out, with a chuckle of relief. The guy's eyes widened in alarm, and he looked over his shoulder like he was afraid someone might walk into the restaurant and hear me outing him. "That's awesome! I was worried you guys were a church group or something." He gaped at me like I was crazy.

The man self-consciously adjusted the collar of his shirt in an attempt to hide his swinger symbol tattoo, visibly uncomfortable. He neither confirmed nor denied my observation, but the look on his face told me I'd hit the nail on the head. Not ravers, swingers. A new customer segment to explore. Brilliant.

I could see he was uneasy, but that didn't mean I couldn't find a way for us to work together. I just needed to assure him that he could be open to negotiating with me, without any worries about his group's privacy. "Hey, I'm not looking to cause any trouble for you guys. I'm all about supporting alternative lifestyles, too," I smiled. "What's your name, sir?"

"I'm Beaver, and my answer is still no!" I tried hard not to chuckle. He looked like he wanted to shove me out the door and end this conversation immediately, his face beginning to flush with embarrassment. I don't think he was used to having people speak with him about his lifestyle choices quite so frankly.

"Listen, Beaver, I understand your concerns. I've actually learned a lot about groups like yours, and I have no problem with how you live your lives. In fact, we would love to be a part of your party, if you're open to it. We could even pay for the space here for you for a few weeks, as a show of gratitude for letting us be involved."

He began to shake his head disapprovingly. Then I said, "Ecstacy, Beaver."

"What?"

"There, I said it. I am in the Ecstacy business. Look, I know the supplies have dried up world wide—and no, I can't get you the good stuff that I am sure your "clients" are used to—but I think I can do one better. Share the space with us for a couple nights, and I'll make sure you have a supply of our legal version of ecstasy that's all the rage right now. I 100%

guarantee they will love it, no side effects and it's 100% legal. That's the best part!"

Beaver suddenly became more attentive, his wariness slowly giving way to curiosity. People usually do that when you mention money and/or drugs. "And what exactly is it that you do?" he asked cautiously.

"We're an international brand with revolutionary, completely natural products. We were in town for the Natural Products Expo, but the organizers took issue with all the beautiful models we brought to sell our supplements at the event, so we decided to host our own, here, at The Jolly Roger," I explained, and Rob held out one of our flyers for Beaver to take.

As he cast a thoughtful eye over the newspaper-style poster, I knew I had him just where I wanted him. So, I continued. "Beaver, I perfectly understand what it's like to be considered unconventional, and to not be accepted by those around you. I belong to an immigrant family, and I've gone through a lot to get to where I am now. But being a social misfit didn't stop me from building a multi-million dollar company, and it shouldn't stop you from doing what you want, either. I'm just saying, I don't see why we can't both pursue our way of life, without being a hindrance to the other."

By identifying with his pain, I had landed the final blow in the negotiation. Beaver let out a sigh and replied, "I suppose we can work out some kind of arrangement. Tell your people they can set up shop in the hall—we'll decide later what to do at midnight. But son, I expect you to make good on your promise."

"You bet, Beaver." I repeated, trying hard not to laugh.

With the venue secured and the swingers knee-deep in Herbal Ecstacy, I formally invited Beaver to attend The Other Expo. He agreed to stay for a bit to check it out, and we shared a table in the hall as the doors opened and the public started pouring in to make their purchases. As we watched the stream of eager local twenty-somethings and older herbal products buyers alike filling the restaurant, Beaver and I actually became friends. I told him about the rave scene and my run-ins with the LAPD as a kid, and he told me about swinging and how he'd built this private group to escape the judgmental persecution of his neighbors in the community. We both had some crazy stories to share, given the nature of the work that we did.

As it turns out, Beaver had actually heard of Herbal Ecstacy before, but he was pretty surprised to find out that the man behind it was really just a young guy who never even went to college. That kind of blew him away, but I could also see that it gave him a newfound respect for me, long-haired kid or no. All the hot models certainly made an impression on him, too. Before long, he invited all of us to stay for the Alternative Lifestyles event after the show. Rob dropped some acid and real ecstasy and ran in, making me promise not to mention it to his wife or girlfriend.

Once midnight rolled around, though, I was exhausted. We'd spent the whole day putting on this last-minute event, and the whole afternoon furiously selling product, but I felt inclined to hang around at least for a little while to check out the swingers' meet-up. I relieved some of the staff and pretended I worked the booth. I sold products face-to-face. It was the most fun I'd had all year. With the fog machines and party lights going, no one recognized who I was for the first time in a long time, and the feeling of making cash, person-to-person sales was glorious. I was just a kid, working a job, selling stuff behind the booth. Beaver was going to be my customer, after all, so it was the least I could do.

Without exaggeration, it was the most insane group of people I've ever seen, and the fact that they were now on Herbal Ecstacy only compounded the insanity to new levels. Fifteen minutes was enough for me to see that the product had been admirably well-received, as had the models we'd brought with us, and then, laughing off Beaver's coaxing attempts to get me to join in the party myself, I managed to slip out and get back to my hotel room safely.

Our little experiment had turned out to be a greater success than anything we could have imagined, because, despite getting kicked out of the main expo, we still managed to sell just as much as we had that first day of the week. The Jolly Roger could only hold so many people at a time, and so we had a huge line of people curving around the building every day, waiting to get inside and try our product for themselves. The packed parking lot and the crowds of people out front served as a better draw than our own promotional efforts ever could, and people kept turning up off the street just to see what all the fuss was about.

We sold millions of dollars' worth of pills that week, and I got regular orders from Beaver for the next few years, usually accompanied by a little note, thanking me for helping to make the world of swinging an even brighter place. That event opened the door to sex shops, like Larry Flynt's Hustler store, The Pleasure Chest in Los Angeles, and thousands of others around the world that started to carry Herbal Ecstacy. In the changeover from VHS to DVD (and then to digital), I was told that our pills were the only thing that kept their businesses afloat in those days. It just goes to show that failure—like getting booted from an event or being flat-out rejected by a potential partner—can actually turn into an amazing opportunity. There's almost always a way to translate a challenge into a success, if you're willing to find it.

And that's how it was for us at Herbal Ecstacy. Maybe I'd become adept at influencing people, like Jim and Beaver, to work with me, and I was even better at influencing customers to buy from me. Our marketing still cost us basically nothing, compared with what we were making in sales, but the show-stopping way we went about things brought us more customers than we could even handle. Money was coming in so fast that I couldn't deposit it in the bank fast enough. There were always bags and bags of it laying around the house, the office, in the trunk of my car—and it was only just getting started.

Journal Entry: Reality Distortion Field

	Sell the Sizzle, Not the Steak	Building Partnerships
What is it?	Sizzle over Steak means you should focus on building the buzz and excitement around your product, more than on perfecting the product itself.	Building partnerships is finding people who can benefit you on your journey and establishing lasting relationships with them.
Why is it important?	Because the feelings and ideas that are associated with a product are what attract customers to you for the first time. It doesn't matter how good your steak tastes—if they don't smell it cooking when they walk down the street, they'll never even know it exists.	Anyone can tell you that a good network is at the heart of all success—in life and in business. The more partnerships you have, the more opportunities there are to make more money (and more partnerships, and so on and so forth).
How to win:	By generating a huge amount of word-of-mouth or viral interest in your product. How? By playing to people's senses, desires, and existing associations. Link your product to something they know and love, and then design all aspects of your marketing and packaging to reinforce that association (and grab their attention). Worry about what's inside the package last.	Having a great network isn't just about being friendly or outgoing, it's about being able to intuit what's important to the person on the other side of the table and deliver on providing them value. Show your worth, and you'll earn a loyal partner that can consistently bring you business opportunities for years to come.

CHAPTER 9:
MAKING MILLIONS

"It's not red, you dumbass! It's Rosso Corsa." I said proudly to my friend as he mocked my "small penis" (mainly out of jealousy) for getting a red Ferrari. "Rosso Corsa is the fucking international motor racing color of Ferrari. It's Italian, asshole."

That was the color of the car in that coffee table book Kal stole for me for my 13th birthday. Like most 13-year-old boys, I remember drooling over those cars—much like the *Playboy* centerfolds, which I knew I had no chance of ever touching either.

I always wanted that car, but truth be told, if you had told me a few years earlier that I would be sitting inside a fancy restaurant eating (rather than doing the dishes while some big wig lived it up), with that exact car parked outside waiting for me, I wouldn't have believed you.

Now, I finally had it. My first Ferrari—brand new, shiny, Rosso Corsa red. I even had a beautiful blonde in the seat next to me, to top it all off. Things were going good—better than I ever could have imagined, really. Then I had a moment that made it even sweeter.

It was the mid-90s, and my model date and I were heading out to a new restaurant opening in L.A. When I pulled up in front of the valets and the small crowd of paparazzi gathered in front of the restaurant we were going to, I got out of the car, and there was this guy just staring at me, kind of frozen with a mix of disbelief and reddening fury. I was taken aback by the intensity of the hatred in his eyes, and then I suddenly realized where I knew him from, and why he looked like he was about to start foaming at the mouth with rage. It was my old boss—the same comic book-like tyrant that had beaten me with his cane when he found me sleeping behind the copy machine in the middle of the night.

Here I was, driving a car that's worth more than what he'd ever make in his life, and he just despised me for it. I was some no-good, vagrant kid in his opinion, yet I'd somehow managed to achieve success in an unbelievably short period of time. You could see the incredulity mixed with his rage. He probably thought I stole the car, and was debating whether or not to try beating me with his cane again.

He was a tyrant, who enjoyed being able to play God in his own little world, and he'd loved using that power over me when I was at his mercy. You know, like when you go to the post office, and you just have a simple task to do, like mailing something, but the postal worker holds the key to that, so, in the Post Office world, they are automatically God. And they take that little sliver of power that they have in their own limited sphere, and they milk the shit out of it. Until you take them out of that environment, and then they're confronted with the reality of their own impotence. That's what happened, and fuck did it feel good.

He couldn't make sense of what he was seeing. It just wasn't computing, and he was turning red, like he was about to explode. I looked at him, and everyone else was staring at him too, at this point, but he was frozen there, just not moving.

So I turned around, walked up to him, shook his hand, and told him my name, all with a broad smile on my face. He remembered who I was, all right, but I had just wanted to make *extra* sure.

The tyrant said nothing. He just sputtered wordlessly, his hand numb with shock when I gripped it and manually waved his arm up and down for the handshake. His eyes kept darting between me, the Ferrari, and the model, then back again, but he still couldn't manage to formulate so much as a "hello."

Then, I handed the keys to the valet, held out an arm to my date, and walked inside.

It was at that moment that I knew I had arrived.

This was the summer of '94, the company was doing great, we had so much money pouring in that I'd ceased even trying to keep track of it all, and I could look around at what I'd achieved and feel pretty proud of this insane empire I'd become the king of. But that wasn't even the peak of our climb. After we did Lollapalooza, that's when things started to really snowball out of control.

Lollapalooza music festival had debuted in 1991, and was a huge success throughout the country, drawing tens of thousands of teenage misfits and oddballs, who all flocked to the event to get messed up, see their favorite bands, and flail their limbs to the music. Naturally, when the tour came to Los Angeles, the party-loving youth of California all descended upon the festival for the weekend. Everyone, from metalheads and punks to ravers and hippies, was there— in other words, all of our typical target customers. I saw it as a great opportunity for me to put my product in front of a huge audience, most of whom would no doubt be eager to get their hands on a pill that would help them keep thrashing in the mosh pits all day.

We got a booth in the heart of the festival grounds, amongst all the other vendors who were lazily hawking their wares, most manned by scruffy pubescent rocker dudes who barely had the energy to glance up when a customer stopped to browse at their shop. That's kind of the standard practise when it comes to selling stuff at festivals. Of course, that's not at all how we were going to do things.

I wanted a sure-fire way of capturing everyone's attention, and getting our product out to as many of the festival-goers as possible in the two days we were there. To do that, we had to create a sizzle, to pre-sell the product in a way that would have all these people beating down our door.

In my opinion, selling is all about influencing people—convincing them to buy your product. One of the best guides I've found on how to do this is Robert Cialdini's *Influence: Science and Practice.*

In this book, Cialdini teaches the skill of exploiting the human psyche in order to succeed in any business. He talks about how human beings generally make decisions based on a common set of psychological factors, and how knowledge of these factors can give you an unfair advantage when it comes to marketing your product. In the book, Cialdini goes through the six principles of influence that help you use human psychology to your advantage in business, and I highly recommend it to anyone who wants to learn how to persuade or better yet as he says "pre-suade" people to buy your product like crazy. One of his principles, in particular, was really influential for me: social proof.

Social proof is based on the psychological phenomenon of normative social influence, which states that nothing attracts a crowd quite like a crowd. People have a desire to fit in, to be a part of the newest "big thing" that all their peers are doing, so once your customer sees other customers buying and loving your product, they're already predisposed to buying and loving your product, too. Even if they've never seen your ads, or your product in real life. Their peers are what give them their first impression of what you're selling.

At Lollapalooza, we used social proof so well to our advantage that it almost backfired. We pre-suaded people to buy our product so effectively that we actually had more customers than pill-packed pyramids to sell.

The people visiting the festival were hearing some crazy stories about the impact of this totally herbal product from those who had already tried it, so they were eager to find out for themselves. Just like at The Other Expo, people lining up to buy our product acted as social proof for those who weren't yet aware of it. We had more attractive models circulating through the festival grounds in the early hours of the first day, bringing more people to our stall to try Herbal Ecstacy, and the line grew even more.

The whole thing was carefully constructed to produce a buying frenzy amongst our customers. However, even I was surprised with the response we got at Lollapalooza.

The massive line created a knock-on psychological effect, one which Cialdini also discusses in his book: the impact of scarcity. When customers perceive that a product might not be around forever, they suddenly need to have it, now, before stocks run out.

People thought, with the volume of customers coming in, they had to grab their spot in line as soon as possible, and once they made it to the sales counter, everybody bought as much as they could afford on the spot. Some even booked orders to take back with them after the weekend, and paid over-the-top prices, since we had a markup to account for the festival's cut of the sales.

Then, all of a sudden, we saw a group of angry beer vendors crowding around our stall, elbowing their way through the queues to come shake their fists at us and complain. At first, I was like, *What's going on here? Why are they so angry?* And then I realized what it was that had gotten them so upset—nobody was buying beer anymore. The line in front of Herbal Ecstacy's stand literally wrapped around the main stage, almost encircling half the stadium, and meanwhile, the beer tents looked like a ghost town. It was insane. I told the beer vendors that I wasn't really sure what they wanted me to do—stop making so much money? I wonder how they would have responded if I told them that on their busiest sales day ever.

The only problem was that we weren't actually prepared to handle that level of traffic. I'd known we were going to sell a lot, so we had thousands and thousands of pyramids with us, but all of them were sold out within a few hours. To keep our doors open and prevent the long line of customers from turning into an angry mob and attacking our stall, I had to send people back and forth to our warehouse all day to restock our supplies. However, we only had one truck with us, and the journey took more than two hours round trip, so by the time they returned with the new pills, we were already completely sold out of the units we had with us in the booth. We needed more trucks, immediately, so I gave some of my employees a bunch of cash and told them to go out and buy us a few used RVs. Then we had several vehicles all traveling between the festival and the warehouse, and our stocks never ran out, no matter how much people bought.

That whole weekend was a total blur. I was buying RVs, sending people with duffel bags full of cash one way and duffel bags full of pills the other way, and I didn't have a moment to count any of it, but I think we must have sold more than $2 million in that weekend alone.

To top it all off, we had all-access backstage passes for the whole weekend, so I spent most of my time around the main stage, selling pills to the bands and roadies who were headlining the tour.

I remember walking in at one point and the Beastie Boys were there. They had brought a group of Tibetan monks with them who were all backstage in their saffron robes, chanting away while everyone was high on Herbal Ecstacy. This was during their Buddhist phase, if you recall those days.

"Shaahin, man," the band's roadie exclaimed when he saw me, stumbling over to throw an appreciative arm around my neck. "This stuff is *amazing*. I've got to get some more from you before you go."

"I'm here all weekend, my friend," I chuckled, patting him on the shoulder. "You know where to find me."

One of the roadies suddenly broke in, disrupting our business chat. "Dudes, help me convince the monks to try this stuff!" He was waving a pyramid of Herbal Ecstacy in his hand.

"Pretty sure Buddhist monks can't consume anything that alters their state of mind, bud," I informed him. He was high on pills and gripping a massive blunt in one hand, and I don't even think he noticed my perfectly reasonable interjection. The roadie bounded off, almost knocking over a few Tibetan singing bowls as he went to go try and shove some Herbal Ecstacy down a disgruntled monk's throat.

Anyways, it was a truly insane week, with us following the tour to all of its California dates, and by the end of it, I'd made a bunch of new connections with people in the music industry, which opened up a whole new avenue of sales possibilities for us around the globe.

> **"Absorb what is useful. Discard what is not. Add what is uniquely your own."**
> **Bruce Lee**

Why can good childhoods and decent upbringings still lead to selling drugs?

The answer is simple: aside from the lure of fast and easy money it's because there's so much demand for drugs, and insane profits to be made. However, there's also huge risk involved. Getting caught means you give up your whole life. That's why you need a hack. A hack is a workaround that increases productivity and efficiency in all walks of life. All these mega-stars, the multi-billionaires, the successful entrepreneurs are, in fact, hackers. They entered a system and hacked it. I was minimizing the risk in pushing pills, while multiplying the profits. I found a hack to get around the laws.

Lollapalooza was a kind of a watershed moment in the whole Ecstacy operation. Our underground popularity was at an all-time high, and now we were about to hit the mainstream market in a very big way.

A friend had managed to arrange a meeting with the managers for one of the bands that was performing at Lollapalooza. They were traveling back to Europe, where they were from, and where they had quite a following in the European rave scene. They wanted to buy a huge amount of our product, so that they could introduce it to the parties and nightclubs back home.

But rather than merely sell them the product outright, I saw an opportunity. At the meeting, I convinced them to become our official European distributors, and within a few weeks, we had orders from overseas pouring into our mailbox faster than we could open them. It seemed as if the Europeans had taken to our product even more rapidly than customers in the U.S. I ended up hiring a whole team of people just to deal with the new orders coming in, and to handle shipping these increasingly vast quantities of pills to the band in Europe.

The huge success of Herbal Ecstacy in Europe encouraged us to apply the same techniques in the U.S.A., so I had Julie reach out to another Lollapalooza band again. They were back in the area performing at another event, and she arranged for me to go there to meet with their manager in person. He agreed to take our product on tour with them and sell it at their concerts, and before long, our pills were getting snapped up by festival-goers from all walks of life, not just kids from the EDM and rave scene.

It didn't take long before the European band, who were in no way equipped to take over handling something of this size, and who mostly spent their time on the road or in the studio, got completely overwhelmed by how fast the whole operation was expanding. The ever-increasing popularity of Ecstacy overseas forced me to fly out to the Netherlands in order to find more local markets, and find multiple distributors who could sell the product locally in different regions.

I remember it was really strange, because we were there for the High Times Cannabis Cup, and yet we almost didn't get let through customs at the airport with our product. We used to advertise in *High Times* magazine, which is a publication dedicated to all things marijuana, and the company holds a big showcase event in Amsterdam every year, where traders can come sell their products and growers all compete for the title of best strain. I brought Rob and a small team to man a stall at the event, and meanwhile I was going to go around the city, meeting with distributors from various European countries, all of whom had gathered in Holland for the *High Times* show. In addition to weed, they also have magic mushrooms and other kinds of psychedelics for sale at the Cannabis Cup, because a lot of those things are legal in the Netherlands, so we saw other companies coming through the airport with bags of marijuana or shrooms, and the customs agents would hardly bat an eyelid. They just glanced it over and waved them through. But then, when we came through, they held us there for over an hour, making us provide all of this documentation to prove what our pills contained, and running tests, and debating whether they were going to let us in, or if they were going to destroy all of our product and arrest us.

Fortunately, we managed to convince them that all we had was ephedra tablets, and they let us through.

Our trip to Amsterdam was, after that incident, a roaring success. Word spread fast of this young American kid promising crazy returns on his 100% legal product, and soon I was showing up to meetings with people already fully aware of who I was, probing me with questions about how I'd managed to start such a huge company on my own. They were shocked when I came in with my long hair and my briefcase full of cash and pills, but they always signed the paperwork once they heard the kind of profit margins I was offering them. By the end of the week, we had deals to sell our product in nearly forty countries in total, including North America and the other countries we already operated in.

> **"The First Law: Performance drives success, but when performance can't be measured, networks drive success."**
> **Albert-László Barabási,**
> ***The Formula: The Universal Laws of Success***

In his book, *The Formula: The Universal Laws of Success*, Professor Albert-László Barabási talks about the two things needed to become a successful person, based on all the research he's done into success and different individuals who were all incredibly high-performers in their own fields.

You know what he found? The two most important things for success, according to Barabási, are performance and network.

Take the art world, for example. If we look at someone like Jean-Michel Basquiat, who's one of the highest-selling artists in the world now, and the highest-selling American artist ever, what is it that made him so successful commercially? Is it because of his performance, his extreme talent? Well (and excuse me if I'm pissing off any art experts here), no, it's not. His work is cool. It's interesting to look at and we can appreciate it, but it's not the best of the era, right? Barabási actually goes through and compares Basquiat's work to a bunch of other artists from that time period, and shows that, talent-wise, there were others who were almost certainly better performers than Basquiat was. Yet one of his paintings sold for $110.5 million a few years ago, and for an artist who came up in the 80s, that's completely unheard of. His more talented peers? You can pick up one of their works for a mere $15,000 today, which is a pittance in the art world.

So, if it's not talent that determines success, what does? Network. Now, as we've seen, you need to have at least *some* talent for this to work. But in an area where performance is lacking, network alone can be enough to catapult one person way above the rest. And that's what I did from the very beginning, and I was able to succeed, even without really knowing a thing about business. I didn't know about branding, or packaging, or products, or formulation, or pills. But I went out there, and I hustled to build the right networks to distribute my product, the right networks to talk about my product. And as I built that network out, my performance improved too. So network really is more important than performance, in my view.

A lot of what I did—building a network, seeking out the right people— I did instinctively. I saw it as chasing the best opportunities, but it's only really in retrospect that I realize how important those relationships were to the kind of astronomical success I achieved at such an early age.

For example, after I met the Beastie Boys and the people of Lollapalooza, their people introduced me to another band, and I ended up spending a few weeks on tour with these types of bands, and from there we went on tour with a prominent EDM foundational band who was touring with Prodigy and many others. Herbal Ecstacy became a fixture at these great concerts throughout the 90s because of this network we had built. Similarly, through our relationship with *High Times*, we ended up working with *Playboy*, *Penthouse*, and even *Rolling Stone*, whose editor at the time turned into quite the fan of ours, and used to write lengthy articles about us—advertising our product to the magazine's huge audience, totally for free. All of that success can be attributed to having the right network. Then, with time, our skills and tactics got better, too.

I ended up staying in Europe for a few more weeks, touring around with the bands and making new distribution deals. Turns out, bands who tour know lots of people who like—no, *love*—pills! No one was servicing these folks, and I had just gotten a direct connection to this avid customer base. At that point, I was creating this amazing business network, without even really having to try, because I was fully immersed in what I like to call "the flow."

When you're in the flow, other people who are also in the flow seem to have a way of gravitating toward you and the things that you are doing. Now, a lot of this may seem like woo-woo, and I'm sure that there isn't a whole lot of science behind this, so, for me, this is really something that falls under the category of following your gut.

The Walkman used to always tell me that when you start on a new journey, things are always going to be rough. Stuart echoed this to me later. Uncertainty is never easy but you have to make yourself okay with it. You're going uphill, you're climbing the face of a mountain, and there's going to be a lot of fog, visibility is going to be low, and you won't be able to see two feet in front of you, maybe even a foot in front of you. But you have to have this unflinching belief in yourself. That belief is more important than having a clear view of where you're going.

And that's what I did. I always had this unwavering belief in myself, and, even though I couldn't see what the future held, I had this resolute belief that I was going to make it, no matter how many times I got knocked down. So what if I couldn't see two feet in front of me? I couldn't see one foot in front of me, but I kept moving as if I could, and I kept carefully climbing that mountain, one step at a time. I would put my hand in one hold, and see that the rock would crumble and fall away, so then I'd put it in another one. Find another way up.

Obstacles will always come as you progress, but it doesn't really matter. Because, at the end of the day, I somehow felt it in my gut, and I knew that I was going to make it. It was more than just cockiness or confidence—it was a commitment that I had made to myself that, no matter what was going to happen, I was going to succeed. As long as you have that, you're going to be alright.

So I made the climb, 1 foot, 2 feet, 10 feet, 100 feet, and it was all uphill at first. Things didn't make sense. Failure happened daily, constantly. I would bump my head up against a brick wall every day, but I kept going at it. I took each failure and used it to learn. I carved into my journal this phrase: "I love not knowing what comes next. I embrace uncertainty."

Synchronicity

> *"With one breath, with one flow, you will know synchronicity."*
> **The Police**

But as I climbed, there was a point where I reached the peak.

Now, I'm not talking about the peak of success, I'm talking about the peak of my climb, which are two very different things. When you peak in terms of success, there's no way to go but down. But when you peak on your journey, you reach the top of that journey. It's a different story. Now, you can glide down, and that's what I did. So then, everything became visible once I reached the top of the mountain, at the height of the Herbal Ecstacy phenomenon. We had made over a billion dollars by the time I reached the top of that peak, and I looked and I was in the flow. Something had happened, seemingly instantaneously, but really took me over, you know, a few years to build up to that point that anything I touched seemed to turn to gold.

That was the absolute peak, and there was a certain kind of electricity that came along with being in the flow like that. There was a magnetism that evolved during that time, so that even when people met me, this young dude who had made hundreds of millions of dollars, and they absolutely hated me for it, they still wanted to work with me. They'd still bring deals to me.

So how did I get into the flow? How did I get into that synchronicity, where things seemed to come to me without trying? After Lollapalooza, I spent less and less of my time in California. I'd get a phone call and suddenly find myself on a private jet to Europe, getting wined and dined by a potential new customer, or getting invited to some celebrity's yacht party in Ibiza. Everyone wanted the long-haired "Ecstacy kid" at their party. All because I was the guy peddling the potentially "dangerous" (or maybe not) pill that everyone was leery of, but still eager to try. I was famous as the Herbal Ecstacy guy, this anomaly that had taken over the party scene all over the world. I had made my dent in the universe, and that dent was only getting bigger. How did that happen?

One day, I was on a train, sitting in the First Class cabin on my way to Paris, when I had one of those perfect moments of being in the flow, which I think sums up pretty well how the effect of synchronicity really works. I was reaching the peak of my success, and that was like a force field, drawing in even more success to revolve around me. I'd been at a Prodigy concert in a little town in northwestern France somewhere, and was heading back to Paris to catch a flight to the U.K., and the train journey was a few hours long. The whole time, I was sitting across from a smartly-dressed French guy who was reading the paper, and at one point, he flipped the page, and I couldn't believe what I was seeing. I don't speak French, but I could clearly see a picture of myself staring out at me in black and white from the newspaper, probably in an article speculating over whether or not our products should be banned in the EU, or something like that. The press in America certainly loved to talk about that.

Anyways, as it happens, the guy sitting to the left of me was a businessman who was headed to Paris to look for distribution deals for his employer, and as soon as he saw that picture, he struck up a conversation with me like he'd known me his entire life. We hit it off, and he ended up taking me for dinner in the city once the train arrived. By the end of the night, he'd become my distributor for Paris and a few other regions in France.

What are the chances of that? That a kid in his early twenties from Venice Beach happens to be in Paris, happens to be on the train, and all this stuff unfolds at once? Slim, but success makes them possible. My success at Lollapalooza had led me to the bands, which had led me to Europe, to that First Class train cabin, and it had also led to the media wanting to run stories about me in the paper. That, in turn, attracted even more people to me, and helped grow my success even more. That's the magic of being in the flow. It's the magic of synchronicity. It's the magic of following your gut.

I am still not sure how it works. It's almost like you're swimming upstream, and, all of a sudden, the flow changes in your favor. Everything changes in that moment. Whereas one area of the water is perilous and holds imminent danger and disappointment, another is filled with life, sustenance, abundance and leads to even more flow. Sometimes it was just a matter of switching lanes or moving a bit to the left, and other times it was making a complete life change. Whatever it was at that time, I always found a way to recover and get back into that moment.

Eventually I learned that having this unwavering belief in yourself, and remembering that that belief is not just a false kind of hope. I had a resolution, that no matter what it takes, no matter how I was going to have to do it, that I would succeed.

And if you have that, if you have that ambition, mixed with a commitment to make it happen, there's a very strong chance that you will make it. Now there's other things that need to be done alongside that, but for me, that's really what it was.

Even when you're in the flow, though, things will inevitably still happen that mess with your flow. Those handholds come tumbling down, you know? But you just have to keep climbing.

So, while I was on this tour in Europe, one of the bands that had been distributing for us was meant to meet me and give me the cash for all of the sales they had done over the past few months. I had fronted them somewhere in the region of half a million dollars' worth of product, and the day I showed up to collect, they told me they had nothing to give me in return. Not one penny.

It turns out, at the end of their tour, their manager had skipped town, taking with him all the money and the remainder of the unsold pills. None of the band members said they knew a thing about what had happened, but they did know that he had also taken all of their profits from the tour when he left.

I actually managed to track the guy down in London, and he also claimed to know nothing about my money, or the missing pills. He said the band must have been the ones who took it.

My suspicion at the time was that it really was the manager who was to blame, but, you know, those were crazy times.

While I was traveling around Europe, I ran the rest of the business operations remotely—believe it or not, mostly using fax machines. There were these giant, clunky cell phones that we all had, but they didn't have easy international calling capabilities yet, I believe, so I was trying to organize my whole team in California all through the use of faxing alone.

I had Rob and Borris there to hold down the fort while I was away, but I could never trust them to keep as firm a hand on things as I did. And even I didn't have that firm of a grip on it all, in those days. Despite my best efforts, people were still stealing from me. I felt like every time I turned around, they were picking all the meat off the bones of my company, and each time I returned from a trip like this, I came back to an even bigger disaster than the time before.

I felt pretty hurt by it all, because in my mind, I was giving these people awesome jobs, paying them way more than they were qualified to earn, and entrusting them with a lot of responsibility. I was giving them autonomy to run an entire department by themselves, or whatever, and I felt like these were great opportunities for people who I'd met on a street corner in front of a warehouse rave at 3 AM, so I expected that to kind of inspire loyalty. Again, part of my naivety at that young age.

Of course, people took advantage of me. Why wouldn't they? I was giving them all the freedom in the world to run around California with trucks full of pills and money, and then fucking off to go party in the canyon or jet off to Europe for a couple of weeks, and assuming that everything would just be okay. But in the end, I could never trust a single financial report or sales order that came across my desk—I always suspected it had been tampered with before my employees gave it to me, or that the right numbers had never been recorded in the first place.

A good chunk of my profits were stolen. Everyone had their hands in the till (unbeknownst to me). Another hefty sum was constantly being put toward "legal fees," much of which was spent bailing my half-baked attorneys out of trouble, and fixing business mistakes—like covering my $500,000 loss from the band in Europe. At the time, I had this philosophy that any problem you had could just be fixed with more money. Suicide margins were my quick relief for all my fuck ups. I had turned the Ecstacy tap on and money flowed easily. It was easier for me to make new money than to chase the old. If your ship bursts a leak, get a newer, better ship.

Now, I try to think upstream—like how can we fix these problems to work better in the future—but back then, I just thought, as long as I could keep making more money, I could afford to fix all of those mistakes with cash. It was an unfortunate choice, and one which cost me more than I even cared to calculate at the time, and that became part of the problem.

Journal Entry: Reality Distortion Field

	Pre-suasion	The Flow
What is it?	Pre-suasion is essentially Cialdini's version of the Sizzle—a way of grabbing your customer's attention and having them sold before they even come to you.	The flow is the state you enter when you're achieving your highest productivity and success, and because of that you keep attracting even more opportunities for success.
Why is it important?	Because effectively pre-suading customers to buy your product means they will seek you out, rather than you having to go to them.	You have to be able to recognize when you're in the flow (or not), so you can take full advantage of the opportunities gravitating toward you.
How to win:	Get people to want to buy your product before they've ever laid eyes on it. You do this by architecting their interest prior to them seeing the sales proposition. Do it by creating a buzz—like using social proof or media attention to spark interest amongst new customers. Once they've heard about you from their friends, FOMO kicks in and they rush to buy (all without ever seeing an ad).	If you're not in the flow, focus on how you can get there. Make it a priority because it is in that state that success will find you. Find the source of what last put you in a flow state and try to duplicate that. The book Flow by Csikszentmihalyi is a great place to find ideas.

CHAPTER 10:

THE YAKUZA AND ME

I once turned on the TV, and Jordan Belfort (a.k.a. the Wolf of Wall Street) was on the news being interviewed by some famous reporter. The interviewer asked something like: "So, Jordan! Did any of that stuff actually happen? Was it really exactly the way you describe it in your book?"

Jordan took a brief pause, and then answered. "Not only did it happen, it was much, much crazier and more intense than that."

I remember the reporter being stunned. But I wasn't. I thought back to when I first saw the movie they made of his life story, with Leonardo DiCaprio playing Jordan. After watching it, I just sat there, thinking how insane it was that so much of what he experienced actually resonated with me. My life had taken a similar trajectory: a meteoric rise to fame and fortune, followed by a stunning fall from the top, back down to the earthly realm of relative obscurity.

And, just like the Wolf of Wall Street, my journey was filled with insane, out-of-control, drug-fuelled stories—a lot of which, when I tell them to people, earn me a stare a lot like the one that the reporter gave Jordan during that interview. You know, the one where you can clearly tell the other person is thinking, "what a load of BS." I know how unbelievable it all sounds, but the truth is, it all happened—sometimes even crazier than the version I usually tell people. Even I sometimes wonder how deep the rabbit hole actually went.

The English equivalent for the term "yakuza" is "gangster," meaning an individual involved in a Mafia-like criminal organization. The yakuza are known

184

for their strict codes of conduct, their organized fiefdom nature, and several unconventional ritual practices such as "yubitsume," or amputation of the left little finger. Members are often described as males, wearing "sharp suits" with heavily tattooed bodies and slicked hair. This group is still regarded as being among "the most sophisticated and wealthiest criminal organizations."[3]

One day, a mysterious man comes to my office, carrying a suitcase with a million bucks in cash inside. He was offering to buy the exclusive rights to distribute our Herbal Ecstacy cigarettes in Japan, but there was a catch: I would first have to meet his bosses, in person, for them to give their blessing to the partnership.

So the next thing I knew, there was a private jet waiting to take me off to Tokyo.

I called my partner in Japan, Hiroshi, and told him about the unexpected meeting, assuring him that I'd send all the details about where to meet once I'd landed in Tokyo. He sounded a little alarmed, but I didn't think much of it. I just assumed he was nervous about the possibility of someone else taking over his distribution role, or thought that I was really flying out there to check up on him and how he was running the operation.

As it turns out, he had good reason to be worried. I just hadn't figured out why yet.

The mystery man and I shared a comfortable, and quiet, flight from L.A. to Tokyo (he didn't speak much English, and I knew only a few words of Japanese). I was still a kid, but I'd grown accustomed to flying all over the world first-class or in private planes— almost always on someone else's dime. It just came as part of the territory. When the jet touched down and a glossy black limousine was there to meet us on the runway, I assumed it was meant to take me to the hotel that my prospective partners had arranged for me for the weekend. Nothing

---

3 "Yakuza," Wikipedia (Wikimedia Foundation, January 8, 2021), https://en.wikipedia.org/wiki/Yakuza.

out of the ordinary here—just another wealthy businessman trying to woo me so he could get in on the viral growth that Herbal Ecstacy was experiencing at the time. I'd seen it all before—or at least, I thought I had.

The limo driver didn't take us to a hotel. He drove for what felt like hours, into the heart of the city and back out the other side, taking us deeper and deeper into the suburbs that sprawl outwards from Tokyo for miles in every direction. I remember getting a little nervous then. Were they taking me directly to their warehouse? Had they told Hiroshi where to meet us, like I'd asked? I tried to put these questions to my taciturn companion during the long drive, but he just grunted noncommittally in reply and lit another cigarette.

Finally, we arrived at our destination. It was a minka—one of those classic Japanese houses with wood-and-paper walls and the iconic curved roof—tucked down a nondescript street in an equally-nondescript residential neighborhood. No one had even told me the name of the man I was here to meet, but suddenly I was being ushered inside. I glanced back over my shoulder at the quiet street and the limousine parked in the driveway, and noticed that there were some shady-looking guards posted around the property at regular intervals. Strange, for a sleepy little suburb like this.

With my shoes left at the front door, I was given some sandals to wear and led down a hallway to a large, traditional Japanese tatami room. The mystery man nudged me through the door and then shuffled away hurriedly, leaving me to face his bosses alone.

There were two tatami mats spread out on the woven floor, rice paper walls and thin sliding doors separating the room from the hallway and those adjoining it. Inside, slender women in typical Geisha dress served sake and little dishes of food to the thirty or forty men who were sitting around the edges of the room, all puffing away at their cigarettes. These were not normal-looking men, by traditional Japanese standards. Nearly every inch of them was covered in tattoos. I could see the bold black outlines and colorful patterns of even more ink through the fabric of their starched, white shirts. Something else I noticed, which was definitely out of the ordinary, was the fact that a few of them were missing fingers on their hands.

Looking around the room, I spotted Hiroshi—pale-faced and almost visibly trembling as he clutched his sake, sitting squeezed in between two particularly rough-looking characters who were nearly twice his size. In these surreal surroundings, my immediate instinct was to flee for my life, and Hiroshi looked like he shared those feelings. But I didn't leave. Not just because I knew I probably wouldn't get very far if I did, but because I was curious as hell to see what was going to happen. I was caught up in the flow, and I could feel it. From the mystery man appearing with his cash-filled briefcase the day before, to finding myself faced with a room full of yakuza-looking mafia bosses, circumstances were once again aligning to bring me to some great new opportunity. I'd just have to survive long enough to see what it was.

We, as human beings, often become so consumed with living that the idea of death never crosses our minds. You never think to yourself, "Today's the day I might die." Especially not when you're still barely legal to drink. But that day, it seemed like a very real possibility that I might not live to see tomorrow.

As day turned into night, I began to realize that no one, other than my business partner, spoke a word of English. The man I was there to meet—apparently, one of the heads of the Yakuza itself— had still not appeared. The women continued to pour sake and serve delicious morsels of the most incredible and delicately-prepared Japanese food I've ever had. The men sat around, mostly in silence, occasionally exchanging words in Japanese and constantly chain smoking American cigarettes.

Hours passed like this, and I eventually asked Hiroshi what was going on. He told me to be quiet, and explained that everybody was waiting for the boss to arrive before discussing any business. So I just kept my mouth shut and sipped my sake, casually wondering if I'd end the evening with some really fucking bizarre new business partners, or buried in an unmarked Japanese grave somewhere.

And then it happened. I heard the door slide open and everybody—I mean everybody—stood up to form a circle around the smoke-filled room, and remained silent as their leader came through the door. He was an older man in a gray suit, with the look of someone who'd been through some grisly stuff in his life and wouldn't be fazed in the slightest if a bomb exploded right next to him. He was flanked by two younger men in suits, even more battle-ready than their ward, their cool eyes scanning the room as if to make sure the boss was being paid the proper respect due to him.

The man's eyes met with mine. It was a pretty awkward moment—I didn't know whether to smile or not, if I should shake his hand or bow. In all our hours of waiting, no one had explained the appropriate protocols to follow when greeting a mafia boss. And the last thing I wanted to do was make a misstep right off the bat. I opted for meeting his cool stare with a blank expression that matched his own, and tried to hide the nervousness I felt.

The boss seemed satisfied by that. At least, he shifted his glare away from me and moved to sit at the low table in the center of the room. Not a word was uttered. One of the girls dutifully came forward to pour him a cup of tea, and quickly retreated again to the safety of the other Geishas, never once looking at the man's face. I sat down again when Hiroshi motioned for me to do so, not knowing what to do. Should I say something now? I got the impression that maybe it would be best to just keep quiet, and wait for the boss to open the discussion.

Nothing was said for the next 15 minutes. And in that room, 15 minutes felt like 15 years.

All the yakuza guys kept smoking in silence, like this was the most normal interaction in the world, but for Hiroshi and me, the tension was palpable. I was imagining the worst of outcomes, like having all my fingers cut off, one by one, or being beaten to death by forty tattooed mafiosos in this quaint tatami room. Is that why they liked to meet in places like this? Maybe it was really easy to replace the woven floors, if they happened to get all bloody. At least I could say I'd had an interesting run, before my young life was snuffed out. And if anyone ever found out what happened to me, it would make for a fucking incredible story.

I kept a straight face, but inside, I was in a complete mire. I kept cursing myself for being there, rehashing the decisions I'd made that had led me to this place—I mean, these were stone-cold killers, and I had practically thrown myself into their laps like an eager puppy. One particular Japanese proverb kept jumping into my thoughts: *"I no naka no kawazu, taikai o shirazu."* It means, "A frog in a well cannot conceive of the ocean," and right then, I knew exactly how that frog felt. I may have been used to handling the small-time drug dealers who operated in Venice's rave scene, but I felt way out of my depths in that room.

Just when I started to think that we were going to spend the whole night sitting there in silence, the Bossman reached over and touched my hand, bringing me sharply out of my thoughts and back into the present moment. He said something to his translator, and I assumed he was explaining the details of the distribution proposal they had for me. Either that, or telling me to make my peace with God.

Instead, the translator turned to me and said, very matter-of-factly, "We will take the company and all holdings in the U.S.A., Europe, and Japan. For this, we will pay you $100 million over 1 year."

And with that, Bossman put out his cigarette, stood up, and left. His wiry bodyguards slid out after him like his mirror-image shadows. That was it.

Is this some kind of test? I found myself thinking.

They hadn't even given me a chance to reply. I guess they assumed the answer was obvious—what twenty-something-year-old kid in his right mind would even *dream* of saying no to one of the most infamous crime syndicates in the world, right?

"Hiroshi-san, what's going on?" I asked, for the second time that night. "I told you, the cigs only, and Japan only. Not the entire company worldwide! What did you say to them?"

The look in his eyes was one that I had never seen him wear before, not even during the hours we'd spent anxiously awaiting Bossman's arrival. It was a look of real fear.

Hiroshi didn't say anything.

Terrified or no, I felt like shaking some sense into him. What the fuck had he told these people that they thought they could take over the entire business? If both of us ended up dead, I was fully prepared to blame him for it. But, of course, it wasn't really his fault. Hiroshi wasn't like me—he never would have contemplated turning down a "request" from the Yakuza, so even if he had agreed to these insane terms, I couldn't really blame him for that. Still, right at that moment, I was pissed. Was I about to die for my company? And had I put myself in this situation by following my own crazy instincts? Well, Hiroshi certainly wasn't helping things, either.

Bossman suddenly reentered the room, with the translator and his suit-clad shadows in tow.

"Do you accept our offer?" the translator asked.

There was a pause. These men were conspicuously armed. Refusing them would be unwise, to say the least. I could feel my business partner's worried eyes boring into the side of my head, hoping that I'd make the smart decision, and we could both escape with our lives and fingers intact.

I smiled. "Yes, we respectfully accept your generous offer. For Japan only."

The translator translated. Bossman listened to my reply, and turned to look dead at me with hard, flat eyes. I just kept smiling, like we were two men having a pleasant chat, and refused to let my show of confidence falter.

After a brief staredown, they all left the room again.

Hiroshi had turned white, and was frantically murmuring something that sounded like a prayer under his breath. We had no idea what was going to happen next.

Another hour passed as we waited to see what reaction my counter offer would produce. Did I even make a counter offer, or did I just sign my own death warrant? We tried our best to relax, drinking the matcha tea, sake, and miso soup that the Geishas kept bringing us (apparently, we were still considered guests—that had to be a good sign, right?), but nothing could take our minds off of the impending doom that lay waiting for us outside that door.

I understood that this was one of their tactics—to use fear and intimidation to coerce the desired response from an opponent. Making us wait was just another layer to that strategy. They thought that if they left us to sweat it out a bit, we'd eventually crack under the stress of anticipating our own imminent and brutal murders, and agree to anything they wanted.

But I also knew a thing or two about the psychology of good negotiation. Their tactics were just static, trying to get in the way of my flow. And right now, the best thing for me to do was say nothing and hold my ground. My friend Chris Voss, a former FBI negotiator, talks about the art of successful negotiation in his book,
Never Split the Difference, which is one of my all-time favorite reads. He says that, in situations such as these, "no deal is better than a bad deal."

I decided that I was going to leave there with a good deal, or none at all—even if "no deal" came with some pretty dire consequences for us.

Although violence was still a real possible outcome here, I was betting that, as long as I didn't succumb to the pressure they were trying to exert on me, we could still come to a profitable arrangement for all parties. And one that would get us safely out that sliding door, without having to ever see these guys again. Besides, I *was* Herbal Ecstacy. Without me, the products and company may not survive.

Then Bossman and his entourage appeared once again, and again the whole room stood when he entered. He motioned to one of his generals to bring a bag over, and the man hurried to comply.

Get ready to apologize and accept whatever they want, I thought, just in case that bag contained a purpose-built finger guillotine. Maybe my reading of the situation had been a little off. Maybe it wasn't a negotiation, after all.

Bossman instructed his general to open the bag with a silent gesture.

You could have cut the air with a knife. I found myself holding my breath, and I could feel the same sense of nail-biting terror emanating from Hiroshi in waves. I just hid it better than he did.

The man opened the bag and took out a wooden box. My eyes were glued to it as he slowly opened the lid and reached inside to remove whatever it contained. And then, to my complete surprise, he produced a fairly large, solid gold statue of a cat and held it out to me. It was a gift.

"Japan." Bossman said in a strong accent. He smiled, revealing a crooked row of tea-and-cigarette-stained teeth.

I finally let out the breath I'd been holding. I thought Hiroshi was going to burst into tears of relief and joy right there on the spot. It seems my gamble had paid off.

That was it. The meeting was over. A single word exchanged, a whole lot of awkward and nervous silence, and now we had a deal. Just like that—there was no written contract, no paperwork, no agreement, no nothing. The deal was: they were going to tell you what the deal was. You're welcome. Nothing about what had just happened made sense to me, but nothing about that trip made any sense at all.

Hiroshi later told me that he had never seen anyone refuse them, and that in the eyes of the bosses this move was one that commanded respect. I told him it was because I didn't "refuse" them. He finally smiled.

The men all disbanded once Bossman took his leave, and we were led back outside to the waiting car. The driver opened the door for me, and I climbed in the back as gracefully as I could while still holding a large gold cat in my hands.

The cat was likely worth $250K or more (and likely purloined from someone who owed them). How the fuck was I going to explain *that* to customs once I got back?

Once inside, my partner explained that everything had turned out as good as we could have hoped for: their "organization" would now take over the sole rights to our Herbal Ecstacy cigarettes, one of our biggest products in the Japanese market, and would have zero ties to the rest of the company.

I sat back in my seat and stared down at the cat in my lap, shaking my head and smiling softly to myself. I was still in disbelief at how close we'd come to getting killed by a mob of angry yakuza members, and more than relieved that we wouldn't have to do business with them in the future. Selling them the rights to the cigarette product in Japan was a fair trade for not having to be associated with that kind of stuff (and the deal was really with Hiroshi who would act as the intermediary and not directly with us)—I mean, we were drug dealers, but we were *legal* drug dealers. And despite that, we still had federal organizations so far up our asses that we could taste them in our breakfasts each morning. I could only imagine what they'd do if they caught wind of us working with *real* drug dealers. But if we just sold them the product outright and washed our hands of it, the feds couldn't use that against us. Or at least, I hoped not. I made a mental note to check with Tom about that later.

The limousine took us to my hotel room, and we were met there by one of Bossman's two shadows. He was holding a large duffel bag, which he left on the foot of my bed before walking out again— of course, never saying a word the whole time. Hiroshi unzipped it after the shadow left, and inside was a little over $1,000,000 in cash. He said it was their way of solidifying the deal. We both stood there, looking at the absurd amount of money in front of us, and I personally was just glad that we were taking the Yakuza's jet back to California, because we would have had a hell of a time explaining this one to airport security. I pictured the customs form that said "Anything to declare?" Gold cat—value $250K, Cash—$1 million dollars, incense, matcha tea and cigarettes.

There was still another day until our flight back to L.A. , though, and the night was still young. So I did what any rational human being would do who's just narrowly escaped a mafia deal gone wrong and is on an all-expenses paid trip in Tokyo with a duffel bag full of cash and a gold cat worth more than most homes: we went out partying.

We called up a couple of friends in the city and a crazy night ensued. The group of us drove to a secluded onsen in the suburbs. We sipped sake as we sat in the natural hot springs, talking business and toasting to our successful brush with death, and every once in a while, wild snow monkeys would jump down and bathe in the steaming waters with us. It was a pretty magical experience to be a part of, and made the day we'd just had seem even more surreal. It's also one of those stories where, when I tell it to people, I can see them looking at me in the same way that the interviewer looked at Jordan Belfort—like I'm completely full of crap. But I can assure you, I'm not inventive enough to make up something this crazy. From staring down a Yakuza boss while getting served matcha tea and sake by Geishas to sharing a drink and a hot mineral bath with macaque monkeys, it was definitely one of the weirdest and most wonderful days in my life.

As another round of sake was poured into our cups, I looked around at my peaceful surroundings, at the monkeys splashing themselves in the onsen, and my thoughts drifted back to the insane deal we'd just made. Had I dived in too deep? Was this going to come back to bite me later on? Following my business instincts had gotten us out of immediate danger today, but where would it lead to tomorrow? I couldn't see to the end of the road, but I knew I would never stop traveling until I got there.

Throughout the night, I kept turning these thoughts over in my mind, but every time they came to the surface, my apprehensions were quickly drowned in cups of sake. The million dollars I had sitting in my hotel room certainly helped to dispel any lingering doubts, too.

Journal Entry: Reality Distortion Field

	Don't Let Fear Conquer You	No Deal > Bad Deal
What is it?	Conquering fear is having the courage to face terrifying odds, or seemingly crippling self doubt, and find a way to win in any environment.	'No deal is better than a bad deal' is one of Chris Voss' key principles of a successful negotiation.
Why is it important?	Fear stops you from being able to act in your own best interest and gives the upper hand to your opponent.	Negotiation is crucial for almost all kinds of success. If you're not a good negotiator (e.g. you give in to what the other party wants, to your own disadvantage), you're not going get very far in pursuing your own goals.
How to win:	Say nothing and stand your ground. By keeping control of your fear you maintain a strong position. Portraying confidence and certainty disarms your opponent. If you are having trouble not showing your fear, fake it till you make it.	Know what you want before going into the talk, how you plan on getting it, and where your limit is. Never be pressured into doing what the other party wants. It's okay to walk away, rather than accept a deal you're not happy with. Take the time to revisit it later, and you can always reopen negotiations at a later date. Then you'll be even better prepared, and ready to secure even better terms.

CHAPTER 11:

FAST LANE

"The interesting thing is how one guy, through living out his own fantasies, is living out the fantasies of so many other people."

Hugh Hefner

You give a teenage boy millions of dollars, and you naturally set him up for a crazy ride.

Ed's influence had exerted a tempering hand over my actions in my earlier years. He had taught me the importance of discipline, and made me be rigid in how I conducted my business and took care of my body, but the more money I made, the less disciplined I felt in my personal life. I stopped doing martial arts every day, and started to indulge in travel with increasing frequency. I mean, I had the power to finally fulfill every one of my desires, and of course I was going to explore that. What young man wouldn't?

The stress of those days was sizable. Like Atlas, I held the weight of the world on my shoulders. The feds, thieving employees, disloyal girlfriends, harsh deals, the press, the local governments, lawsuits and competitors. Everything always came at once. Travel for me was both exploration and avoidance. On one hand, I could get lost in a new country and culture and feel myself assimilate into another world. On the other, I was hiding from the sad reality back home that everyone was stealing from me and that the house of cards was moments from falling.

The money was pouring in, and except for wondering how much of it was being pocketed by my employees before it hit my bank account, my problems were all "high quality" or so I thought. So, with Lisa away for the day at a photoshoot and a bag full of cash in the back of my car, I drove up the Pacific Coast Highway from Santa Monica.

It's a beautiful drive up to Topanga Canyon. The shoreline curves around the bay and the mountains lean in toward the sea, making it a stunningly transportive pathway to the place which, to my mind, has preserved the true, 60s spirit of California unlike anywhere else. Its laid-back, Bohemian charm was enough to convince me that this was the place for me to live the first time I visited there, and now that I had the means to make that dream a reality, I intended to do just that.

The calm of Topanga is the perfect antidote to the hustle and bustle of L.A. Its spectacular mountain views and the scenic cloud cover add to the magic of the place. Mix in the flavor of Hollywood, and you've got yourself a recipe for the quintessential rock star lifestyle. I felt like I could use a peaceful escape from the everyday insanity at Herbal Ecstacy, and a place to fully let loose with the parties that I threw. My neighbors in Malibu had been complaining, and I was tired of the police constantly showing up at my house.

So I couldn't resist when an old haunted hunting lodge came on the market. It was huge, and could easily host the number of people I planned on inviting around, and it was built right into the cliff face, blending in seamlessly with its rocky, wilderness surroundings and overlooking the full sweep of the canyon below. It even had its own waterfall. It only took ten minutes of walking around the property for me to make up my mind.

"I'll take it." I told the broker confidently.

"I haven't even told you how much it is," she replied, squinting at me in confusion.

"Doesn't matter. I'm moving in tonight. Just get me a deal. You said it's vacant, right?" She nodded, eyes wide. "Cool. That's all that matters."

The house was for sale by owner—an old school Jewish doctor. She somehow managed to arrange an impromptu meeting with him immediately. I handed him a deposit bag with a large sum of money in cash inside, and the broker assured me we'd sort out the paperwork as quickly as possible. When I drove back down to Santa Monica, I already had the keys in my pocket.

When I got back to Malibu, I packed a few bags and went to collect Lisa from her gig in town. She was shocked to see the backseat filled with suitcases and kept asking me where we were going the whole way there. I just smiled, and told her she'd see when we arrived.

She couldn't believe her eyes when I handed her the keys and welcomed her to our new home.

Over the next few days, Lisa and I went on a spending spree. Maybe more like a spending rampage, actually. I bought properties all throughout town, a few of my favorite exotic cars, a couple of jet skis, and a speedboat. I hired a Hollywood stereo guy to install a surround sound theatre system, with one of those screens that went up and down automatically. I wanted my music to play seamlessly in every room, too. He made it all happen.

I wasn't big on furniture, but Lisa was adamant that the Topanga mountain retreat was not going to remain freakishly vacant, like my Malibu house had, so she hired interior designers to come fill the place with furniture. My own idea of decorating was to have meteors and fossils everywhere and wild animals as pets, and Lisa was insane enough to let me do that, so I guess it was only fair that I let her have her chaises longues, or whatever. In the end, the house turned out looking like the inside of a 90s Banana Republic store— think Indiana Jones meets Natural History Museum.

We'd only been there for a few weeks, but I was definitely making a splash in the neighborhood with my extravagant spending. I had made a few celebrity friends who lived nearby, and was constantly throwing parties that the whole city seemed to hear about within an hour of me deciding to organize it. The parties kept getting crazier and crazier every time. Topanga was famous for its hippie chicks, and these events were full of them. They would show up at my door in the middle of the night, whether invited or not, and within minutes, another event would ensue. Often, things got totally beyond my ability to control them, and often, Lisa was the one spurring on the insanity. She and the hippie girls would all take drugs and invariably end up in the jacuzzi, and even if I begged her to put some clothes on in front of our guests (like when potential business partners came round to visit), she would shout something at me about how her free spirit couldn't be tamed, and then dive defiantly back into the hot tub.

There were a lot of crazy nights there, where I still am not quite sure what actually happened. One night I do remember, though, was when Lisa got so messed up that she had to excuse herself to go puke it out in the bathroom, leaving me alone with our female guest. I didn't want to be a bad host, so I carried on the fun without her, naturally.

When I woke up, Lisa was standing over my bed, screaming bloody murder at me, while the slender redhead from the night before made a run for it as fast as she could, taking my sheets with her as a makeshift dress. Standing there naked and trying to dodge the random items Lisa was throwing at me, I tried to tell her that I didn't really see what the problem was—I mean, I had assumed Lisa was going to be back in just a couple of minutes to join us, once she was done purging herself.

"I think it was just a bit of a misunderstanding, that's all," I told her, but she certainly didn't see it that way. She ended up going back to her own apartment for a few weeks, where I heard she was going off on some kind of bender and blowing off work to snort coke with Krissy all day. I knew she'd be back, once she got over my perceived betrayal.

I have to admit, I wasn't always faithful to Lisa. She knew that, I think, she just didn't want to be confronted with it in person. What I did when I was on my own, however, was another thing.

One night while she was gone, I was alone in the house, and I had sent the staff on leave so that I could have some real time to myself, when the doorbell rang. I opened the door, and there were a group of young women standing there smiling at me, ready to prompt the start of another party. They had seen me on the news and managed to get my address from one of my employees on the beach. Inventive as they were, they had tracked me down and were excited to meet me. As soon as I opened the door, they came right in, uninvited, and before I knew it, they were all in the spa and beckoning me to join them.

I could see that they were all high on something, and they tried to offer me some of whatever it was they were taking. It was a common perception in those days that I used a lot of drugs—my unconventional appearance, the nature of my company, and the kind of people I associated with definitely gave that impression. The truth was, I still didn't feel comfortable with taking drugs myself, and I had never even caved into Lisa's multiple attempts to get me to try them with her. So instead of joining them, I kind of awkwardly went back inside and started reading a book. I wanted a quiet week to myself, and that's what I was going to have, damnit.

But the girls had other plans. Two of them came in, totally naked now, and started pleading with me to come outside with them. Admittedly, I had been sort of struggling to focus on my book, with all these beautiful women all squealing and giggling in my pool, and I think they saw the slight uncertainty on my face, because they pounced on that moment of weakness like lionesses on a gazelle. Unable (or unwilling) to defend myself, I let them drag me out of the house and back to the patio, peeling off my clothes and giggling even more as they went. Then one of them offered me a single, white capsule of pure MDMA, straight from the source. A circle of women surrounded me, all pushing me toward the pill and assuring me it would be the greatest thing I ever did. Talk about peer pressure.

I'm not sure if it was the trouble with Lisa, or the stress over work, or the feeling of wanting to escape from it all for a bit, but for some reason, I gave in. That was the first time I ever took real ecstasy.

As someone who had never taken any kind of "serious" drugs before, trying pure MDMA for the first time was a pretty eye-opening experience, to put it mildly. We were in the depths of the wilderness, surrounded by peace and nature, in a setting as different from an underground warehouse rave as it was possible to be, but as soon as I started coming up on the Molly, I felt like I was standing in the thick of a writhing crowd of ravers.

My heart raced as the drugs kicked in, and with every pulse of blood through my body, I could feel this intense, tingling sensation growing stronger and stronger, spreading over my skin and through my muscles. The music playing from the speaker system completely took over my entire consciousness, until I could even see the notes moving through the air like technicolor, dancing patterns of sound swimming before my eyes. The baseline seemed to animate me against my will, because my limbs started moving all by themselves, my hands waving as they traced the moving, flashing lights of the music in front of me. I knew then what all of my clientele were so possessed by when they went to those raves. Right then, I must have had the same delirious, far-away look on my face that the crowds at parties always had when they were lost in the beat of the music on the dancefloor. I completely understood how they felt. It was like becoming one with the music.

At the same time, every one of my five senses had been turned up so high that I didn't think I could physically contain all of the phenomena I was experiencing. The girls were touching me, and the feeling of their fingers on my skin was like pure electricity, sending shockwaves all throughout my core just from the slightest graze of flesh on flesh. They were giggling about how far gone I was, but I barely registered it at all. I was too fascinated by the way the hot water of the tub and the cool night air played against each other on my skin.

A drug-fuelled evening ensued, and I'm not even sure how long it was before the girls finally left. Maybe one day, maybe two, but it wasn't until I woke up alone one morning, lying in my backyard, that I realized I'd completely lost track of the date. I sat bolt-upright, feeling around for my phone to see how many messages I'd missed from my staff.

I had no luck finding my phone, but I did find a discarded bikini top laying over the arm of my lounge chair and a half-smoked joint stuck to my thigh. With a groan, I dragged myself through the wreckage of the past few days' partying and stumbled inside to throw a robe on and continue the search for my mobile. I went to the door, and saw that there was a small manila envelope sitting on the front step, so I cut it open and saw that it contained a notice from the Federal Trade Commission, the FTC. They wanted to open an investigation into the sales of ephedra (our key ingredient and what gave our Herbal Ecstacy its kick) in the United States, and were filing an action against us regarding some of the claims we made about the safety of our products.

I may have been slightly out of it, but I still had enough sense to think, *Holy crap! I need to call my attorney.*

> *"Sometimes adversity is what you need to face in order to become successful."*
> **Zig Ziglar**

Rob and I usually got along great—we were friends, as well as colleagues—but our relationship started to deteriorate when the media learned that he wasn't really the man behind the whole operation.

For months, he had handled all of our interviews with the press, and I was so grateful to him for that. With his actor's background, he was great at taking on the role of CEO and presenting a powerful image to the world, but eventually, word got out that an image was all it was. A few news outlets were digging into our backgrounds, trying to find out more behind this company that was attracting so many lawsuits, and even more hungry customers, and one of them had figured out that it was actually me, and not Rob, who was the owner of Herbal Ecstacy. Then they found out how old I was, and my time of enjoying my anonymity was officially over.

The media became less interested in Rob, who they now saw as just an employee, and wanted me to be on camera more and more. The first time this happened, I thought Rob might quit his job right there and then.

He'd just finished primping in the mirror, perfecting his suited Mr. Clean look for the cameras, and walked out into the lobby where a TV crew from a local news station was setting up, preparing to do an interview about the legal high phenomenon and Herbal Ecstacy's role in popularizing it. All of us had been expecting Rob to be the one on camera that day—myself included—but when he walked over and started introducing himself, all smiles and charm, he was soundly rebuffed by the show's producer.

"We were told we'd be speaking to the owner of the company," the pinch-faced woman told him flatly.

Rob visibly recoiled, looking like he'd been punched. "I'm the CEO!" he cried. "That's not good enough for you?"

"You're the CEO, but not the owner, correct?" she shot back, just as levelly as before.

"Well, I—er, no, but I—"

"Then you're not the one we're here to interview," the producer cut off his stammering curtly, then turned on her heel to peer at me. "You're him, right? Shaahin Cheyene?"

I glanced quickly at Rob, who was giving me a threatening look, like he expected me to lie and say I was an intern or something. I shrugged my shoulders at him and spread my hands, as if to say, *Sorry, man, what do you want me to do?* "Um, yep. That's me."

"Excellent. Let's just get you to stand here for a sec to check the lights, okay?" She was ushering me over in front of the cameras before I had a chance to reply. Rob, looking like he was ready to howl in indignation, spun and marched out, his hands balled tightly into fists by his side.

I had hesitantly agreed to that first interview, but then after a while, I started to get more comfortable with the idea of having my face out there. This meant that Rob was thrown increasingly into the background, and for someone who craved the limelight so much, this was simply unacceptable to him.

We started to fight a lot—not just about who was going to do the interviews, but about completely unrelated things, too. I tried to work things out with him several times, but it only seemed to keep getting worse. In the back of my mind, I knew that the situation was probably heading toward disaster, but at that point, there wasn't much I could do about it.

Despite the trouble brewing between him and me, and the number of enemies in general that I was accruing at that moment, I was also having a lot of great things happen to me. Because I was in the flow and exponentially building on my success, I attracted a lot of incredible opportunities without even trying, and managed to stumble upon others seemingly by accident a lot of the time. But, because of how ignorant I was of the business world at large back then, there were also a lot of opportunities which I could have taken advantage of and didn't. One of those was the chance to take the company public, which I completely blew, because I wasn't even aware that it was happening at the time.

I was sitting outside a small beachfront café on the Venice boardwalk when a loud, shrill ringing started coming from my bag. It was my new cellular phone. It was the size of a shoe box, weighed 10 pounds, and consisted of a corded phone, attached to a box with a massive antenna that you had to fully extend in order to get a signal. It was a monstrosity of a device, but it was a rarity in those days, and I remember being quite proud when I first bought it. It's hard not to laugh, thinking about it now.

However, my number was unlisted, I'd just recently bought the thing, and only a handful of close associates had the number, so I was surprised when the call turned out to be from a complete stranger.

It was the secretary for a top executive from one of the country's largest financial investment firms, although I didn't know that at the time.

"Hello, I'm looking for Shaahin Cheyene of Herbal Ecstacy, please," said the professional-sounding female voice on the other line.

"You got him."

"Please hold for Mr. Brown."

I sat waiting for about 2 minutes before the secretary finally connected me, and found myself speaking with an older, gravelly-voiced man, who sounded like he'd spent a lot of years berating subordinates or smoking cigars, or both. He came across as very professional though—much more frank and serious than the usual clients I was used to dealing with in California.

"Shaahin, Tom Brown here. I got your number from our mutual friend, Jonathan. I just arrived from New York. I'd like to speak to you in our office. Are you available to meet today at noon?"

"I could be," I said, still not sure who this guy was or what he wanted.

"Great, we'll send a car for you."

I told him to organize the details with my secretary and hung up the call, before paying my bill and lugging my 10-pound phone with me back to the office. Mr. Brown had cut straight to the point, but in our 40-second call, he hadn't actually mentioned what our meeting was for.

Back at Ecstacy HQ, I probed Julie for more information on the mystery caller.

"He's a Wall Street guy. From Bear Stearns," she explained.

What the fuck is a Bear Stearns? I thought to myself, but didn't want to ask Julie to clarify, since the way she'd said the name sounded like she expected me to already know. *Sounds like some kind of Jewish animal control company.* Instead, what I said was: "Wall Street? Well, I don't want to buy any stock." All of my money was going into my company at that point, and I didn't know the first thing about the stock market, so investing in it was pretty far down on my list of priorities back then.

"Yeah, I know, but uh… maybe that's not what he's after? If he's sending a car for you?"

Julie had a point, but I still suspected Mr. Brown was just trying to sell me something. Nevertheless, I was intrigued, so when Julie called into my office just before 12 and told me there was a limousine waiting outside for me, I grabbed my heavyweight phone and briefcase and headed downstairs.

The limo took me to a sky-rise building near Santa Monica, and when I got out of the elevator on the top floor, I quickly realized that the entire penthouse seemed to be dedicated to Mr. Brown's office alone. The wide room was set up like one, long runway, leading right to his desk.

His secretary was all smiles as she motioned to me to follow her and sat me down in one of the plush leather chairs opposite Mr. Brown. He was warm and friendly when he greeted me—something I hadn't expected from our brief phone conversation, and a detail which instantly put me on guard about the whole situation. Then three people came in, carrying tea and detox juices and a whole bunch of vegan hors d'oeuvres, and I really got suspicious. They'd clearly done their research on me. This was a perfectly orchestrated sell, if I'd ever seen one.

I eyed the food warily, but it was actually delicious, so I begrudgingly took a few bites while Mr. Brown warmed me up with a bunch of small talk. "You know, bud, I actually grew up with a lot of Persian friends!" he told me, trying to assure me of his multicultural outlook in that way that only people with very few ethnic friends do. "In fact, one of my best friends is a Persian named Fred." A Persian named Fred? Really?

Misguided attempts at empathizing with me aside, he did a relatively good job of trying to build a rapport with me and get me talking about my company. *To his credit, he's feigning interest in the business really well,* I thought, taking a sip of tea.

"So, I heard you're doing several million in sales a month?" Mr. Brown asked. His expression hadn't changed, but I sensed that we were getting to the part where he tried to get me to buy a boatload of stock through his company.

"Yeah, we're doing good," I said elusively.

He kept asking more questions about the company—what was our founding team like, how did we see our growth projections for the next few years, what markets we were expanding to—and to each one, I gave the most unspecific reply I could think of. Mr. Brown never mentioned stocks, but I started to get the feeling that he was sussing us out for some kind of corporate takeover, instead.

After a while, I think he got the idea that I wasn't interested in whatever he was offering, and we just cordially shook hands and went our separate ways.

With the meeting finished, I got in the limo and went back to my office in Venice, still wondering what the hell had just happened.

When I walked in, Julie immediately asked me how the meeting had gone, and I said something like, "I don't know. It's just some asshole trying to sell me stock. If he calls again, tell him I'm not interested." And that was that.

Mr. Brown's office did call again. And they kept calling back, multiple times over the next few weeks, but we just kept ignoring them.

I never really thought much about it again after that, because I was wrapped up in running my company, so I didn't have time to dwell on a weird corporate meeting. But looking back on it now, I think he was feeling me out to see if we were a good fit for them to take us public. And I think Mr. Brown was very interested in the company. But I didn't even know what that meant. I had no idea what going public meant—I'd never traded a stock, owned a stock, none of that stuff. So I just kind of assumed that he was trying to sell me stock, or that he wanted to be my stock broker or something.

That's how unsophisticated I was. Had I been a little bit more open to the idea, sought out expert counsel, or even had an experienced mentor at that time, things could have been very different— Herbal Ecstacy could have been a publicly traded company. Maybe I would have decided it wasn't the right choice for us, and would have chosen to remain a private enterprise, or maybe I would have waited and gone public later. Maybe I would have made multiple billions of dollars, and been able to actually track how much my company was really worth. Who knows?

My company was huge, and it was only getting bigger. There was no other supplement company that had experienced such a meteoric rise in such a short period of time. In those days, the supplement companies that made the kind of money that we did had all been around for ages, and they had big names and established brands behind them, whereas we were a brand-new company. Before the internet, information took longer to get from one space to the next—influencers weren't able to influence masses of people with a single click, it took time to build a following. So the fact that Herbal Ecstacy became a global phenomenon, seemingly overnight, really speaks volumes to how impactful that product was. I assume that viral effect is what had the people at Bear Stearns doing heavy research into who we were and how the company worked.

But I was cocky and I was arrogant. I turned that opportunity down without ever really exploring it.

If I'd had a good mentor, I might have avoided some other problems, too, like the many lawsuits that were starting to be filed against the company. And I soon did find another mentor, although he was far from the traditional one you might imagine.

Journal Entry: Reality Distortion Field

	Explore Your Options	Waiting
What is it?	We know the more choices we have the better decisions we can make. Exploring your options is always assessing every opportunity from all angles, rather than dismissing the seemingly-uninteresting ones offhand	Waiting is what gives you the time to explore your options and decide on the best course of action.
Why is it important?	Wealth is a result partly of access to options. If you reject opportunities without taking the time to fully consider the possibilities they present, you could be missing out on new paths to success (or deals, or revenues).	Just like 'no deal is better than a bad deal,' sometimes 'a deal later is better than a deal now.' So it's important to wait for the right opportunities, rather than blindly seize whichever ones present themselves to you..
How to win:	By having as many options as possible to choose from. By always questioning everything, including your own assumptions about people and situations. Ask yourself: How could this be useful to me? What benefits would this bring? What are the risks? If you're unsure, find out. Don't let your ignorance stop you from spotting a potential opportunity. Seek counsel.	Knowing when to act and when to wait is the key. You need to act and not overthink, especially when it comes to starting your business. The ability to take decisive action is the mark of a successful leader, but so too is knowing when to sit and wait. By judging the playing field, and not jumping to hasty decisions, you can set yourself up for a win in the long-term.

CHAPTER 12:
WILDE TIMES AT ECSTACY HIGH

"**A** man called to sell me a plot and funeral insurance the other day. 'That's the one thing I am getting for free. I will be dead in the hallway and they will have to come haul me away for free,' I told him. Spend money on my own death? I think not," Stuart Wilde once told me, when we were hanging out together in the woods somewhere in Ireland. "Instead, I'll take that money to the pub, where I can buy something useful, like a pint of Guinness." Death was one of Stuart's favorite topics when he was shit-faced and/or wasted. He was hilarious, sober or drunk.

Stuart wrote one of my favorite books of all time, called *The Trick to Money is Having Some*. If you don't have a copy of it, I strongly recommend it. This book has a particularly special meaning to me, because it was written by a very dear friend and mentor of mine, but it's also got some interesting insights in general. He wrote it in the late 80s, I believe, although it really started to gain popularity in the early 90s.

In his book, Stuart talks about something that he called the "metaphysics of money." When it comes to money, very few people talk about how it really works, especially in a language that's palatable for the masses. I loved *Think and Grow Rich*, but it was also very old-school, and not written in a way that spoke to modern people in the 90s. I had read virtually every self-help and business book that had been released in more recent years, but Stuart's *The Trick To Money* was the first of them that really spoke to me. He had managed to encapsulate the spirit of guerrilla entrepreneurship and spirituality all within one work. He argued that—far from being some selfish, evil enterprise—making money was not only okay, it was godly.

That struck a chord with me.

On top of that, his writing was brilliantly refreshing. He was irreverent. He didn't care what other people thought, and he certainly wasn't your average, new-age group leader. He had told me that he was the "Guru to the Gurus." According to Stuart, Wayne Dyer, Deepak Chopra, Anthony Robbins, and countless others all called upon him for advice. In that world, he was a legend. I devoured his book, and now I own multiple copies of it, but the first one I bought is filled with notes, and nearly every page is highlighted.

Now, here's the thing. And I think this is a very interesting point to consider. When you're thinking about money, money is attracted to money. I learned that myself during the Ecstacy days, when I noticed the synchronicity and the external alignment of events that kept happening to grow the company's success more and more. So when I read Stuart's book, I knew I had to seek him out, because here was this guy describing the exact same phenomenon that I'd witnessed over and over again in my own life.

So, in typical, barely-legal millionaire style, I hired a jet to take me to one of his seminars in the mountains of New Mexico. It was just the kind of thing that Stuart himself would have approved of.

When I met Stuart, I gave him a bag filled with Herbal Ecstacy, Ecstacy cigarettes and about a dozen other products from our line, and within five minutes of introducing ourselves, we were roaming around the mountains of New Mexico together, with Stuart high as a kite on my pills and whatever other drugs he was already on at the time. I remember giving him another product we had, called Magic Mushrooms, which came in a little mushroom-shaped bottle, and he just lost it. He loved it so much. I took that as a real compliment, since apparently (and hitherto unbeknownst to me) he was somewhat of a connoisseur when it came to his drugs and debauchery. But that is what I loved about him. He never pretended to be a perfect white knight of the new age movement. He was their scoundrel stepson that they all loved and wished they could be like. He represented what real uncensored freedom could be like.

We became fast friends for years to come. I saw Stuart as a mentor, but I was also a huge fan of his, and just felt honored to be around him, most of the time. For the first time since the Walkman walked away, I had a hero of sorts to look up to. He sadly died a few years ago, but he had a huge impact on my life, and I'll never forget him.

Stuart was really an interesting character. He did this lifelong dance around money, and loved to explore how money worked, but he was also a master at putting himself at the center of lucrative deals and in situations where he would win. And that was the amazing thing.

Like many other iconic cult figures, Wilde was a rebel, and a savvy entrepreneur. He warned against the dangers of organized religions and cautioned against blindly following gurus, even though he himself amassed his own loyal following of people prepared to spend their money and their lives in any way that Stuart told them to. Also, like many other enigmatic leaders, Wilde was a contradiction.

He had started out as T-shirt and jeans designer in the U.K. at the height of the raging 60s counterculture movement, before he decided in the 1980s to leave the business world behind and follow a spiritual medium named Marshall Lever. Lever had a small following as a psychic and claimed to be "channeling" an entity from another dimension, which he called "Old Chinese." As time passed and Lever made the criteria for his followers more rigid, people began dropping out until there were only two people left in his little clan—one of which was Stuart. Lever soon retired, and Stuart decided to start his own movement by writing books and conducting seminars. It was the start of the New Age revolution, and he was at the forefront of it all.

Especially after the success of *The Trick to Money is Having Some*, Stuart's own following began to grow and become increasingly more fanatical. Despite his own warnings against demagoguery and the hidden agendas of other cult figures, he soon also started to fall victim to the temptations that came along with the power of his position. He divorced his Australian wife, moved in with a supermodel in the U.K., and began living a lavish lifestyle off the proceeds of his book sales and followers' "donations," amongst other schemes.

As his lifestyle became more extravagant, so too did his expenses. In a brilliant ploy to keep up with the ever-increasing costs of being a New Age guru, Wilde began a series of seminars, called *Warriors in the Mist*. He charged $5,000 per person, and regularly drew crowds of up to two hundred people per event—adding up to about a million dollars a day.

Soon, other New Age gurus were following in his footsteps, trying to milk people seeking self-improvement for all they were worth. Most of them even consulted with Stuart about the works they were publishing. He had become a sort of "guru to the gurus." He also started collecting information and stories on many of the top figures in the industry, and told me that drugs, prostitution, gambling, and strange ritualistic ceremonies were just the beginning of the weird things he knew that were going on in other New Age groups. He used to joke with me that one day, he would publish the stories and expose them all for the hypocrites they really were.

But I saw that Stuart himself was becoming the very thing that he once campaigned so strongly against. He liked to drink, shall we say, and by normal human standards, he was definitely an alcoholic. Stuart also loved women—many women. His seminars usually consisted of Stuart getting drunk and high before going on stage, after which he would sleep with one of the many desperate and seemingly "damaged" females he described as "broken birds" that attended his events, and emerge late in the evening to deliver some half-coherent teachings. But few got to see this side of Stuart. Only the inner circle ever glimpsed behind the curtain—most just saw an eccentric English gentleman with some wild ideas.

Despite all of that, though, I learned a lot from him. The fundamental principle of his philosophy is really, for me, "Life is NOT serious. Money is NOT serious. Seriousness is a disease of the ego. You have to be able to laugh at everything. Money is just a form of energy. It is not scarce, unless you make it so. Choose to be wealthy and abundant. Don't judge other people's experiences. Let them have their wealth or their poverty. Most importantly, detach. DETACH, DETACH, DETACH. Don't push. What is "yours" will come to you. You create your life, your energy, your excellence, and the world will beat a way to you. The more you push outward, the more what you want will move away from you. Don't major in minor things. And if you don't have a major, fake it till you make it."

These were critical things that he talked about. He said: "If you don't have it, don't lose heart, hang on. In the meantime, you're going to have to work on your energy. For at this level, currency is energy, nothing more. As you raise your energy, people show up and buy. Now you'll be comfortable billing them. It's nothing more complicated than that. As you get stronger, it gets easier and easier."

So he wasn't talking about energy in a scientific sense, but in the sense that energy can be defined as your general vibe, how you look at the outside world, and how your actions are reflected in the environment around you. I don't think that's woo-woo at all, actually, if you think about it, and what Stuart talked about mostly was how to change your attitude and act like you were wealthy.

So when I was a millionaire and reading his books, I thought about being a billionaire, what would it be like if I made a billion dollars, and I tried to materialize that reality in the way I was living my life. I went on yachts and partied with celebrities and spent insane amounts of money, and somehow it attracted the right people and the right deals to me. And at the same time, I got to have an amazing time. Maybe I was in the flow. Maybe I just got lucky, I don't know. But something about the principles in his book worked for me.

Giving It Away

Another thing Stuart talks about in *The Trick to Money* is the idea of giving money away to get even more money back. So, if somebody asks you for money, or if anybody asks you for anything, really, he says just give it to them. What an outrageous concept, right? I read that part in the book—in fact, I highlighted it—and I thought to myself, *I'm gonna do this. All of what he's saying has worked for me so far, and I want to go from millions to billions. So I gotta go all in. Let's make it happen.*

I decided it would be best if I didn't tell anybody about this new resolution of mine, so that people didn't decide to take advantage of my new, principled generosity, but I did start saying yes immediately to any request that came my way. The first day of this new regime, a friend of mine showed up in my office, and he said, "Shaahin, I want to start a band."

So I said, "Let's hear the music."

He played his demo for me, and oh my god, was it bad. It was the worst music I'd ever heard. This guy had no chance of ever making it in the music industry, ever. I wanted to purge my stereo after listening to it.

My friend watched my face eagerly for a sign of my reaction, then mercifully hit pause on the track. "So, what do you think? We need all new equipment to get this thing off the ground, and I only need like $10,000 to make it happen. Would you lend us the money, maybe?"

I had to grind my teeth and cringe, but I had said I was going to commit to this, and so I had to do it. I went off and wrote him a check, and he thanked me over and over again, telling me that it was just a loan and I'd get my money back, plus interest, in no time, but I just smiled and nodded, knowing I'd likely never see that $10,000 ever again. I told him, "Don't worry about it. I don't give out loans, it's just an investment."

Unsurprisingly, I never saw that guy again.

The next guy that showed up in my office wanted to go skydiving in Hawaii, and he needed $5,000 for a trip for him and his family, and I wrote him a check, too. This happened again and again—I must have given away a couple hundred thousand dollars before I eventually changed this philosophy. As it turns out, it didn't bring me back a lot of meaningful returns, but I did learn something key from my time spent wilfully throwing away money all the time:
money is just a vehicle, and detachment from it brings freedom.

That realization, that moment of kind of emotionally detaching myself from money, brought me back to what Ed had told me the very first time I met him—that buying and selling is what makes the world go 'round, and that being able to influence people to make these transactions is the most important part of being successful. Money is just one vehicle of that influential ability. There are other ways to influence people, too.

When you can cultivate that detachment—and I'm not recommending that everybody should go and give away hundreds of thousands of dollars—but if you can detach from the minor things, it becomes a lot easier to focus on the big picture. At that time, that amount of money was a small thing to me, and I learned that even larger sums of money would come and go. But when I learned to detach from the power that money traditionally holds over people, and understood that it was a vehicle of influence, like anything else, and that it wasn't so serious, and I could always make more, everything changed. When I took that piece of information in, and really absorbed it and incorporated it into the way I approached my business, that's when we went from making hundreds of millions of dollars to a billion dollars in revenues.

One weekend, Stuart was in town visiting, and we decided to go up to the mountains with a group of friends to have a bonfire and a small gathering out in the forest. So about ten or twelve of us were sitting around the fire, drinking beers in the wilderness and talking life and business and money, when suddenly Stuart took out a pile of cash, and started waving it around, daring us all to throw it in the fire.

For me, the very notion was sacrilegious. But that was exactly the lesson that he was trying to teach us—how to detach from chasing money, and relinquish the power you give it over yourself. None of us jumped to accept the challenge, though, so he started throwing hundred-dollar bills, one by one, into the fire.

Most of the people there didn't have a lot of money. Everyone was totally shocked, and even once they started throwing $20s in themselves, they gasp, "Oh my god!" Whenever they watched one go up in flames they were all giggling nervously like naughty school children.

Then came my turn. Everyone turned to look at me, except for Stuart. He just kept calmly committing $100s to the flames, almost never saying a word. Just burning his stack of cash methodically. Now, I was an extremely money-conscious person at the time. I was obsessed with it, and with making more of it, so the idea of just burning it for no reason was incredibly hard for me to swallow. But Stuart had a sort of indescribable effect on people, a little like the way the Walkman had, and somehow, he managed to convince me. Eventually, I just said, "fuck it," and took out my wallet.

So there we were, a group of buzzed wayward souls, sitting around a fire in the middle of the wilderness with our wacky spiritual guru, burning all of our money together. We must have burned through ten grand that night.

Setting my cash on fire for no reason was just another one of the crazy things that happened in those days. We all laughed, and I never thought much about it again. But what the whole exercise really was, looking back, was an affirmation that money wasn't real. I mean, it was real, but it didn't mean anything.

At the same time as I was burning through money in the mountains, the company was hemorrhaging it. The suicide margins were serving us well, because we definitely would have been dead and buried by that point without them.

Legal fees were starting to mount up. We were getting slapped with actions and suits left, right, and center, by private entities and public agencies alike. Product was inexplicably going missing. In a largely cash business, we had duffel bags full of thousands and thousands of dollars moving around the office all the time, and I knew that opportunists were going to take advantage of that. I got regular financial reports from Kirby, but I didn't even believe the numbers I was seeing. We had so many millions of dollars coming in that it felt like the well would never run dry, but it was hard for me at any given point in time to judge just how deep the well truly was.

My staff was now close to two hundred people, but I felt like I couldn't trust any of them. I thought every single one of them might be stealing from me.

I figured they were all pretty loyal to me, because I was paying them three times as much as most of them could have gotten anywhere else, but in retrospect, that's probably not why the majority of them hung around and worked so hard to please me. They didn't want to lose their jobs, because that would mean losing access to our warehouses full of pills and the sacks of cash they were being asked to transport. That was where most of them made their real money.

At one point, I started noticing that certain people were buying cars, expensive watches, or even houses, that I knew they definitely shouldn't have been able to afford. I mean, I was paying them well, but not that well. It made me wonder, where the hell was all that money coming from? The answer seems so painfully obvious to me now, but at the time, I guess the reality hadn't fully sunk in yet.

Still, I was suspicious, so I started to dig a little deeper into what was going on, and I found out that a lot of my employees had been regularly helping themselves to product, cash, or both. I started hearing stories about people selling Herbal Ecstacy on Venice Beach on the weekends and pocketing the profits, and entire truckloads of pyramid boxes disappearing off the logbooks. It seemed like everyone was in on it—one person would steal some money, another would cover it up in the records, and someone else would smile and lie to my face about the whole thing.

It didn't feel like just an attack on the business, it felt like it was almost personal. I thought I'd been a good boss—well, I mean, I wasn't a very personable character all the time, but I had Borris for that—and I had given these people a chance to make great salaries and work at this fun, exciting company, and all they wanted to do was stab me in the back. They all wanted even more for themselves than what I was giving them.

That feeling of paranoia soon spread out into my other relationships, too. I started to question Lisa's motives, even though she'd given me no real reason to.

She used to clip out the articles and ads for Herbal Ecstacy that she found when reading through newspapers or magazines and save them in a folder. It was little things like that which made me really crazy about her. Sure, I was still traveling the world, meeting different women and having some wild private afterparties, but when I came home, she was the only one I wanted to be with. Usually. There were also times when we'd fight like a pair of angry cats trapped in a sack, and she would storm out for weeks at a time without me seeing her. It was a tumultuous, on-and-off relationship, but it was the closest thing I had to stability at that time.

She didn't care about all that stuff. The money, the fame, the glamour—none of it really impressed her. If I bought a new car, she'd make some joke about men always trying to overcompensate for something. If I offered to take her anywhere in the world she wanted to go, she'd choose her favorite pizza place in town, not some five-star hotel in Bali. Lisa was different from all the other girls. She actually loved me for me, not because I was the king of the Herbal Ecstacy empire.

That meant a lot to me, back then. Still, my trust issues had gotten so bad that I couldn't help but wonder if it was really authentic or not. Was she only with me because I helped her get modeling gigs, and let her stay in an awesome mansion?

When I asked her as much, she threw a shoe at me.

Staring at the nickel-sized hole the heel of her stiletto had put in my wall, and how close it had been to my head, I rounded on Lisa, ready to lay into her for almost taking out my fucking eye with her Louboutin, but before I could open my mouth, she laid into me.

"Is that what you think, you fucking moron?" Her Jersey accent always got sharper when she was angry, and right then it was the strongest I'd ever heard it. "You think I'm some fucking whore who's just using you for your money?"

"I—"

Lisa carried on shouting right over me, so I snapped my mouth shut and let her continue, watching carefully to make sure she didn't reach for the other shoe. "So when I tell you I love you, you think I'm lying? I'm just full of shit, right?" She was shorter than me, but she lifted her chin to try to square off with me, her eyes defiant as they met mine. "You L.A. guys are all the same, you know that? Thinking every single girl is just some evil gold digger. I thought you were different, but you're just a self-absorbed fucking asshole, like all the rest of them."

She raised her arm, maybe to slap me, but I caught her wrist before I could find out. I let my hand slide down to lace my fingers in hers, and released a breath I hadn't realized I'd been holding.

I could see she wasn't just pissed at me for thinking the worst, but it really hurt her, too. If she was putting on an act, she was doing a hell of a convincing job of it. "Maybe I am," I sighed. "I've just been disappointed every day for the past year, it feels like. Everyone's stealing from me—my employees, my competition, my friends—and it's started to mess with my head, you know? I'm sorry. I know that's my issue, and I've got to deal with that, but I shouldn't put it on you."

Lisa's fierce expression melted into a huge grin in an instant, her perfect teeth all on display. "No, you shouldn't," she nodded in agreement, giving my hand a squeeze. "But you shouldn't let anyone fuck with you, either."

And just like that, the fight was over. That was how it was with Lisa. She could be just as mercurial as me, especially when she had a few drinks or lines of cocaine in her system, and that meant that things could quickly flare up into white-hot arguments between us, and just as suddenly cool and solidify once more.

She was right, of course. Lisa may not have known the first thing about business, but she was a tough chick, with a fair amount of street smarts that she'd picked up from her youth in Jersey—something which, from the few stories she'd told me, had been pretty rough, peppered with abuse, addiction, and trouble with the law. All of that had given her a cutthroat attitude that would have served her admirably well, had she ever decided to become an entrepreneur herself.

So Lisa actually frequently gave me great advice like this, without even meaning to, necessarily. I shouldn't let anyone fuck with me, and I was going to start making sure it wasn't so easy for anyone to screw me over ever again.

I had a business to run, an empire to build, and I couldn't let leeches jeopardize that, or distract me from the task at hand.

The next day, I went into the office, and made everyone go outside and stand in one long line all down the beach in Venice.

I had one rule as a boss, and that was that, if I fired someone, I was going to do it face-to-face. So I walked down the whole row of people and fired every single one of them—two hundred people, one after another. There was a line of people all wearing glow-inthe-dark Ecstacy butterfly shirts, going all the way down the block and around the corner, each waiting for the axe.

"You're fired," I said, then moved to the next. "You're fired. You're fired. You're fired." And so on and so forth. All in all, I think it took me less than an hour or two to fire them all. One guy, who had just started with us, remained. It was his first day. His name was Ben, and he was from Ghana, West Africa. We met through the Walkman, and I had hired him, unsure of what role he would take in the company. Since he had just started, I did not fire him. Ben ended up being the only person I hired in those days that did not take advantage.

That day most of them walked off, and I never heard from them again. But a lot called and left messages over the next few days with me or Ben, asking why they'd been included in this mass layoff. Because everyone on the team knew that a lot of theft was taking place, too, except (unlike me) they probably knew exactly who was responsible for all of it. So the ones who were shocked and hurt at having my suspicions extended to them, I hired back.

I felt like, having done this huge housekeeping of my staff, I could now have a lot more faith in the people working for me. These were the loyal ones, I reckoned, the people who had been honest all along. Nevertheless, I did also hire a private investigator, whose sole job was to make sure there was no more stealing going on, and he still continued to catch people at it—either helping themselves to some cash before tallying up an order, or overpricing product and pocketing the difference, or just taking whole boxes of pills to sell on their own somewhere.

I never really solved that problem—in fact, it only got worse as time went on. Part of that was the half-assed way that I'd gone about assembling my crazy team, and part of it was the fact that even I still didn't know how much money we were actually making. Lisa was right—it was inevitable that people were going to take advantage of that.

After that, I started hiring new people, and I decided that, this time around, I was going to do a better job of it. I didn't have time to interview every candidate myself, but I told Borris and Rob to find the best, most trustworthy people they could to fill the vacancies created by my mass firing session on the beach.

One of the people Rob found to be a new distribution manager was this guy, Steve. Steve was an old friend of Rob's, but also an ex-convict, as I later found out. He didn't have any formal managerial experience, but he had run an interstate drug trafficking ring in his earlier years, so he did know a thing or two about moving pills. I ended up paying to put him through night school to get his business management degree, and rented a house for him and his family to live in close to the office. I thought doing things like that would help buy his loyalty—like I was giving away money to get something back, just as Stuart had taught me—but in the end, it didn't exactly work out like that. Maybe I wasn't doing it right.

Journal Entry: Reality Distortion Field

	Currency is Energy	Trust & Loyalty
What is it?	The idea that money is just a form of energy is one of Stuart Wilde's core teachings.	Trust and loyalty are the foundations of every successful team.
Why is it important?	Because seeing money as a vehicle, rather than as an end in and of itself, is part of being in the flow and attracting increasingly better opportunities to you. You have to detach from the monetary value of currency, and instead see it as a means to achieving greater and greater success.	You have to be able to share your "secret sauce" with your team, without fear of them selling it to the competition. But, more importantly, you have to trust the people around you to consistently deliver amazing work if you want to be sure your business will run smoothly. Team building is one of the tasks that should never be delegated or abdicated by a leader according to my friend Marx.
How to win:	In Stuart's words, "Create your life, your energy, your excellence, and the world will beat a way to you." Don't chase having the money—chase having the energy that having money brings. That energy will magnetically attract money (and people) to you, anyways.	Cultivate trust first by hiring experts who you can rely on to do their jobs well, and then by having full transparency (and a system of checks and balances) within your organization to keep everyone honest. Cultivate loyalty by being generous (but not too generous), fair, and giving people autonomy. Remember as a boss it is your sole responsibility to build the team and inspire them to win for you.

CHAPTER 13:

THE 350-
MILLIONDOLLAR SCAM?

In December of 1996, we seemed unstoppable. Ecstacy was selling huge in every market we were in, and even though cheap copycats had sprung up, trying to grab a piece of our market share, we were untouchable. We'd established our brand so firmly that no competitor was going to have an easy time dislodging us from our position at the top. We were Coke and there was no Pepsi. I was throwing wild parties almost every day, and thanks to our connections in Hollywood, not only were many celebrities our customers, they also regularly turned up at these drug-fuelled soirees, getting high on our pills so they could fully let loose at my mountain lodge in Topanga.

All of them knew me, and whenever I'd walk into a room, people would do a little cheer for the kid who had made the whole evening possible—the one who had built this insane world for all of us to enjoy. I started to feel like quite the celebrity myself. In the Esctacy rave scene, people treated me like a rock star, and more and more people from the outside world were beating down my door, dying to catch a glimpse behind the curtain of my weird and wonderful empire.

I was starting to get a little more comfortable with life in the limelight. I still didn't like taking photos and avoided cameras as much as possible, but it was nearly impossible to escape the media attention when I was in Malibu. A random photo of me leaving in my Ferrari or Porsche or dining with some model often made the back pages of the L.A. rag magazines, usually with some caption speculating over who this mysterious young millionaire really was, and where he'd come from.

When I needed time away, I'd drive up to Topanga and have a quiet weekend with Lisa (we were "on-and-off" at that stage), without turning on my phone once the whole time, but inevitably, when I drove back from the mountains, I always descended back into the chaos that awaited me down below. Rob was gleefully willing to handle all the interviews while I was away, but as soon as I was back, the press always demanded me instead, and I think having his spotlight constantly ripped away from him forced a bigger wedge between us than ever before. My assistant was informing me about calls from different reporters every day, asking for a comment about the latest lawsuit that had been filed against us, and I felt like Tom and I were constantly attached at the hip, hammering out the details of the next case we were trying to win.

So when I got a call from a "journalist," who worked at *Details* magazine, telling me that they wanted to do a huge cover piece about me, I wasn't too surprised. I did, however, think it would be the perfect marketing opportunity for us. Any publicity is good publicity, right? And the media gave us endless amounts of free publicity in those days.

Details, in particular, was a great fit for us. They were a music publication—I was going to share the cover with Chris Cornell, the lead singer of the band Soundgarden, who were huge at the time—so it was an ideal way for us to reach new customers in different music scenes, just like we had at Lollapalooza. The people at *Details* knew how popular Herbal Ecstacy was with concertgoers and music fanatics around the world, so we were a good choice for them, too. It seemed like it was going to be a great synergistic relationship.

You could say that Rob didn't take the whole thing very well. He kept trying to brief me on what to say during the interview—I think he was worried that I'd screw it up and make the company look bad—and at one point, he even said that he was going to write a script for me. That's where I drew the line. "You do know that you're my spokesperson, right? Not the other way around?" I finally snapped at him during one of his long, pre-interview grilling sessions. I must have hit a nerve, because he got up and walked out, and he didn't say another word about the *Details* article again, after that. Every time it was brought up, though, he'd just sort of silently stew in the back of the room. I could tell that he wanted it to be him on that cover. How could I tell him that, if it was, we wouldn't be getting this cover story at all? People were interested in me because I was young, alternative, and an enigma—nobody would have cared half as much if our CEO was a middle-aged bald guy who came from a well-to-do Jewish family.

Still, Rob had a point. Most of the media attention we got was negative, and there was a good chance that this feature could turn out to be the same. It made me pretty apprehensive going into it, but The *Details* Reporter kept assuring me that it wasn't going to be a hack job—their readers were just interested in my story and how I'd managed to build the company from nothing.

He and I did a series of one-on-one interviews, and he also shadowed me at work once, so that he could do a kind of "Day in the Life" segment for the article. As it turns out, he was even worse than your average, douchebag journalist. The moment he had his tape recorder running, he fired derisive comments and outrageous questions at me non-stop, and I could almost see his upper lip curling in disgust and disdain when he took down notes on whatever I said. I know that's kind of a reporter's job, to ask the tough questions, but he was so arrogant in the way that he did it, speaking to me like I was some filthy kid who had no right even being in the same room as him. He didn't ask much about the company at all, really—all he wanted to know was who I was sleeping with, what drugs I did, whether or not our strategy was to get young kids hooked on our product so they'd be customers for life, things like that. He seemed to think every rumor he'd heard about me, and about Herbal Ecstacy, was true, and wanted me to address each one of them. I felt like it was a complete waste of time, trying to defend myself against insane accusations, like that we were smuggling cocaine from South America, and that's where our real profits came from. At the end of the day, he was just a failed writer, putting out third-rate articles until *Details* gave him this opportunity. He knew that the story which would sell the most copies was the one with the most drama, and that is what he crafted.

With that fiasco over, they then flew me out to New York, where the magazine had rented out an old castle to be the backdrop for the cover shoot, and when I arrived, my paranoia only grew stronger.

The guy they'd hired to take the photos was David LaChapelle. He was (and still is) one of the best photographers in the world, and is most well-known for his groundbreaking portraits of celebrities, like Rihanna, Michael Jackson, and Leonardo DiCaprio.

LaChapelle is known as the "Fellini of photography," thanks to his completely unique, otherworldly aesthetic. He mixes colors like he's trying to transpose a Warhol painting onto the real world, and creates these insane alternative universes with the way he stages and composes his incredible images.

Now, at the time, I had absolutely no idea who the guy was. It wasn't until later, when I saw the final photos and started looking into his other work, that I realized how perfect of a choice he'd been for this particular cover. If I'd known who he was and how epic his photography was, I would have been over the moon to work with him. But I didn't, so instead I took out all my paranoia on him.

I grilled him for hours before we started shooting. "You're not gonna make me look stupid, are you? Or make me look like a drug dealer? I don't want to look like a drug dealer. You know we don't actually sell drugs, right?"

"Really? That's a shame. It'd be cool if you did," David finally said, taking me completely off-guard. "Look, if I were you, I would listen to what 'they' are saying and just own it."

I was totally freaked out, and suspicious of every little thing 'they' did. But David was so cool about it all, and so reassuring, that he managed to put me at ease before the shoot finally began. He's an amazing, energetic guy to be around, so it's hard not to get along with him. Plus, we were hanging out at this stunning estate, and there were swimsuit models all milling around the property to be extras in the photos, so it was bound to be a good time.

And that's how I was convinced to put on a pink robe and sit on a neon throne for an article entitled "The King of the Thrill Pill Cult."

Despite my nerves, it turned out to be a pretty fun weekend. I quickly realized that David was sort of a big shot, and that the production team from *Details* weren't able to really tell him what to do. He has this unbelievably creative artistic vision, and he wasn't going to let anybody stand in his way of executing it the way he wanted to. That made me feel much more secure about the whole thing—knowing that he was 100% focused on delivering amazing photos, not pandering to whatever image it was that the magazine people wanted to project.

After we wrapped in the evening, we'd party with the models at the castle, or in New York City's best clubs, and I handed out tons of free samples of our pills and other products, getting lots of interested customers' phone numbers in return.

It was great. I'd already finished the interviews with The *Details* Reporter—that venomous slug of a human being—so now, the whole thing was over. I flew back home, and tried not to worry too much about what the end result would be. Even bad publicity was good publicity, right? Besides, it was out of my hands now.

~❖~

A little over a month later, in January 1997, the issue was released.

I had just ended a business meeting with a buyer from New York, when Julie came storming in. Normally, she was the picture of British reservedness, but today I could almost see smoke coming out of her ears.

"I just came back from the newsstand, and I have the first copy. You're not going to like this," she said, her lips drawn tight into a thin line. She was clutching a rolled up copy of the magazine in her white-knuckled fist like she was ready to beat someone with it. Julie had been against the whole idea from the start.

"Why, what's wrong? Did they not give us enough coverage?" They had said it would be a feature and a cover shoot, but maybe they'd relegated us to a tiny column on page 46—who knows?

"That's not the problem. The article is five pages long, and you're on the cover," she sighed.

"Okay, then… what's the problem?" I asked hesitantly, not sure if I wanted to hear the answer. I already had an idea of what she was going to say next.

"Well, it's the heading on the cover. They have a really amazing photo of you, but it's accompanied by the title, 'The 350-MillionDollar Scam,'" Julie blurted out, like she was trying to get the bad news over with as quickly as possible. She unrolled the magazine and held it out for me to see, watching me uneasily for any sign of a reaction.

"Does it say what the scam is?" I took the magazine from her and looked over the cover, my brows drawn together in confusion. "Are they trying to say the pills are fake, or that the revenues we're reporting are inaccurate, or… ?"

"That's the thing. I've read through it, and it doesn't actually say anything in the article about a scam. It's just the headline they chose, probably to get more readers. What they do, though, is make it seem like all of your money is blood money or something, by painting you as some kind of drug lord," she explained nervously, and there was a halting stutter to her voice as she swallowed hard and continued. "It says you're the King of the Thrill Pill Cult." Julie seemed shocked when I didn't freak out screaming or anything. I just nodded and took the magazine from her, then left the office for the day. I wanted to be alone when I read it, not surrounded by all my employees. Then, if I did freak out, at least no one would see.

I called Lisa to tell her I was going out of town for the night, and drove up to my house in Topanga.

A five-page exposé piece done on you can have a pretty serious psychological effect. This was a point in my life where my cockiness was at its absolute maximum, yet despite my apparent arrogance, my confidence was at an all-time low. After that article was published, it plummeted to altogether new depths.

Lisa was the only one who knew how self-conscious I secretly felt. I'd started out sleeping in the back of my car under a freeway overpass, and had ended up making over a billion dollars from my loyal following of raving customers, but I still suffered badly from Imposter Syndrome, and the sensationalist *Details* article only made me feel even more like a fraud.

I read and re-read the article alone in the lodge, and at one point tossed my phone over the balcony to silence for good the endless calls I was getting from people asking for a comment on the story. I was still trying to let it all sink in.

It seemed like the whole purpose of the piece was to discredit me in any way possible so they could sell more copies. They presented stories out of context, and the tone of the article was totally antagonistic. You could tell how much the *Details* reporter hated me from the language that he used. The headline was certainly controversial, but reading the article, I soon realized that Julie was right—they provided no evidence to support the claim that Ecstacy was a scam. They just relied on half-told truths and blackening misrepresentations of my personal life to paint the picture they wanted of me. For the most part, the reporter focused on my aggressive business tactics and metaphors that aligned me with gangsters, to show my domination of the natural supplements world as akin to someone running a crime syndicate.

Yet, as hard as they tried, it seems they couldn't find any real, damning information about me. The reporter had called Stuart Wilde, as well as a few other celebrity friends of mine, to get a quote from them for the story, and afterwards they told me that the journalist had been trying his best to press them for some gory details he could publish. Of course, all of these people were regular fixtures at my house parties and die-hard fans of my product, so I think they all gave me a glowing reference. Needless to say, few to none of their positive comments were included in the story.

The only good aspect of the article were the photographs. They really were incredible, and I thought that David LaChapelle had kind of perfectly captured the strange, psychedelic world of excess that I inhabited back then. That's why I chose it to be the cover of this book.

Still, as I read through the article for the third or fourth time, I panicked and self-deprecating thoughts started to race in my head. I thought that nobody would like me or associate with me anymore. I thought that my friends would all disown me. I imagined my life being over, and my business ending, all in that one moment. The credibility that I had built through years of hard work had taken an immense hit.

Time went by and the magazine got around. I think at that time the distribution of that magazine was likely in the millions or at least in the hundreds of thousands. As the magazine traveled from person to person and around the world, I noticed something very different from what I had expected.

~❖~

In his latest book, *Unreasonable Success and How to Achieve It*, bestselling author and serial entrepreneur Richard Koch lays out a roadmap to success. In it, he claims that:

Successful people typically don't plan their success. Instead they develop a unique philosophy or attitude that works for them. They stumble across strategies which are shortcuts to success, and latch onto them. Events hand them opportunities they could not have anticipated. Often their peers with equal or greater talent fail, while they succeed. It is too easy to attribute success to inherent, unstoppable genius.

At the top of the list of key attitudes and strategies that can propel one to new heights of accomplishment is: self-belief!

I remember what Ed had taught me. You can never allow anyone else's opinion of you shape your belief in who you are. It was true. Every time I doubted and faltered from my seemingly unshakeable beliefs, and every time I allowed others to shake me out of my own reality distortion zone, I faltered.

Marriage proposals, alliances, friendships, business proposals, deals (big ones), lawsuits, and (even bigger) unwarranted sexual harassment lawsuits ensued.

Everyone seemingly wanted a piece of me. A few women who had worked for me for a short time in the early 90s suddenly came out of the woodwork. Some of them, I don't even think I'd met personally before. The truth is, I wasn't in the office long enough at that time to harass anyone. I wasn't a harassing boss. If anything I was an absent one. They falsely accused me of everything under the sun but when they realized that wouldn't stick they said that the workplace environment in itself was threatening to women because we had porn magazines (like *Playboy*) littered around the office. But they weren't there to serve a practical function, if you know what I mean —they were there because we advertised in those magazines! It was totally insane, and I was completely unprepared to deal with accusations like that. Luckily, none of them had any real evidence, so Tom was able to close those cases relatively easily, but there were even bigger problems we had to worry about. What could possibly be worse than a bunch of false sexual harassment suits, you might ask?

At the same time, we had a federal lawsuit brewing against us. We'd been sued by several states before, but now the FTC was starting a huge investigation into ephedra, and Tom told me that a coalition of state governments were getting together to slap us with a huge lawsuit of their own. When I tried to find out how serious of an issue this was going to be for us, he said he still didn't know how big it would end up being. Then, I walked into the office one day and Kirby told me we'd done a billion in sales revenues. Suddenly, I realized just how much I had to lose, how unwieldy of a beast my company had become, and how feeble of a master I was to tame it.

It was all too much for me to take. I drove up to Topanga again, just to be alone. It was something I was doing more and more these days, and this time, I felt like I never wanted to go back to the real world again. All I wanted to do was shut myself away and drown out the roar of the maelstrom that was constantly swirling around me.

I went out and sat by the hot tub, staring at the water and the patterns that the ripples made, casting an unearthly, shifting blue light around the garden. The artificial strangeness of it fit my mood.

Lisa had been staying at her apartment in the city for a few weeks, working on a series of swimsuit shoots that had kept her too busy to come to Topanga, but she was back now. She listened to me talk about the article and all the messed up half-truths it contained, and all my worries about the impact it would have on my business life.

"I'm just not sure that anyone even likes me for me. I mean, I've never had a lot of friends, and I'm okay with that, but it's just crazy feeling like everyone you meet is out to get you, or get something out of you."

"I know. Sometimes, you're not even sure about me," she said dryly, rolling her eyes. "But seriously, I can't even imagine what you must be going through. If I were in your shoes, I'd be completely overwhelmed. There's no way I could manage all those people, all those orders, events, press briefings, lawsuits—I don't know how you do it, honestly, babe. You've got a lot of stuff going on right now, and I know it seems like the whole world is against you, and you have to fight against them all yourself, but just remember you're not totally alone here, okay? I'm always there if you need me. And I'm definitely not out to get you." She shifted so that she was straddling me and planted a kiss on my lips.

"I know, I know," I chuckled, running my hands over her hips. "I guess I'm just feeling a little insecure, that's all. I'm supposed to be this badass business mogul now, but a lot of the time, I'm like, 'Fuck, I was sleeping in the back of an old Lincoln a few years ago—how have I managed to fool all these people into believing I'm legit?' You know? I feel like a fraud." I had never admitted that to anyone before.

"You are not a fraud," Lisa huffed, jabbing her finger into my chest. "You are a badass business mogul. And most of the time, I think you really believe that. I mean, look at all the things you've done!" She gestured around at the house and the property we were sitting in. "Look at what you've built for yourself. Who fucking cares if you came from nothing? That just makes you even more of a badass, in my opinion."

"And you think everyone else sees it the same way you do? Like they don't see just an ignorant little kid who they can take advantage of?" I challenged her.

"No one thinks you're ignorant, they're just dirty fucking vagrant opportunists, that's all. And maybe they're not the real problem." She arched a knowing brow at me.

I gaped up at her. "What, so the problem is me?!"

"You are really generous —too generous, if you ask me. Maybe you should stop giving away so much stuff for free."

"But that's part of how this whole thing works, Lis. I do these favors, and then they owe me. The universe will bring it all back around," I assured her.

"Yeah, okay." She didn't sound convinced in the slightest. "But what about the people who just think you're an easy target? Like, 'Oh, Shaahin is so free with his money, he won't mind if we just take some for ourselves.'"

"I make it pretty fucking clear at the office that stealing won't be tolerated. I fired two hundred people, remember? All at once."

"And yet, people are still stealing from you?"

"Yes, all the time!"

"Is the company still doing well?"

"Yes, we're making a boatload of cash. Lisa, I found out the other week that we made a billion dollars in sales. A Billion. Isn't that messed up?"

"Messed up? That's incredible, baby! So why aren't we celebrating right now?" She hopped up and down on my lap, then started looking around, like she might find a handy bottle of champagne laying somewhere nearby.

"It's messed up, because I don't have a billion dollars. I can't account for anywhere near that amount. So there could be people stealing from me who I don't even know about. There could be something bigger going on. I have no idea. That's what's messed up," I sighed. Lisa looked back at me, clearly shocked by that, but I couldn't bring myself to meet her eyes. She was the only one who was really proud of me, and suddenly I regretted being so honest with her about how out of control I really was.

"Why don't I have Adan make you something to eat, and we can put on a movie or something?" she offered, and gave me another quick kiss before hopping up to go find the chef. I watched her go and then buried my face in my hands.

At least things with Lisa were great—she was here for me, no matter what, and didn't ask any questions about the girls I saw when she was away. But it still felt like it was all spinning wildly beyond my control.

I ended up retreating from it all for a couple of weeks.

I was trying to run my company, but it felt like the whole world was against me, everybody was stealing from me, and I didn't understand why. You know, when you're in it, it's hard to see what your life is really like—it's only from 30,000 feet that you can have a crystal clear view of what's going on and why. But when you're in your own bubble, it's hard to see clearly.

Achieving that level of success at such an early age meant that I never knew if people wanted to be my friend for me, or if they wanted the notoriety and luxury lifestyle that came along with hanging out with me. I didn't know if girls were interested in me as a person, or just wanted my money and to be around the buzz that circulated around Herbal Ecstacy. I didn't know if people really wanted to work for me, or if they just wanted to be around the madness and take advantage of the crazy way things were run to steal as much as they could carry. People are opportunistic. I felt like I couldn't trust anybody.

Yet, in a weird way, I was also so concerned about what other people thought about me. I was a self-made millionaire when I was just a teenager, and that was actually a very scary place to be. Because I had all of this confidence that got me to where I was, that unerring belief in myself, but what that mostly boiled down to was "fake it till you make it," right? I thought, Okay, I don't know a lot of things, but I'm gonna pretend like I do, and I'm not gonna let anybody else know how clueless I really am. But then the side effect of that was that I was always constantly worrying, *Oh my God, what if I'm found out?* What if people knew that six months earlier, I was sleeping in a vacant apartment that I'd stolen the keys to?

I felt like I was going to explode. I was the one who was supposed to keep this insane ship afloat, while we were being attacked on all sides, and it was all my own fault. I'd brought myself to exactly that point in my life, and I had no one else to blame but myself for the way things had turned out. I knew I had to make a decision about what to do next, but it was all too overwhelming. All I wanted to do was stay home, lock all the doors and windows, and try to think through my options— or avoid thinking about it at all, hoping something would magically change on its own. I spent a lot of time wishing I'd done things differently, lamenting the bad decisions I'd made to bring us here. I spent even more time wishing Ed was still around.

Eventually, though, I did have to go back and face the music. And what I found when I got there was something I had definitely not been expecting.

Journal Entry: Reality Distortion Field

	Self-Belief	Destroying Self-Doubt
What is it?	Knowing and believing in who you are and what your mission is, regardless of what others may think or say of you.	Ignoring others' opinions is owning your weirdness and staying true to yourself and your path. It is the foundation of any decent Reality Distortion Field.
Why is it important?	Because facing problems head-on and with absolute belief and courage is what gives you the grit and experience to continuously succeed, in any environment, even if that belief may seem unwarranted to someone on the outside. When the going gets tough is when real growth happens.	Especially when you're gaining success and gathering enemies, people are going to try to tear you down. But ignoring those opinions is crucial to staying on track for your own success.
How to win:	By standing your ground. Every successful person in the world has, at least once, been faced with a seemingly insurmountable problem. Or been scared or uncertain about their own path. But they only got to where they are now by conquering those obstacles, not running from them. This becomes much easier when you have what Richard Koch calls an 'Unreasonable Self-Belief'.	Stay in your own reality distortion field. Stay strong in your beliefs. Be like the palm tree whose deep roots allow it to shake with the wind but not fall. Remember the line between business and personal. Your competitors (and other jealous people) may not like your company coming in and stealing their profits, but you shouldn't take that personally. Never let others' opinions make you second-guess yourself. Create your own reality distortion field and make it so.

CHAPTER 14:

ME AGAINST THE WORLD

The 350-Million-Dollar Scam feature did nothing to slow down sales, however. Quite the contrary, actually. As a result of the publicity, business boomed to even greater heights, and I was officially thrown into the public eye, with no going back. On the back of that article, we got multiple features on the cover of *Newsweek* and dozens of other publications, were being requested for TV interviews more frequently than ever before, and all the free publicity sent our sales through the roof.

I took over as Herbal Ecstacy's spokesperson, and limited Rob's role to effectively what amounted to being an in-office mascot which he hated. To say he was pissed when I told him would be an understatement. He hurled his thick Motorola flip phone (a massive thing in those days) across my office so hard it took a chunk out of the wall, and told me, in no uncertain terms, that I was a snake and a liar, and that my self-obsessed need to control every aspect of the company was going to be my downfall. Then he stormed out, and didn't show up to work for the next two weeks.

That was the beginning of the end of my relationship with Rob. Not long after, I had to let him go from the company, and Steve left along with him. I thought that would be the end of it, but I underestimated how much Rob craved the limelight, and the lengths to which he would go to get it back again.

Despite what Rob thought, though, I was far from pleased to be stepping so firmly into the public eye. I'd never been a showman like him, and now that 90% of the questions I got from the media had more to do with my age and lifestyle than with Herbal Ecstacy or the success we'd achieved, most of the time, doing interviews was anything but an enjoyable experience.

Reporters lined up in front of the house to catch a glimpse of the guy who was allegedly selling drugs all over the world, but still, nobody could touch him. Newspapers were rife with speculations over my past and my present. Fabricated stories of me having connections with Mexican cartels and other drug lords often made the front pages as people grasped desperately for some kind of explanation behind my age and the unbelievable life I lived. These weird and wonderful stories seemed to grow more elaborate by the day, and they even overshadowed all the thousands of words that newspapers were printing about the lawsuits being brought against us by various different states.

I was shocked by how many people we offended.

Parents and parent associations hated us, because they felt we were corrupting their innocent children by exposing them to drugs. The anti-drug activists hated us, because we were "promoting drugs." They were all calling our product a gateway drug—which, as I later found out, wasn't a good thing. It meant that Herbal Ecstacy was acting as a bridge toward much harsher, more damaging drugs. But originally, I remember hearing the term and thinking, *Wow, that's kind of a cool name.* I just didn't have a clue what it really meant until the harsh reality of people's hate mail started pouring into our inbox on the heels of that *Details* article.

The pharmaceutical companies were equally upset because we were taking up their market share and we were mostly unregulated—unlike them. The natural products people despised us because they felt that we were bringing undue attention to the natural products industry, and they didn't want it to end up getting regulated because of that. Herbalists hated us because we weren't using the traditional formulas in the traditional ways. All manners of government agencies were out to get us because we had slipped under their

radar and found a loophole that allowed us to operate in the way we did. The religious people were upset, too, for whatever reason. The manufacturers of cheap, knock-off pills wanted to tear us down because we dominated the market with an iron hand. Even the outcast psychedelics community hated us because we were slandering their "sacred psychedelics" and turning their holy sacraments into a money-making venture. It really did feel like it was me against the world.

In the end, I basically got painted as some kind of dangerous, criminal misfit—a menacing evil that was perpetuating the deleterious effect of drugs on society. Editors often called me out, telling me that I should be ashamed of myself for not acknowledging the harm I was inflicting upon our great country.

I kept telling myself that, if I was making this many enemies, I must have been doing something very right. And there was one group which not only liked us, but loved us: our customers. So I tried to focus on the image of 200 million Herbal Ecstacy fanatics, all happily raving in their respective corners of the globe thanks to what I was doing, and let the sound of their acclaim drown out all the other noise.

> *"While you are sleeping, your enemies are planning your demise."*
> **Shaahin Cheyene**

Still, it was hard to hear, and I was still that kid inside who couldn't bear to back down from a fight, so I wasn't about to let them slander me in the national news without some kind of pushback. I designated Tom to deal with it, and he promptly served the newspapers with defamation notices. I barely even kept tabs on all the different lawsuits we had pending with them, since I had so much other stuff on my plate at the time, and I was starting to feel a little overwhelmed by it all, to be honest.

The world, almost unanimously, hated me. Rob wasn't speaking to me. Even Lisa was getting pissed over all the photos of me with other women that kept appearing in the papers, and she'd been threatening to move out for good. I had millions of dollars' worth of legal fees piling up, and the stream of lawsuits didn't seem likely to let up anytime soon. I felt like I couldn't trust my employees. The media was constantly digging for information on me, trying to find any weakness which they could exploit to sell more copies of their papers, and I was subconsciously terrified that they would find out who I really was. I had nightmares in which reporters asked me about the time I got caught squatting in an unfinished condo, or brought out my old boss from the copy shop to re-enact him beating me with his cane on live TV. I felt like a fraud on the verge of being exposed.

I suddenly thought about Ed one day while I was driving up to Topanga alone in my car. He would have told me to use the media to my advantage, not to let them use me as material for their eye-catching headlines.

I started to hatch a plan, and out of sheer coincidence, it wasn't long before the opportunity to put it into action dropped right in my lap, disguised as another challenge.

Tom called me one day and told me that I'd been requested to appear before a government panel on supplements, with the specific purpose of deciding whether or not ephedra—our key ingredient— was to be banned for commercial sale.

I didn't want to go, at first. I was still reeling from the *Details* article, and I didn't feel like I could handle another grilling like that in the public eye, so I kept putting off their calls and hoping the whole thing would just go away. I tried to tell Tom that I wasn't going to attend, but he wasn't having any of it. For once, he actually put his foot down with me.

"Shaahin, we need to talk about this." He had burst into my office without knocking, waving the summons letter around and disturbing my morning meditation ritual.

"There's nothing to talk about, Tom," I told him curtly, trying to focus on my meditation. "It's going to be a room full of stuffy old farts, all eager to tear me a new asshole. Sorry, been there, done that. I'm not interested."

"Look, if you don't do this, we won't have a voice at the hearings. If we don't have a voice, they'll all gang up and throw us under the bus, and there will be nothing we can do to defend ourselves. We don't want to be the sacrificial lamb. I need you to do this for me. For the company. Please." I cracked an eye open to look at his imploring face, and sighed.

Tom always had a way of convincing me to do the "appropriate" thing. It wasn't that he was a great attorney, but rather, it was his skill at relating to people. Tom was a peacemaker. His hippie sensibilities always led him to the path of least resistance. For a 39-yearold who lived in an attic with his insane girlfriend and all of her chickens, he was a remarkably wise and intuitive person sometimes.

"Fine!" I grumbled, and Tom happily marched out to confirm my appearance at the panel, before I had a chance to change my mind. Meditation spoiled, I clicked off my peaceful music and started preparing what the hell I was going to say in front of all these lawmakers.

I flew to Washington the next day.

When I walked into the panel meeting, the room was filled with all manners of lobbyists and government types, as well as all of the other heads of the big natural products companies, and everybody else that was involved in the manufacturing or sale of ephedra-based supplements. They were there to make the case for not restricting ephedra, because I wasn't the only person at that point making millions of dollars selling that ingredient. It was my competitors—the other herbal products businesses—that had asked me to come and speak in front of the panel. I think their plan was to throw me under the bus to save themselves. My competitors reckoned something like, "Let's give them the kid. He's selling drugs. We're selling vitamins—we're the responsible ones. Congress should just ban the long-haired anarchist guy, and leave the rest of us to make millions off of scooping up his customers."

It was a sea of browns, grays, and blacks in that room. Everyone was in their stuffy, buttoned-up shirts and suits, with their identical black briefcases, and when I came in, in my technicolor Ecstacy T-shirt and hospital scrubs, I think they all must have done a mental victory dance. Like, this is going to be too easy, right?

Wrong.

Tom and I had been prepping my statement and rehearsing responses non-stop since I agreed to attend, and when it came my turn to speak, it all went surprisingly smoothly. I gave my testimony to the lawmakers and politely walked out after we were done.

Outside the building, I was approached by one of the heads of the other supplements companies. He was an older man in his sixties, with a thick white beard and an even thicker Southern drawl.

"Son, I want to thank you for coming out here. But I need to ask you to do something for us, for all of us. We want you to take your product off the market voluntarily. Now, I know that might seem tough, but the truth is, it's giving us all a bad name. We all feel that the FDA won't push through with the ban, as long as we tone things down a little, and, well," he gave a little chuckle, "you're not really the toned-down type." The man clapped a hand on my shoulder like he was an old friend, rather than someone trying to tear down everything I'd worked my whole life to achieve. "Now, if you go along with this, we can make it worth your while. But if not, you might just find out what the consequences are of throwing stones around when you live in a glass house."

Clearly, my competitors weren't ready to give up on their plan of using me as a scapegoat, even if they hadn't been able to make me look bad in front of the panel.

Normally, my fighting spirit would have had me bursting at the seams to take all of these corporate clone fuckers down a few notches, but at the time, I really wasn't feeling like my usual, scrappy self. My crisis of confidence had gotten the better of me, and as Tom and I went to grab some lunch and sat together in one of D.C.'s parks to eat, I was uncharacteristically quiet, lost in thought and a gnawing sense of worry.

"What do you think I should do, Tom?" I said finally, while my attorney finished off the last of his granola bar. "They don't seem thrilled with us. If I'm not mistaken, that sounded like a threat to me. Should we consider listening to their offer, you think?"

Tom was pensive for a minute. Then he turned to look me straight in the eyes and said, "Throw some stones. Take the house down. Glass houses are fucking stupid, anyways." I'd never seen that look of steely determination on his face before. It gave me the boost of confidence that I sorely needed at that moment.

"Yeah! Who lives in a freaking glass house in the first place! Let's get to work."

I immediately set about turning the media circus to my advantage. Networks across the country were talking about the ephedra panel, and they were all eager to have me on a guest to talk about the controversy surrounding the issue. Instead of running away from all the attention, I decided I was going to face it head-on.

What I thought was a PR nightmare ended up becoming our most successful marketing campaign yet.

By the time I landed back in Los Angeles, my phone was ringing off the hook. I told Julie to book us as many television appearances as possible, and one of the first ones we landed was on *Nightline*. Sam Donaldson was to do the interview himself, and David Kessler, the presidentially appointed head of the FDA (and now my personal archnemesis) was to be on alongside me as an opposing viewpoint. Kessler refused to appear at the same time as me, so they had to film him in D.C. and me in Venice.

It was time to take the glass house down.

The next appearance I did was on *The Montel Williams Show*. The day before I was scheduled to do the filming, some anonymous source called me up and said, "Shaahin, don't go on. They're going to ambush you."

Now, there were a lot of people at that time who didn't like me, so it made sense that they would use the show as an opportunity to try to take me down a few notches. My unnamed friend told me that they planned to have a bunch of my usual enemies—big pharma, the government, other natural products people—come on as guests to attack me, and tell a bunch of terrible stories about natural highs. The show's producers hadn't told me any of this, of course, so the plan was clearly to catch me off guard and watch me sweat it out on national TV while I tried to respond to all of these stories.

The goal, I think, was to change public perception surrounding our products and our company. They didn't actually attack Herbal Ecstacy itself, so much as tried to paint the whole legal high movement as a danger to kids and society in general, and that's a tactic that could have worked out really well for them, if I hadn't been prepared with my own narrative.

Richard Rumelt, in his book *Good Strategy/Bad Strategy*, highlights how important it is to have a well-formulated plan of attack for any situation you're going into. It's not enough to have goals—you need to have a coherent strategy for how you plan on achieving those goals. In this case, my goal was to not only make it through the show without making my company look bad, it was also to use this opportunity to our advantage. My strategy for doing that was, to use Rumelt's words, to formulate a "cohesive response to an important challenge."

When I got that call warning me, I could have easily refused to go on. But I saw this as an unprecedented opportunity for me to get our product in front of millions of people—the perfect chance for me to use the media to my advantage, for a change.

They did try to attack me on the show, but to no avail. I had prepped tirelessly in the lead-up to the taping to make sure that I could counter every possible claim they could make with pure, hard facts. And they made my job easy, because none of them had really done their research very well. They tried to say the key ingredients we used were dangerous, but they hadn't even gotten the names of some of them right (like thinking ephedra and ephedrine were the same thing, which they're not), and I was able to school them on live television, in front of the whole country. I knew what was in my product, and I knew all the studies that had been done on all of my ingredients, and every case wherein someone had experienced complications from taking them. So, despite the fact that I was the youngest person in the room, I ended up sounding like the most well-educated one there. None of them were able to say much in response, once I'd laid out the actual facts, and by the end of the taping, I walked out of that studio feeling totally fucking victorious.

But I also had another trick up my sleeve.

While my enemies were busy plotting their attack, I was orchestrating my own (much bigger) offensive. The whole time they were arguing with me on air, I waited patiently for the perfect moment to unveil my master plan. They had no idea it was coming, and I felt like I was going to burst with anticipation, but I held it all in and fielded their questions calmly. Just waiting.

Then, the moment finally came.

"Do you really think people want to buy this product, knowing the potential 'risks'?" One of them sneered at me.

"You tell me," I shrugged, and unzipped my jacket.

The moment I peeled it off, revealing a Herbal Ecstacy T-shirt with a huge hotline number on it, visible from 100 yards, the entire audience suddenly did the same. Hundreds of hoodies all came off at once, each one hiding a Herbal Ecstacy shirt underneath.

You see, I *had* planned ahead.

With only a few hours to go before I had to be at the studio, I printed up as many T-shirts as I could find, with our 1-800 number emblazoned across the chest and back. I gave them out to everyone in the audience, along with free pills, as long as they agreed to wear the shirts live on the show. I told the whole audience to wear them underneath a sweater or something, and only take off their jackets when I did. So the cameras started rolling, and we had this big reveal, with the Herbal Ecstacy logo and our number displayed all across the studio. It was the best free PR we ever got.

My opponents were dumbfounded. They looked like they'd just found themselves tricked into coming into the middle of a rave cult lion's den, and they were desperate to find an escape.

It was all I could do to keep from throwing my head back and laughing.

See, I knew that, no matter what happened that day, it was going to get people interested in our product. Whether they slammed me and made our pills out to be the worst thing in the world, or it went miraculously well and they had only nice things to say about me and my company, the result would be the same. People enticed by the idea that our product was in some way taboo or dangerous would want to try it, and people who heard the positive things I had to say about it would also have their interest piqued. And I was absolutely right. Our phone lines started ringing off the hook the moment the show aired, and we sold more product off the back of that one broadcast than we had in the last few months combined.

We ended up making over $10 million from that one show, and the avalanche of new orders and revenues that came crashing down on us in the weeks and months that followed was truly remarkable.

Ed would have been proud.

Journal Entry: Reality Distortion Field

	Get Some Enemies	Control the Narrative
What is it?	Getting enemies isn't a bad thing—it's a sign that you must be doing something right; not just because you're pissing someone off but because you have struck enough of an emotional cord to elicit a feeling. This is true influence at work.	Like in the martial arts. Use your enemies momentum to win the battle. Controlling the narrative is using the media's (or the public's, or even your competitors') voice to your own advantage. It's inducting them into your reality distortion field.
Why is it important?	Generally, the more enemies you have, the more successful you are. And the louder they complain about you, the more disruptive your business likely is to your industry.	Because, you don't want to let a perfectly good enemy go to waste. You can use their momentum to propel you to a win.
How to win:	Make it your goal to misbehave regardless of what people think of you. This is what it means to be a true disrupter. No, seriously. "Well-behaved (people) rarely make history." So go out there and step on some toes, in the same way that Airbnb stepped on the hotels' toes, and now they'd all love to stab them in the back. Find a way to disrupt and do something new that people did not expect. When enemies show up and have a strong reaction to it, that's a pretty good sign that you know you're on to a winner.	First, ask yourself how any seemingly confrontational situation can be used to your advantage. Seek the advice of those who know more than you. Mentors often tell you what you need to hear, rather than what you want to hear. Don't let your need to be right get in the way of seeing their advice for what it is: an intelligent perspective from a trusted source that should be mined for all possible insight. Ideally, find many mentors. The more perspectives, the better.

CHAPTER 15:

THE BATTLE BEGINS

In the aftermath of *Montel*, the company officially reached its peak. We did more sales that year than in any year previous, and it looked like we would be doing billions of dollars in revenues from then on out.

In short, my competitors ended up cutting off their noses to spite their faces. Their plan to make me into the entire industry's scapegoat had completely backfired. Herbal Ecstasy was now selling more product than ever before, and the FDA moved forward with considering a wholesale ban of ephedra sales across the country, regardless of anything any of us did to stop them. They even issued a warning about the effects of the ingredient, to show how serious they were about cracking down on everyone in the industry.

The ride was getting crazier and crazier, but little did I know, I was also quickly running out of track.

In the background of all this success, there was a storm brewing. Tom told me that the big legal case against the company was now officially pushing through, and that it was seven states in total who had joined in the action.

The big issue at the heart of the states' lawsuit was the fact that we were claiming Herbal Ecstasy was not dangerous, and had no adverse side effects. In almost ten years of running the company, we had zero problems with people getting harmed by using our products, although of course, there were always some cases where people took way too much and ended up getting sick because of it.

The same can be said of any mind-altering substance.

Nevertheless, MTV, CNN, all the major networks at the time were running stories saying that our product was dangerous. Some of that was down to the FDA's interest in regulating or banning ephedra, and some of it was because of a common confusion between ephedra and ephedrine—the latter of which can have some pretty serious side effects. That was the same misconception I thought I'd put to bed on *Montel*, but reporters kept repeatedly making that mistake. In fact, I think MTV once did a feature where they showed a tombstone next to a picture of our product, and they said that some people had dropped dead at a rave while taking Herbal Ecstacy. But it wasn't even our pills that they were taking, it had been some other legal high product.

We sued some of these networks for libel, and won some pretty large settlements out of court, because they didn't actually have any proof to back up the claims they were making about Herbal Ecstacy being dangerous. But, remember what I said about one big success cancelling out a lot of small failures? Well, it works the other way, too. And our small wins in these suits were not enough to offset the huge loss we were about to take in the biggest court case yet.

The other issue was that they felt we were intentionally advertising to kids. We bought a package of late-night TV commercials, which ran across several networks, and one of them happened to be Nickelodeon, a kids TV network during the day but showing solidly stoner content after hours. Now, the commercial ran at 2 AM or something like that, when Nickelodeon shows black and white series and adult-oriented cartoons, but they still tried to skewer us over that one.

And I was defiant to the very end.

I could have just backed down. I *should* have just backed down, paid the fine, and walked away with my company intact. But that wasn't who I was then. And while I'd have made a different choice if faced with that same decision today, it still isn't who I am now. A part of me will always be a fighter, a child of that 1970s rebellion waged in the cradle of civilization, and while I would sign the check now if I could, I'd still have a bitter taste in my mouth afterwards, knowing that I backed down. When bullies come after you, is that what you do? Do you just throw your hands up and surrender? Sometimes, in the business world, that's exactly what you should do, no matter how roughly it grates on your soul, but I didn't see that at the time. I wanted the fight.

I remember the moment that I realized I had that fighting spirit inside of me.

Get up.

So there I found myself, 13 years old and on the ground under a bench on the playground. It was them against me, and I was outmatched and outnumbered. I was bleeding from a cut on my scalp and from my nose, and I had one hell of a headache.

"Get up, you little towelhead!" A boy about five years my senior prodded me roughly in the side with the toe of his boot.

"He's a Jew, you dumbfuck. I don't think they wear towels," his more culturally-conscious associate corrected him, his impish little face curled into a permanent sneer.

"I don't care! Whatever he is, we're gonna fuck him up," replied Boy #1, landing another kick in my ribs with his boot.

In that moment I made a decision that would change my life forever. Because right then, I decided not to run. I decided not to stay there, curled up under the park bench, waiting for these bullies to do to me whatever they were planning in their vicious adolescent brains. Instead, I felt something change inside me. Anger, fury at the injustice of my situation suddenly swelled up in my chest, and I felt zero desire to sit back and let myself be the victim of their onslaught. I wanted to fight. I wanted to wipe those sneers right off their fucking faces.

"Fuck you," I snarled, with all the vitriol I could muster.

Then I pulled myself up to my feet and removed my belt. I wasn't exactly sure what I was going to do with it, but I thought that swinging it around seemed like a semi-tough thing to do.

Boys 1 & 2 rushed me, and their group of cronies jumped in.

Everything was happening in slow motion. I started swinging, brandishing belt and fists, and I still remember the look of dumb shock on Boy #1's face when my belt buckle first connected with it. That shock quickly turned to anger, though it wasn't much of a bludgeoning device. It certainly caused more annoyance than meaningful injury. Kicks flew into my ribs, my face got pummeled even worse—at one point, I couldn't tell if I was on the ground or still standing. But never once did I stop swinging.

Blood flew across the playground, peppering the wood chips with blood splatter from the gash on my head. They were kicking the stuffing out of me, but I started to realize that I was actually causing some damage, too—or, at least, it felt that way in my adolescent head.

I kept getting knocked down, but I kept getting up. Charge after charge, battle after battle—to me, this was war. I was ready to die that day, if that's what it took. I wouldn't let these assholes win. Not today, not ever. It didn't matter that the odds were against me and I was less than half their size—I would go down fighting.

One of the boys got hit hard in the mouth and left. The smaller one got tired out eventually. It takes work to keep beating down a guy that won't die.

"This guy is nuts. Let's go," I heard one of them say finally as they all stared at the insane gaze and smile on my bloodied face.

At the end of it all, I was the last man left standing on our playground battlefield, clutching my belt in my battered fist and clinging to the park bench to stay upright. My face looked like last Thursday's cold pizza.

By the look of me afterwards, I wouldn't say I won that day. But I can tell you one thing: I didn't lose. I had given it everything I had. I hadn't run away. It felt right.

The thing about fighting the federal government is that they'll always have way more money than you do. You're always going to be outnumbered, and fighting against kids who are bigger than you. So many people (Tom being the most outspoken amongst them) warned me not to go up against them, but I just couldn't back down from the fight. I burned through a lot of money in lawyers and legal fees, but I didn't care. I was going to take them all on.

I felt like I was in the right. I was David, and here was Goliath, coming to try to destroy everything I'd built. We were operating completely freely, but the powers that be wanted to come in and take that all away, and I was prepared to do anything to stop that from happening.

So we went head to head with the U.S. governments, the big pharma companies, the supplement companies, and more. We were battling seven states, the FDA, and the FTC, so I knew it wasn't going to be easy, but I also felt this burning desire to win. It was fight and win or die, and I was ready to die to keep the company alive.

We put together a rock-solid defense. My lawyers gathered together every shred of evidence we had that our products were safe, that we had never purposefully advertised to children, or that we'd ever made untrue claims about the dangers associated with ephedra (which were basically non-existent). We had doctors, chemists, pharmaceutical consultants, advertising lawyers, herbal products manufacturers, and even alternative medicine experts all lined up to give testimony on our behalf. We had hundreds of boxes of files and paperwork that we sent to the courts to prove our case, and I was sure that, with the mountain of evidence we'd accumulated, there was no way they were going to be able to stop us.

Oddly, though, my lawyers didn't share my enthusiasm. I think they knew that, no matter how good of a case we put together, the government's would always be better. On top of that, Tom kept pointing out that, even if we won the suit against the seven states, we still had the FTC to contend with. They were pushing to make our products illegal, and if they succeeded, nothing else we did would matter. My attorneys' concerns kind of messed with my confidence at the time, but mostly I just shook them off. I was going to push ahead with fighting back, no matter what.

The battle for my company's survival had begun. Or was it the beginning of the end?

In the midst of all of this craziness, I still had to run the company, though. Now that Rob was gone, I had to do it all on my own. Truthfully, not having his manic, drug-addled, mad energy around was a relief in many ways, but I did miss him. I was flying all over the world, meeting with clients and distributors, striking new deals, and exploring other products that we could branch out into.

During one of my tours of Europe in the late 90s, I visited Stuart Wilde at his home in one of London's wealthy suburbs. Stuart was dating a famous supermodel at the time, who was living there with him, and the two of them took me to Ireland for a few days to meet another business mogul friend of Stuart's, a multimillionaire named Gordon who knew even more people than Wilde did. He thought it would be the perfect chance for me to network and make more connections with European retailers, but that's not exactly how the trip ended up working out.

Gordon threw some crazy parties at his house in Dublin, with the most eclectic mix of guests I'd ever seen, from Deepak Chopra and Allen Ginsberg to Naomi Campbell, George Michael, Bono, and Elton John. I was in the middle of a 21-day fast, where all I was consuming was water, because fasting was something I was really into at the time, but it definitely made the strangeness of that week even weirder. I was happy to hang out around Gordon's townhouse and talk philosophy and spirituality and business with this insane mix of people, and I was nearly as messed up off the lack of nutrients as all of them were on drugs and the Herbal Ecstacy I'd brought with me, so needless to say, it made for some pretty interesting conversations.

But Stuart, who was more outrageously drunk and high than any of us, had other ideas. He decided we were going to take a bunch of hallucinogens and go to the Irish countryside to "see the fairies." That's right, ladies and gents. It was a literal Fairy Hunt. Grownass people in the 90s, doing drugs in the Irish forest and trying to catch fairies.

A group of us ventured out of the city to a forest, where there was this old abandoned castle. Apparently, that's where we were going to meet the Druids who are the "carriers of the Fairy Liquid," and they would lead us on a sort of quest through the woods on something called a fairy walk, in order to track down the mystical little creatures. At this point, I was still sober, if not a bit giddy from my fasting high, so I just thought it was all some sort of role playing thing that everyone was in on. With that said, Stuart's reality distortion field was next level and he really did have us believing it all.

When we got to the woods, the Druids actually showed up.

They were... well, Druids. The men had long beards that looked inspired by Merlin himself, and wore long, dark cloaks that brushed the forest floor when they walked. Each carried a long walking stick ("This is my staff. I take it with me wherever I go," one of them solemnly corrected me when I called it that), and held a torch high in the air as they led us through the woods, chanting softly together in Gaelic. Their leader had a bearskin over his head, his face peeking through its gaping jaws like he was wearing a hoodie. I followed dutifully, caught between bursting out laughing in disbelief at how strongly in character these guys were, and letting myself be won over by the hushed, sanctified feeling in the air. It felt like we were going somewhere crazy, somewhere magical.

Finally, they brought us out into a small clearing, and motioned for us to stand around in a circle while two of the Druids lit a campfire in the center of it. The others were still chanting, their voices growing louder and louder as the head Druid came around with this bottle of Fairy Liquid, offering some to each of us to drink while they performed their ceremony. Only then, they said, would we be granted access to the Fairy Land. They passed the bottle around in a circle, and when it got to me, I just drank it quickly, without giving it much thought. It tasted bitter and a bit musty, but I downed it so fast that I didn't have to bear the taste for very long.

Then, I suddenly heard someone say, "Holy shite."

"What?" I asked sharply, looking around at a bunch of halfdrunk, half-high faces, all staring at me in shock.

"You're supposed to *sip*," Stuart's girlfriend told me, her mouth hanging open a little. "You're supposed to have *one* sip, not drink the whole bottle!"

It was like the moment she said it, the Fairy Liquid started to hit me. It was my first time on real psychedelics, and I had just taken a mega-overdose. They later told me that what I'd consumed was equivalent to a pound or two of mushrooms, or something like that, and I believed them. As soon as that potion kicked in, the world changed.

First, I saw the fairies, just as promised. I was hallucinating sparkly little fairies dashing around the undergrowth of the forest around us, twinkling in the trees overhead, as the Druids led us on the fairy walk. I could see the flutter of wings all around me, hear these little fairies laughing, and it was starting to really freak me out. The only thing that kept me from losing it entirely is the fact that all the others were saying that they could see them, too. So I thought,

Okay, I'm not crazy. I guess the Fairy Liquid just works this way for everybody. But I was a lot, lot further gone than the others. I'd started to hear voices in my head.

Some Irish gypsies (also known as Travellers) showed up at one point, literally driving a covered wagon that was pulled by a stout little pony. These gypsies got out and started a fire with the Druids—I guess they were friends—and took out an animal skin with the head still attached, and one of the head Druids put it on, and they all started beating drums and speaking in Gaelic as they danced around the fire with their staffs. That part, I did not hallucinate. That really happened. But it definitely made my trip feel even stranger.

One of the fairies suddenly appeared again, holding out a glowing hand to me and beckoning for me to follow her. She started leading me off into the forest, and I just got up and left the others behind at the fire, walking off into these dark woods all by myself. I think Stuart wobbled over and tried to stop me, but the Druids held him back, saying something like, "he needs to go on this journey alone."

And what a strange journey it was. The deeper we went into the forest, the more out of it I became. Eventually, I walked right out of fairy land and into a world composed entirely of projections from my own mind. With every step I took, it was like I was traveling through time, walking through different moments in my life like a ghost, watching it all from this psychedelic, detached standpoint.

In one scene, Ed was looming over me like a giant, shaking his huge finger disapprovingly at me. "You're on your own now," he whispered, but it came out like a gust of wind that threatened to blow me over. Then he walked away, the whole world shaking as his truck-sized, sandaled feet marched him out of sight forever, leaving me alone in an empty, endless white space.

In the next, I was a teenager again, getting beaten by my boss with a cane, while reporters all stood around me in a circle, jeering and flashing their cameras.

Then, I was standing at the cliffside in my backyard in Malibu, staring down at the waves below, and Lisa ran up behind me, giggling, and playfully pushed me over the edge. As I fell, I looked up and saw her standing up above, waving and smiling, her petite frame shrinking smaller and smaller by the second.

I opened my eyes, and I was swimming in a sea of money. The surface of it was churning like the open ocean during a storm, and I was struggling for my life just to keep my head above the cashline. But in the midst of that fear for my very survival, for some reason, I had this overpowering need to count it all—like I knew that, if I didn't count it, the storm would never end, and I would die. So I kicked my legs as hard as I could and tried to grab as many dollars as I could, whenever a wave of them came crashing into me. But no matter what I did, I kept losing count. I knew I had to start all over again, and I had this sinking feeling of utter and complete despair, knowing I'd never finish. I'd never make it out.

Then I'd suddenly come out of it, and be back in this insane fairy dimension, being led through the forest by these incredible creatures. The next moment, I'd be stepping back into a dreamlike memory, witnessing all the bad decisions I'd ever made in my life play out like some Salvador Dali-inspired nightmare.

Next thing I knew, I was waking up inside the abandoned castle. The Druids had found me passed out in the woods and carried me there, to what looked like a pretty robust mushroom-growing operation. The damp old building was apparently perfect for growing this particular fungus, and the whole place was filled with row upon row of mushrooms. I was lying on a makeshift cot in the corner of a big, stone hall, with Stuart and all the others crowded around me in a circle.

"How long was I out for?" I asked, as soon as they explained what had happened.

At first, no one spoke. Even the Druids, who were holding burning torches to illuminate the room, were silent.

"It's been two days," said Stuart, after a long pause. "You were pretty out of it, kid."

That was an understatement. I had had so many intense revelations during my trip to that alternate dimension in the fairy forest.

What was going on in my life? What was I even doing? How had it all gotten so messed up? Coming back to the real world after all of that felt strange. It was reality, but now I wasn't so sure what was even real anymore.

Over the next few days, they nursed me back to health with Kerrygold butter and homemade bread and, you know, care. After that fast, I broke my veganism and was just vegetarian for a while, and I think it was a good decision, because I swear, that butter was exactly what I needed right then.

And finally, I was okay. We went back to Stuart's place in England, and I stayed with them for about a week before flying home. And that was just one of my adventures with Stuart. We had a lot of adventures like that.

But that trip was also the end of an era for me, in many ways.

In London, I slept in Stuart's meditation room, and during that time I saw that all of his self-destructive habits were gradually getting worse, and beginning to take a serious toll on his mental health.

I'd already seen some of this unfolding back in L.A. As Wilde's alcoholism, drug use, and womanizing ways reached new heights, the seminar piggy bank began to run dry. On two separate occasions, he had walked out, after the event's promoters chided him for being drunk on stage—leaving them to deal with issuing refunds to his hundreds of angry fans. He started to accumulate large debts, and by then, Stuart had discontinued the seminars altogether and retreated to England to pursue writing full time.

I was worried about him. The man I'd been so inspired by seemed to be falling apart before my very eyes, but the heaviest blow came when I

walked into his office one day and found him chatting to a young woman who was typing out the manuscript for his next book. I couldn't believe what I was seeing. I always assumed he had written all of his own books, but when I questioned him on it, all he said was, "Everyone does it. You think Deepak and Wayne write all their own stuff? They got all their best lines from me! And even
I had help."

I guess I can't blame him for outsourcing, but it definitely disappointed me. It made me feel even more disillusioned with his whole school of thought—wondering, *were any of those things he'd said to inspire me even his ideas?*

Just like other gurus before him, the life of Stuart Wilde was a mixed bag. He managed to bring the philosophy of spiritual abundance to the mainstream over 20 years before the film "The Secret," but in the end, his hard-hitting lifestyle may have caused him to prematurely pass. He was only 66 when he died, and while I stayed in intermittent contact with him throughout the remainder of his life, I never held him in the same regard again after that trip.

In the early 2000s, Wilde came to visit me in Los Angeles. But something had changed. This was no longer the dynamic and charismatic personality I had known and loved. He was older, tired, in poor health, and no longer making much sense. He had begun to walk with a limp. He talked about UFOs and reptilians taking over the government. He had a beautiful but haggard transsexual in tow as his partner and was trying to score some "Ekkie," as he so elegantly requested from me. I advised him that I only ever sell Herbal Ecstacy and had no intention of fetching actual MDMA for him.

That trip was a strange one. Stuart stayed at a high rise on Sunset Strip and outlined the work for another book in a drug-fueled week, which nearly landed him and his cohorts all in jail. It was all so very "Hunter S. Thompson meets The New Age."

After that, Wilde made a beeline for the Amazonian jungles, where he found some Ayahuasca and began to take it regularly, seeking some new level of spiritual enlightenment. The drug seemed to validate his existing metaphysical beliefs, and he took to taking it regularly. Then, he told me, he met someone who he called "a bent shaman." Apparently, the shaman had spiked his usual Ayahuasca potion with a poisonous datura seed, which is known to often bring about permanent psychosis and paranoia.

After this, Wilde never recovered. His blog posts went from friendly to paranoid. He began suspecting that extraterrestrial and supernatural entities were "controlling him and his followers." Things got weirder.

Ever the consummate entrepreneur, Wilde had a solution to this terrifying dilemma. He began to offer healings (for several thousands of dollars a pop); selling small, magical flashlights that could blast evil (for a couple grand more); and hawking equally-expensive holy water, which was blessed by none other than himself. He also began to do smaller seminars in Italy, where starstruck followers would pay up to $20,000 to hang out with him for a week. Wilde also started to solicit donations from loyal followers in exchange for hanging out with him. Long gone were the days of teaching about money mastery and personal development.

How I feel about Stuart now is also a mixed bag.

He was a friend and mentor, but he was also, in my opinion, a fraud and a snake oil salesman. He did lead an extraordinary life and inspired millions of people—for that, I give him credit. But toward the end of his life he became exactly the person he railed against in his younger years, and the epitome of everything he stood against.

For me, the realization that Stuart was an inherently flawed individual— just like all humans are—was a major revelation. I looked up to him as an almost larger-than-life figure, just like I'd once viewed Ed, and I think it had never occurred to me before that either of them could have their own issues or shortcomings as human beings. For a moment, accepting that my mentors had all been human, and therefore, necessarily flawed, nearly undermined all of the faith that I had in the things they had taught me. How can an imperfect person give perfect advice? I felt like they had to be shining examples of everything I aspired to be, in order for their words of wisdom to hold any meaningful weight.

But then, I came to also realize how unrealistic those expectations are. No one person can be a font of perfect knowledge. Everyone has their own perspective and their own way of approaching life, and it's up to us to decide what parts of that approach resonate with us. Stuart could be flawed and still have a lot to offer me—I just had to exercise my own judgment and caution when it came to applying that in my own life. Just as the Walkman had taught me in his enigmatic way, I ultimately knew that I had to be independent and learn to stand on my own two feet. Mentorship was critical, but it wasn't a crutch that I could rely on entirely to guide me.

It had been a crazy, strangely sobering trip to Europe, and one that opened my eyes to my revered mentor in a totally different way. But I had also undergone some strange and deep revelations on that Irish Fairy Walk with the Druids… . It felt like something big was shifting in my life, but that it was happening just beyond the edges of my perception, always stuck in my peripheral vision but never fully in focus. The fairies had been trying to tell me something, I just wasn't sure what that was, yet.

When I got back to the U.S. is when I had the real wake-up call.

Journal Entry: Reality Distortion Field

	Humans are Flawed	Keeping Control & Perspective
What is it?	That all people are flawed is just a fact of life, and one we all need to accept, not just in the pursuit of success.	Sometimes things seem out of your control. That is when you need a new perspective, and to gain control by either taking or not taking some action.
Why is it important?	When it comes to mentors, this helps you sort and choose the information they give you. With other people, it helps you manage your expectations of what they can do for you.	Because our minds seek certainty and we operate best when we have that feeling of certainty. Few people can operate optimally with uncertainty. The good news is you can reach this optimal state simply by changing your perspective.
How to win:	By managing your expectations to avoid disappointment, and being able to separate the valuable from the invaluable when it comes to accepting advice. If you know an imperfect person, they can still give you golden insights into certain things, so don't discredit someone just because they don't fit your idea of perfection.	When things seem out of control, seek perspective. This may be talking to one or more people who can show you an angle you don't see yourself. Then take an action, or make a decision to take no action. This will give you control (or at least the feeling of it) so you can be back in the flow.

CHAPTER 16:

A GRAND HEIST

Jeff Bezos to an exec after a product totally flopped: *"You can't, for one minute, feel bad."*

Imagine being the guy that reports to billionaire Amazon founder Jeff Bezos that you just lost $170 million because of the Amazon Fire Phone's failure.

This vignette from Amazon lore gives insight into two of Bezos' key principles for leadership and success.

First and foremost, failure has to be part of growth.

"As a company grows, everything needs to scale, including the size of your failed experiments. If the size of your failures isn't growing, you're not going to be inventing at a size that can actually move the needle," Bezos wrote in his 2018 annual letter to shareholders.

Failure is absolutely one of my favorite topics to talk about. Why? Because we live in a society where everybody is chasing, they're chasing money. They're chasing things. They're chasing material objects. But what they're not chasing is discomfort. And it's really discomfort that brings us to discipline, and discipline is what makes us succeed, even when we fail—perhaps especially when we fail.

If you've already burned the fleet, and then you lose a battle, now you really find the discipline in yourself to turn things around the next day, and make sure you never lose another one again. That's the kind of do-or-die mentality that I was chasing when I moved out of my parents' house and went to live on the streets.

Even once I'd made it, and I was in the flow and experiencing a lot of success, that didn't mean that I didn't still experience failures. For people who are extremely successful, those failures are quickly forgotten, but the lessons learnt from them aren't. You've probably heard, "if you lose, don't lose the lesson," or, "if you fail, don't fail on the learning." These things are self-evident to those sitting in a comfortable situation, looking at failure from a safe distance. More importantly—as we learn from Bezos—it's essential to fail fast and often in order to build predictable and bulletproof systems that will allow you to reach success.

But when you're in it, and when you're feeling the discomfort of your situation, a failure can seem like a huge setback. And some of them did feel that way at the time, but I learned that it's possible to look at failure in a different way, even while it's happening, and to take something positive away from it in that moment. It's all about perspective.

In the lead up to the big states' lawsuit, the FTC was always buzzing around in the background, threatening to ban ephedra and, in the meantime, sticking their nose in our business as much as possible. The FDA was doing the same, and they even raided our Venice office and our warehouses, taking all the files they could get their hands on and confiscating a bunch of products to take for testing.

Apparently, someone had tipped them off that we were actually putting real drugs in our products (which of course, we weren't). We had deals with several different major manufacturers to produce our pills, so we weren't directly in charge of the manufacturing process ourselves, and that gave me cause for concern. I remember being paranoid that someone at one of the factories was in on it, and was going to set us up, or that the government was going to plant evidence, or something like that, just to see us shut down for good.

As it turns out, the exact opposite thing happened. I hired an independent lab to do our own testing, and we found out, by analyzing all the batches, that one of our manufacturers had been not putting any active ingredients in our pills *at all*. So they didn't have any ephedra, or even any caffeine, in them—it was 100% carrot powder. In retrospect, we were fools not to have suspected something sooner, since the manufacturer had offered us a really low price— way below what the other factories charged us. So really, we should have had the pills tested sooner, but we didn't.

Anyways, I had Tom threaten to sue if they didn't give us a full refund, and we pulled those batches of product from stores and had it all destroyed. The only problem was that one of the orders, which were in the shape of little animals, had already been shipped and sold in Japan, so there was nothing we could do about those ones. It was too late

A little while later, I got a call from our distributor in Japan, and I was mortified, because this is millions of dollars of business. I thought, *Oh man, what are we going to do? What am I going to tell this guy?* So I got on the phone, and I was extremely nervous and still trying to figure out what to say to explain this catastrophe, and then the guy tells me that this was the single best batch he had ever received. He didn't know what we did differently, but could we please make all the batches the exact same way in the future, because people were having the most amazing experience.

Now, up until that moment, I had thought this was a huge failure. I thought we were gonna lose the business in Japan entirely. I was absolutely devastated. But that was just my perspective. Ed had taught me that, in any situation, you have to have two things: control and perspective. And in this particular situation, I had lost control, because the pills had left and people were already buying them. But I had also lost my perspective. I had no idea what this man was going to say on the other end of the phone, or that this could actually be a good thing, or even just not such a big disaster, after all. I just naturally assumed that this was a failure.

But it wasn't.

So, I learned that day, when you find yourself in a situation where it seems like failure, the two things you want to do immediately is seek a way of getting control and a way of changing your perspective. So in lieu of control, you can gain perspective. And when you do that, getting back some control over the situation is usually a lot easier, just because you've changed your frame of mind.

The raid in itself wasn't much of a failure, in the end. The FDA found nothing, and they went away, grumbling, to go regroup and find a new angle from which to attack us.

What was a much bigger problem, and one which I had neither control nor perspective to properly deal with, was what happened the next day.

I came into the office the following morning, and I could immediately tell that something was seriously wrong. I asked a whitefaced Borris what was up, and he just stammered out that I should get to the warehouse as soon as possible. Evidently, he was too terrified to be the bearer of such bad news himself.

I sped over there as quickly as I could, and when I pulled up, I saw a huge crowd of my employees all milling around outside. The warehouse owner was there, as well as some security guards and a few police cars, and I felt my blood run cold. Something was definitely very, very wrong.

Once I'd pushed my way through the crowd and got inside, I could see what it was. The place was basically cleaned out.

What should have been a packed warehouse, with rows and rows of boxes waiting to be shipped out across the world, had just a scant few items remaining on the shelves. More boxes were overturned in the middle of the aisles, their contents strewn across the floor and smashed. Either the culprits had been in quite a hurry, or their goal had been to destroy everything they couldn't carry. And they'd done a damn good job of it.

Millions of dollars' worth of product was missing. We'd been robbed blind.

Now, I was used to people stealing—a box here, a truckload there, a couple thousand dollars sneaking its way out of a cash delivery now and again—but this was something on a totally different level.

Apparently, some rough-looking guy had shown up with some trucks in the middle of the night, and managed to convince the guards on duty that he was merely picking up a shipment on my orders.

I knew immediately who it was. There was only one guy who could pull that trick off at night, Steve.

The guards hadn't gotten the memo that Steve had left the company, so they sat back and let him in. When I asked them why they'd done nothing, even when Steve and his cronies were totally clearing the place out and smashing boxes as they went, they didn't have an explanation. Maybe he'd paid them off, who knows.

We had buyers calling us for weeks, angry that their orders were delayed, even though they'd already paid for the shipment. Our manufacturers couldn't produce the stuff fast enough to satisfy all of the demand, so we were shipping product in from our distributors overseas just to keep the supply chain moving. Meanwhile, I had millions in lawyers' fees to pay to keep our defense going against the states' lawsuit, so the last thing I needed was for our profits to take a hit right at that moment. It was a huge blow financially, but it also struck me to the core emotionally.

I had never felt so betrayed in my entire life. Some people said there was a guy in a car that never got out that matched Rob's description, but others disputed this. I never was able to prove definitively that Rob was involved in the heist, but all of the circumstantial evidence certainly seemed to point in his direction. I had already heard that he had come up with his own knock-off version of Ecstacy called "Rapture," and had started up a new company selling the product under a different name. To make matters worse, his new business partners in this venture were a pair of wealthy Beverly Hills businessmen who were already embroiled in a lawsuit with me. They owned a competing company, and were some of my biggest enemies in the herbal products industry, and when Rob left, he made a beeline straight for them.

The betrayal of someone who I thought was my good friend going to work for my competitors had hurt badly enough, but soon after the theft took place, I heard a rumor that the pills were being packaged and sold under Rob's new brand name. My best guess is that Steve and Rob orchestrated the whole thing together, so that they could sell Herbal Ecstacy instead of their own, inferior product, and screw me over as much as possible in the process. But in reality and for various reasons, I'll never truly know what happened, or who was behind it all.

My paranoia completely took over, after that, fuelled even more by the lack of certainty over what had gone down. I was convinced that someone was following me, either investigators from the FDA or someone hired by Rob and his new employees to spy on us and steal our trade secrets. I would only ever leave my house through the back entrance, and would change cars twice a day to make sure nobody was tracking my movements. Sometimes, I saw the same car sitting at the end of my block for days at a time, or a suspicious-looking guy watching me from across a crowded café, and I was sure it was some detective or agent who'd been assigned to tail me. Maybe I really was being followed—who knows? Maybe it was just paranoia.

When so many people are out to get you, and you're getting sued by so many different agencies, it really takes a toll.

Backed into a corner as I was, I still wanted to fight. I don't think it ever occurred to me that I didn't have a shot in hell at winning any of our lawsuits, or that I wouldn't be able to find those guilty of the theft and punish them. Even if I did know that, subconsciously, that still didn't stop me from trying. So, even though it seemed like the whole house of cards was tumbling down around me, I never gave up my fighting spirit.

That was the beginning of the end for us, but I still wasn't prepared to accept that just yet. Although, little did I know, it wasn't even the most painful betrayal I'd have that week.

Just a few days after the FDA raid and the warehouse clean-out, I came home one evening to find Lisa, and all of her possessions, were gone. I couldn't really believe she would just up and leave like that, without so much as a word. I tried calling her multiple times, but it went straight through to voicemail every time. I started to worry, thinking that maybe the ex-boyfriend from Providence that she'd always said was still looking for her had actually found her, and she might be in some kind of trouble. I even considered calling the cops, but I knew it wouldn't end well for her if I did.

She was the only person left in my life that I felt like I could confide in, and with all that was going on, I needed her then, more than ever. But she'd left me on my own, right at the critical moment. Just that in itself was a huge betrayal to me.

Then I found out what she'd taken with her when she left, and the betrayal took on whole new depths.

Lisa had apparently helped herself to cash, gold, and one of my credit cards on her way out the door, and used it to buy herself and one of my former employees a first-class flight to Miami, as well as tens of thousands of dollars' worth of luxury clothes and jewelry from various shops in Beverly Hills. It turns out she'd been sleeping with the guy for the past few months, and the two of them had decided to run off together. To fund their venture after I inevitably shut the stolen card off, they'd taken some boxes of Herbal Ecstacy with them—as if I hadn't already lost enough product already that week.

I had come to expect that kind of behavior from the people who worked from me, but I never saw it coming from Lisa. It completely blindsided me. Now it made me wonder if she was in on the heist with Rob and Steve. My world was crumbling.

Even though the amount she took on her own was tiny, compared with what Steve and Rob had made away with, it hurt more than any other betrayal that happened to me during the Herbal Ecstacy years. I couldn't believe that I had totally opened up to this girl, let her into my life, given her everything she ever wanted, and this is how she repaid me? Worse still, she knew, better than anyone, how hard it was for me to trust people, and how messed up I'd been over the previous thefts, and she went and did the exact same thing anyways! She seemed the most vicious snake of them all.

Sitting in my house, alone, thinking about her laughing with her boyfriend on some Florida beach, I thought to myself, *How could you have been so stupid?* A betrayal of this magnitude stunned me; however, I learned an important lesson: You are ultimately alone on your path to success. The closer you let people to yourself, the greater the harm they can incur, and the more disappointed you'll be in the end.

It had, without a doubt, been the worst week of my entire life. The FDA raid, the Steve heist, Lisa's betrayal—it really didn't seem like things could get any worse at that moment in time.

Then, I got notice from Tom that we were going to lose the states' lawsuit if we didn't settle, and everything really fell apart.

In the end, the FTC had forced us into a corner, where all we could do was sign their settlement. I had to agree not to sell products with ephedra anymore, and not to advertise in specific places. The seven states were all given judgments to a similar effect, and Herbal Ecstacy was ordered to give payouts to each in the form of fines and penalties.

I had fought as hard as I could, every step of the way. I tried to take the issue to court, refused to sign the agreement as long as I could, and explored every possible option with my lawyers to convince them to change the terms of the settlement. But none of it worked, and my doomed efforts ended up costing me millions of dollars in legal fees.

At some point, you just can't keep fighting.

But the worst part about it wasn't the money that I threw away, fighting a foregone conclusion. It was the freedom that I lost.

It had been an undeniably entertaining 10 years. I got to enjoy the work I was doing—creating, traveling, growing the buzz and the size of this company—and I got to do all the things I'd ever dreamed of as a broke kid on the streets. I lived like a rock star myself, getting to hang out with the most incredible people and be talked about in the media and own all of these fancy things. It was exciting. But the other side of that was actually pretty terrible, sometimes. Not knowing who my friends really were; having people steal from me, because they didn't feel like I'd really earned it; people being jealous of me. So it was a difficult time, even if I was surrounded by money and women and celebrities.

I had been able to live my life in this extraordinary way, being the master of my own destiny and making my dreams a reality, but all of that came crashing down seemingly overnight.

Journal Entry: Reality Distortion Field

	Control vs. Perspective (Part II)	Pick Your Battles
What is it?	In every situation, you either have to be in control, or change your perception of the situation.	Picking your battles is being a clever general.
Why is it important?	Because you can't always be in control of every outcome, but you can control how you view the situation.	You need to decide when to fight and when to back down if you want to reach your goals with as little resistance as possible. Action and non-action can be equally valuable when undertaking intelligently.
How to win:	By always looking for opportunities to turn a negative into a positive, and considering perspectives other than your own. What you perceive as your greatest failure may actually be a huge success in the eyes of some, so just by changing your perspective, you can often find a way to regain control of a problem that once seemed like something you were powerless to solve. You gain perspective by having the conversation that leads you to it.	Conserve your energy for the fights that really count, and be okay with walking away from the ones that don't. Sacrificing your pride is better than risking too much on a battle that isn't worth the effort. At the same time, avoid making unnecessary and powerful enemies if you can avoid it (although you still want to have some). A war can only be fought successfully on so many fronts at once.

CHAPTER 17

THE ART OF STALKING

> *"The very first principle of stalking is that a warrior stalks himself, Don Juan said. He stalks himself ruthlessly, cunningly, patiently, and sweetly. There are four steps to learning it: Ruthlessness should not be harshness, cunning should not be cruelty, patience should not be negligence, and sweetness should not be foolishness. These four steps have to be practiced and perfected until they are so smooth, they are unnoticeable."*
> Carlos Castaneda, *The Power of Silence*

In his many flighty and poetic books, self-styled shaman, author, cult leader and counter-culture guru, Carlos Castaneda, talks about how the warriors of antiquity would master what he called stalking. Today the term stalking has many negative connotations, but to me what Castaneda alluded to still holds true.

I remember learning exactly what it was that Castaneda meant about stalking when I took a trip to the Columbian Amazon. It was pitch black in our camp one night and my guide suddenly suggested with some urgency that we get back into our tent. Something was happening.

I looked around and spotted what had caused the commotion. There was an elusive black jaguar in a tree above us. You would think that seeing jaguars would be a common occurrence in the Amazon. Unfortunately, due to poachers, it is actually a rare sight, and one that I feel quite privileged to have beheld.

At first, we could only see a glimmering pair of cat's eyes in the tree. Then, as it got darker, the whole animal became revealed. In the darkness of the night, the jaguar was waiting patiently for his prey. He wore the darkness of the night like a fine coat. His green eyes nearly glowed in the dark. He was calm, yet he had a commanding presence. It was almost as if he was waiting for his prey to come to him. As the mosquitoes ate away at any unexposed areas on our bodies, we waited patiently inside our tent to see what the big cat would do. I remember that we devoured two thermoses filled with herbal tea as we watched the hours go by.

The big cat barely moved. It just sat there, totally alert. It was almost like it knew, with total certainty, that lunch would come at midnight.

Then, as if on cue, a small wild boar appeared. I looked at my guide and smiled: "Lunch time?" My guide nodded.

Before the boar could snort a second time, it was over. Without hesitation, the big cat had leaped from his perch high above and claimed what was his. The act was violent and quick. It was carried out with surgical precision. Although for us it was a sight to be seen, for the cat it was a non-event. It was as matter-of-fact as breathing. It was collecting its birthright. It was an act of pure intention, manifested through patience.

Ed once told me that the problem with my generation was that we tried too hard to exert our own will over the world. "Many shamans view the world as a predatory environment, made up of predators and prey. They also believe that nature is violent, but this is neither a good thing nor a bad thing—it is part of the natural balance of life. Just as there can be no light without darkness, there can be no predators without prey, and vice versa. It is the natural order of the universe. Part of turning your fear into courage is knowing whom the predator is and whom the prey is. You have to decide which one you want to be. Building up your character along your path will make you strong; and the strong are not preyed upon, so you will not be preyed upon. It is with your courage that you navigate the predator/prey world without getting hurt and without hurting others," he said.

"I'm not sure if I have what it takes to really do that," I told him.

"If you weren't sure, you wouldn't be here," he told me. "The weak fall prey. If you become strong, you avoid falling to the bottom of the food chain. By becoming strong, you can put yourself in a place to help others. And you have what it takes to become strong. All you need is to gain power and knowledge, and that's what you're here to do, isn't it?"

I nodded, but I still wasn't sure what he was really talking about. "So, what's the next action I need to take, then?"

"Be patient. Work on yourself and watch. Patience. That is the essential quality of the silent hunter, who waits in the dead of night for its prey," he said.

Being an impulsive kid, hungry for success, I didn't like the idea of my next action being no action at all. When I told Ed as much, he sighed and looked at me with those dark, wise eyes.

"Don't think so much about the pounce, Shaahin. You need to work on the patience, otherwise you'll always miss your target. Just look at wild animals—you see them pounce, capture, and devour their prey. Society values this. But there is little value given in Western culture to how long that animal has been waiting in the bushes for the right opportunity, for how long he waited, hungry and patient, in the shadows. There is no talk of all the seemingly okay opportunities that were discarded, so that the perfect opportunity could be capitalized on. Everyone lauds the pounce, but no one lauds the patience.

"The pounce is necessary, but, when the time comes, and you are prepared, it is also effortless. It is the patience that is difficult. You need to get comfortable with yourself. You need to cultivate silence and patience. Right now you are bored, because you can't stand to be alone with yourself for 30 minutes. Work on that. Work on your patience," he said calmly.

I still had no real clue what he was talking about at the time, and that was part of the problem. As a young man, I often acted on impulse, rather than waiting and judging for the perfect moment to pounce.

So, if I could go back in time and give my younger self one piece of advice, it would be: If you don't know, don't go. It's okay to make no decision and to wait. It's always better to wait before you speak, and to take time to ask the right questions first or seek counsel, than to jump headlong into decisions without fully considering all the consequences of your actions.

I would tell my younger self always to ask: What am I trying to achieve? Based on those goals, those objectives, then you can formulate a strategy. But for that, you need other people usually— ideally, people who are smarter than you, wiser than you, or more specialized than you. Sometimes it costs nothing to go to those professionals and seek counsel. Then, once you've gotten that counsel, you develop a strategy. With a strategy in hand you can inventorize the tools available to you and develop tactics. You will utilize these tactics to implement your strategy. Your strategy is what guides your decisions, and is the yardstick by which you gauge whether or not it's a good idea to act now, wait, or pass on an opportunity altogether. The required action then comes into place. Knowledge, Courage, Action. The knowledge gives you the courage to act as Wayne Boss often reminds us. Using that framework now has put me in a place of strength, and made it easier for me to consistently make good decisions that are aligned with my long-term business goals.

When I was younger and more hotblooded, I used to make decisions very quickly. Then compensate for my losses later. Which was hard to do, because I was moving so fast that I didn't really watch what was going on, so I wasn't even fully aware of the size of my losses. I didn't watch my money, and I didn't keep a close enough eye on the business, everything was just go, go, go. One hundred percent, full steam ahead. If someone asked a question, boom! Here's an answer. If somebody I knew did something, boom! I needed a reaction right away.

But now that I'm older, I understand that sometimes waiting, or taking no action, is better than giving a hasty reply. Sometimes you have to take time to seek counsel. You have to ask what the implications are of acting now, versus waiting until you have all the relevant information. Oftentimes, things can unfold in your favor, even if you do nothing. But we as human beings always have this need to influence things and act right away. But it's not always necessary. We want to make things change, now; we want to do something, anything, just to avoid inaction—but it's sometimes the deals that we leave behind that make us the most money.

Now, isn't all of this at odds with the idea of synchronicity and being in the flow, you might ask? In my opinion, no. You can be in the flow and be attracting amazing deals and partnerships because of the magnetism of your success, but that doesn't mean you have to snap them all up immediately, the moment they're presented to you. You can let the great opportunities come to you, but still take some time to be patient and fully screen each one before pulling the trigger. A true predator doesn't always need to chase down its prey—he also lets his targets come to him (i.e., pre-suasion), or stalks them patiently, and only launches his attack once he's calculated the risks and is sure that his offensive has the highest possible chance of success.

Patience is learned in the moments between moments. Animals are much smarter than we give them credit for, in that way. Big cats and other predators know that their patience is the difference between life and death, between satiation and starvation. Yet many humans fail to realize the power that patience gives you, namely the resilience to endure and persevere in every situation you will face.

This is also the difference between the way Eastern business and Western business is conducted. When I traveled to Japan or the Middle East, we often would have several meetings and tea together before the topic of business even came up. In Japanese business culture, they realize the importance of patience. Unlike Western meetings, which start with a discussion of the exact business at hand, in Asia the first meetings about large business dealings rarely ever go beyond the "getting to know you" stage. They understand that the destination is a foregone conclusion, and they are willing to wait as long as it takes to earn the desired result.

As Stuart Wilde told me, "You must become a professional waiter." If you want to take the necessary steps to achieve your goals, you have to realize that a big part of the effectiveness of this planning is to have the patience and the perseverance to see it through. You can directly affect the things you have control over. Equally important, however, is being able to wait for the things that you do not have direct control over to come to you.

Patience is confidence. It is the knowing with certainty that lunch will come and when it does, you will own it. This does not mean that everything you expect will become a reality. Rather, when you put conscious and intelligent thought into your decisions and then act with intention and patience, your outcome is assured. Illumination can take time. Patience allows you to face each situation calmly. If you are willing to do whatever it takes and wait, no matter how long it takes, then your outcome is assured. This is the ultimate confidence.

Even if you're itching for feedback from the other side, the person on the other side of the deal, sometimes doing nothing has miraculous effects. Because then pressure builds up on the other side, and they move to take action. It's like playing chess. If you can put off a move long enough for the other person to make a foolish move, then you can take advantage of it—it's the same in the grappling art of Brazilian jiu-jitsu. Younger and less experienced guys will get on the mat with a few moves in mind, and then push those moves as hard as they can, regardless of the terrain. But the pro knows that the best move will depend on what vulnerability your opponent gives you. Your best move is actually to exploit their weakness, which may be an unknown before the fight begins. In this case having a preformulated move will be a losing strategy. Better to wait.

You sometimes look at the higher belts, the people that have been doing it for a long time, and they seemingly relax and fall asleep before a sparring match (we call it before a "roll"). If you watch them, they're not making any moves. They wait for the younger, more inexperienced guys to make their move. But what they're doing is letting the pressure build, and they're letting the other person make a foolish move, to give them something that they can then use their masterful toolset to take advantage of.

So if I could go back and do it all over again, I'd become a better professional waiter. I would be a better stalker. I would wait for better opportunities to come to me, take the time to do my research if necessary, and be a better judge of which battles were worth fighting, and which weren't.

I would have settled with the government right away and maximized the time we had at the peak. As much as it felt good to think that I was fighting for "justice," fighting for the rights of the little guy against big, corporate America, continuing the fight against bullies that I'd been waging my whole life, the whole David and Goliath thing was a bit of a fantasy. I was a kid. I didn't have good legal counsel; I had no idea what was truly required to win a lawsuit of that scale, and couldn't stop thumbing my nose at everyone.

I defied authority every chance I got. I enjoyed defying authority much more than I enjoyed making money, or anything else, so the second the states came to me said, "Hey, you violated this act and this code, now you've got pay these fines and promise never to do it again," I would just give them the middle finger, every single time. My response was never to give an inch, and to try to fight it all out in court, so that I wouldn't have to ever give in to their demands.

Had I known better, I would have negotiated. I probably wouldn't even have ended up having to pay the entire amount they were asking for. I could have given them what was a relatively small sum for me in those days, apologized, signed their agreements, and changed up our tactics a little to keep everyone happy, and it wouldn't have killed me. But instead, I chose to tell the entire U.S. government to go fuck themselves. Hindsight is indeed 20/20.

I am always a disrupter and a hacker at heart, looking for ways to win big in any system. But people who know me also tell me I'm still a scrappy, relentless little kid at heart, even today. I have a keen sense of justice, and I don't like to be bullied. Back in the day, when I felt like the states and the FTC were bullying me, I just gave them the finger. I was getting backed into a corner by all of my enemies, and I didn't care. I just kept challenging them to hit me with the best they had, brazenly defying them to come after me.

It's important to think about your enemies when you're trying to be successful in business, or to, as Steve Jobs would say, "put a dent in the universe." As you move forward toward that goal, if you don't create any enemies, or if you don't have any enemies, you are doing something wrong. The second point is that while you are sleeping, your enemies are planning your demise.

That being said, I wish that I could tell my younger self that it's also good to try to avoid making enemies, when it's not absolutely necessary to do so. Don't worry, you'll develop plenty of them as it is, so there's no need to go out and try to create even more. If you can apologize, if you can smooth things over with people, do it. In Farsi, we call this "coming short," which basically means, you know, put yourself underneath people—put yourself beneath people, and make yourself smaller than them. Humble yourself. Say, "You know what, I'm sorry, my bad. I apologize." If it costs you nothing but your ego to do that, and it's going to pay off for you in the long run, then, by all means, humble yourself. If you do—even if you're wrong—you have a chance to turn an enemy into a friend.

The other thing I would say is that, if you do create enemies, think carefully about how you'll react to the things they do. Generally speaking, a lot of people will be absolutely livid at the fact that you succeeded and they did not, or that you succeeded more than them. And that's okay, you just have to ignore those people. If they do shoot arrows at you, and you can ignore them, it will probably make them even angrier, and fuel their hatred even more, but as long as it doesn't affect you, and you can brush them off, you'll be fine. Now, of course, if you need to defend yourself, that's a different thing. It's important that you stand up for yourself and assert yourself as needed, but ultimately, you really do want to forgive and forget. But in those days, I took things very personally. I didn't just defend myself when it was necessary, I did it even when making peace would have been the better (and simpler) option.

I also should have hired better attorneys. Tom was a great guy, but he was an amateur when it came to federal pharmaceutical cases. As my friend and master connector, Ken Rutkowski, always says, "A professional is expensive, but an amateur costs a fortune." Back then, I didn't want to pay the ludicrously high fees charged by the proper professionals, but it wasn't until later that I realized how costly of a mistake that had been. Had I forked out for the best lawyers money could buy, we probably would have protected the brand a lot better, and it might even still be a viable business today.

I think having a mentor, any mentor, would have been a great help to me during the Ecstacy years. I had Stuart, and he helped me a lot in terms of the psychology and spirit of success, but he wasn't really there to give me guidance on the day-to-day of running my business. That's not the kind of mentor he was. I was still in my early twenties, I'd been betrayed in the worst way by the people closest to me, we were still drowning in lawsuits, and now my company was about to be forcibly gutted from the inside out.

Looking back on it, I was actually doing amazingly well, you know. I just needed to get older people around me who had done this before, use their expertise, manage it closely, and then I'd have been great.

It was a crazy ride, but one that taught me a lot.

I now know how to be a better manager. I have better systems. I hire better people. I'm much, much more disciplined in my approach to accounting—in that I actually know how much money I make. I'm certainly less attached to money in general. Oh, and I haven't had anyone steal from me in a long, long time.

I had an extremely successful company, but it could have been even more successful if I'd gone into it already knowing the things I know now, or with a better team of specialized people around me. And maybe I would have held onto more of that money.

But, although I may have chosen to do some things differently, I eventually realized that I don't actually have any regrets about the way it all turned out. Those were some of the best years of my life, and they'd also been an incredible learning experience. All of the knowledge that I gained from the Herbal Ecstacy days, I brought with me into later life, and that helped make me into the successful (and much more responsible) businessman I am today.

At the end of the day, things still turned out well for me. I have a beautiful family, a very comfortable life, and have absolute freedom to do what I want, when I want, and with whom I want. I no longer get reporters or drug-addled crazy people beating down my door for a comment on a story or a hot tub party. I don't make millions of dollars every day, but I also don't lose millions of dollars a day anymore.

Funnily enough, not too long ago, my good friend Ben—the Ghanaian man who had worked with me at the company and still works with me today—found an old duffel bag in a storage unit I asked him to take over. He returned it. That's always been the kind of guy he is. Inside was about $10,000 in cash and some long-expired pills from the Ecstacy days. The cash was packed in bricks with dried up rubber bands from the 90s. Attached to the first stack was one of my old Global World Media business cards. We chuckled in disbelief when we saw it.

I do wonder, still, though—How much did we actually make? Was it really a billion, or was it more? The truth is, I'll never know.

Journal Entry: Reality Distortion Field		
	Patience	Humility
What is it?	Patience is mastering the Art of Stalking. It is waiting for the right people and circumstances to come to you and knowing that you will make it so.	Humility is knowing when to apologize or back down, even when it hurts your pride to do it.
Why is it important?	Because being patient enables you to be perfectly poised to jump on the best opportunity when it comes along, and to pass on those which aren't worth your time. Remember, it is much easier to persuade than to chase.	Humbling yourself is important when it comes to picking your battles, and also when it comes to building the relationships that will support your success in the long term. Stuart would often say the Ego is a trickster. Always put yourself underneath people.
How to win:	By watching, waiting, and being supremely confident in your ability to get the job done when the moment comes. Once the perfect opportunity presents itself, you have to be ready to strike immediately, with no hesitation. In that way, patience is actually directly linked to the ability to take decisive action in the moment.	By weighing the risks vs. rewards, considering the potential benefit that backing down could bring you, and the potential harm that continuing to fight could bring, and making the decision to humble yourself in service of a greater good for your business (if need be). That way, you can live on to fight another day.

289

Epilogue:

Herbal Ecstacy was officially dead.

Well, not dead—we still had other products that we made that didn't contain ephedra, but the ones that did had been, by far, our best-sellers. It was more like Herbal Ecstacy had been shot in the head, but the bullet had been a few inches off, so the company was just staggering around, half-lifeless and with little chance of a full recovery.

It hurt, but I decided to start selling off the company's assets. I wasn't going to wait around for my mortally wounded enterprise to slowly bleed out.

I remember being terrified for a while. I thought to myself, *I don't know what the fuck I'm doing. I don't even know how I got as far as I did, and I'm not sure if I can do it again. Who am I without Herbal Ecstacy, anyways? Did I even really achieve everything I thought I did, or was it all some big mistake, some extravagant hoax?*

My life had been like a dream. Actually, most people can't even dream of living the way that I did back then, so coming out of that was like waking up to a cruel reality, otherwise known as a normal existence.

I hadn't been willing to humble myself before, when I needed to appease my enemies, but after closing the company's doors, I did feel well and truly humbled. For a while there, I lost all the confidence that I'd once had. I thought to myself, *What the fuck just happened? Was that really the last 10 years of my life, gone?*

I had made an insane amount of money, and then lost nearly all of it. I felt like I was back around that campfire with Stuart, only this time, I'd thrown my entire fortune and my company into the flames and watched it all burn. But I had to rebuild from the ashes. I wasn't going to let that be the final chapter in my story.

I had to figure out what my next move was going to be, and that's exactly what I did, once I got all of the teenage moping out of my system.

It was November 2008.

I turned on the TV, or maybe I saw it as a video online, and suddenly there was a news feature with an announcement from Jeff Bezos about the increasing popularity of Amazon Marketplace. It had launched a few years earlier and allowed all kinds of third-party sellers to sell through the Amazon platform. Until then, all the products which people bought on the site were sold by Amazon directly, but now this huge distribution avenue had been opened up to anyone and everyone who had something to sell.

I had a few other products that I played around with after I exited Herbal Ecstacy. For a while, I invented and produced vaporizers, then a series of legal highs, but eventually I landed on what I thought was going to be my next big thing: brain boosters, or nootropics. I had the idea for a new brain supplement called Excelerol, and I had already perfected the formula and the branding for it—the only thing I hadn't figured out was the most important part: how I was going to sell it. I was looking for the perfect distribution channel for a product like this, but so far all of the avenues I'd explored hadn't had a big enough reach or an attractive option for scaling.

Then I heard the Bezos announcement, and everything changed.

I listed Excelerol on Marketplace before I went to bed that night. I typed up a simple description, uploaded my product photos, and didn't think much of it. I figured I might get a few orders over the next few weeks, and that it would serve as a test group for me to get feedback on how to improve the product.

When I woke up in the morning, I checked my email as I normally did, and almost spat coffee all over my computer. I had thousands and thousands of orders, all from a single night.

Was it happening again? Had I found my next hit? Visions of the Ecstacy days danced in my head.

But just then I remembered: it wasn't the product, it was the distribution.

I had spent all this time chasing the shiny object again, when the real gold was there under my nose the whole time. Now that we could sell almost anything on Amazon, the sky was the limit.

The 10,000-hour rule (popularized by Malcolm Gladwell) roughly says if you practice one skill for 10,000 hours, you'll have a good chance at becoming an expert at it.

With that in mind, I started again.

Appendix:

Journal Entry: Reality Distortion Field

Index:

EXCLUSIVE OFFER

If you would like to get free bonus materials, be there for the re-launch
of herbal ecstacy®, see a special interview with me
and former FBI investigator Chris Voss and to join our online
community then please go to www.thrillpillcult.com and use the
code THRILLPILL.

Success Notes

	Game Theory	Ambition	Weirdness
	Journal Entry: Reality Distortion Field		
What is it?	Game theory is (in short) the study of human psychology when it comes to decision-making in an economic society.	Ambition is what gets you out of bed in the morning, and keeps you striving toward the fulfillment of your goals, even when everything is against you.	Weirdness is what makes you unique. Accepting and owning your inner weirdo makes you invincible.
Why is it important?	Whether it be for making sales or building strategic partnerships, understanding human psychology is critical in business. You have to know how to predict and influence people's behaviors to dominate in your niche.	Ambition is what drives us. The ultimate secret to getting everything you want in life is that you have to be willing to do whatever it takes to get it. Ambition is key to desire.	Everyone wants to keep you in a tidy box that they can understand. Deviate, and you may fall out of favor with their expectations. But embrace the true you, and you become infallible. There is only one person that ever needs to accept you. Look in the mirror.
How to win:	With discipline and loyalty. Think of the prisoner's dilemma: you need the rigor to stick to your guns, even when other people are trying to influence you. Follow your plan, not theirs. Then, you need trust and loyalty with the people in your organization if you want your plan to actually work.	If you don't have ambition, pretend like you do until you get it. If you do have ambition, follow it unerringly. Never give up on your ambitions. Keep them at the forefront of your mind, and always make them the center of every action you take in life.	Embrace your weirdness. Own it, and use it to succeed in your own way.

Journal Entry: Reality Distortion Field		
	Detachment	Determination	Misaligned Expectations
What is it?	Detachment is not letting the desire for material things, or the fear of not having them, impact the way you pursue your goals.	Determination goes hand-in-hand with ambition, but it also involves having grit, drive, and the willingness to do whatever it takes to win.	Misaligned expectations are when you expect people, life, or the world to be one way, and they turn out to be another. This is the source of all anger, in my opinion.
Why is it important?	Because attachments are our safety net. Only without a fallback plan do you really go all-out to achieve your goals and figure out what's truly important to you (and what's not).	Ambition gives you the desire to succeed, and determination gives you the will to see that success through to the end. Without both, you won't make it to the peak of your climb.	Misaligned expectations inevitably set you up for disappointment, because you're trying to bend the world to your will. This disappointment can end up being a roadblock in your journey, if you let it.
How to win:	By knowing what really matters. Truly committing to something is uncomfortable. You have to make sacrifices. You have to struggle. If you're not prepared to do that, because you're too attached to creature comforts, you'll never step outside your safe zone and achieve something extraordinary.	If you don't have determination, cultivate it. If you do have it, let it guide you. Along the way, people will try to discount your ideas and circumstances will make winning seem impossible, but trust in your determination to succeed and you'll keep striving toward your goals.	If you want to avoid disappointment in life and in business, be unrealistic about the expectations you set (but be detached from outcomes)—particularly what you expect from other people.

Journal Entry: Reality Distortion Field		
	Learn by Doing	Mentorship	Knowledge, Courage, Action (KCA)
What is it?	The famous "experiment often and fail fast" Jeff Bezos' Amazon mentality.	Mentorship is having someone to guide you and help you grow in ways you may never have experienced on your own.	Knowledge, Courage, and Action are the three building blocks for getting a venture off the ground.
Why is it important?	You can't learn how to surf from a book. Because iteration is the only way to really figure out the way something will actually work in the real world, and it's the best way to learn your trade.	We're all mirrors of the people we surround ourselves with. Find inspirational, successful, insightful people, and their energy will help spur you on to rise to their level.	Knowledge gives you the confidence in your ideas and abilities. That confidence gives you the courage needed to act, to create something new and strike out on your own. It all leads to action, without which nothing is possible.
How to win:	By acting, rather than over thinking. You can plan your perfect business model for years, only to discover it doesn't work a few months after launching it. Just get started, and worry about perfecting as you go. There are no armchair philosophers who are successful in business—it's the people who act that win. Be smart, seek counsel, but do trust your instincts over all else.	Mentors often tell you what you *need* to hear, rather than what you *want* to hear. Don't let your need to be right get in the way of seeing their advice for what it is: an intelligent perspective from a trusted source that should be mined for all possible insight. Ideally, find many quality mentors. The more quality perspectives, the better.	Do your research. Educate yourself. Know the playing field. The more quality knowledge you acquire, the firmer your self-belief becomes. That confidence is essential when you're faced with challenges and uncertainty—things which may stop you from acting. But with knowledge and courage, action becomes easy.

	Journal Entry: Reality Distortion Field		
	Seek the Distribution	Transformative Experience	Being Observant
What is it?	Seek the distribution is about starting by looking at which distribution channels are out there and what the market demands, rather than creating a product and then hoping to find a market to fit.	A transformative experience isn't always gentle. In fact usually it's hard, complicated, messy, painful, or all of the above, but that's also why it forever changes you as a person.	Being observant is when you pay careful attention to the people and the landscape you're operating in.
Why is it important?	Because it doesn't matter how great your product is, or how many potential customers you have, if you can't get that product in front of them.	Because, in the words of Richard Koch, "following a conventional path won't lead to unreasonable success." But also because comfort leads to armchair mediocrity. It's through discomfort and unreasonable change that we find unreasonable results.	Behind every deal is a human. Behind every human is a motivation. Most people don't consider things in a truly nuanced way, so by being the one in the room who notices everything, you can quickly gain a leg up on the competition. By learning about people, you learn to master the deal.
How to win:	Look at the industry you're in. Mold the product to fit the marketplace and it's specific demands. Find the vulnerabilities in the marketplace and exploit them. Feed the market what it needs. Do not create a product and then scurry to find a market. Ask: How are things bought and sold within that industry? How could it be improved? What about in other industries? Is there a totally different distribution model that could be applied from industry X to mine, to revolutionize this space? Once you know how to get your product out there, you can develop it and target your audience in a way that best fits that distribution channel.	There is one train of thought that says you cannot force an epiphany. It either happens or it doesn't. The hack to this is travel. Get on a plane and leave the country to somewhere you are unfamiliar with. Challenge yourself and be open. I don't know anyone who has done this and who hasn't had a transformative experience. If you've never had a transformative experience, don't sit around and wait for one to come to you.	See the things which no one else does. Pay attention to every detail, and then think about how those details impact and interact with one another. In business, it's all about products and services changing hands. By seeing where, how, and why these transactions are taking place, you'll be able to spot ways to hack the system to your advantage. Follow the emotion. Become a student of people. Cultivate fascination.

Journal Entry: Reality Distortion Field		
	Blue Ocean	Perfect the Product
What is it?	Blue ocean is W. Chan Kim's term for value innovation—being in a space where what you have is new, and there are no rules except the ones you make.	Perfecting the product is going through multiple iterations and user testing (once you've found the right distribution). I like to do this live, by letting the customer be the tester rather than testing before going to market.
Why is it important?	Because the best way to stand out from your competitors is to build your own arena to operate in, where there are no competitors (yet).	Without listening to customer feedback and constantly improving your product to fit their needs, your business will stagnate or get swallowed by the competition.
How to win:	Don't just incrementally improve on products and business models that already exist. Reinvent the system, and then dominate it, before any sharks move into your blue ocean. When they do, be prepared to pivot to stay competitive.	Your first product iteration is almost never perfect. But getting an MVP out there, as fast as possible, is essential for figuring out what to do better or differently next time. This process never stops—you should always be perfecting your product and your process.

	Win Bigger than You Fail	Specialized Knowledge	Systems over Goals
Journal Entry: Reality Distortion Field			
What is it?	Make sure that the size of your cumulative successes is greater than the size of your cumulative failures. This can be one big win or (more likely) several good-sized ones.	Specialized knowledge is the opposite of general knowledge, and is one of Napoleon Hill's 13 principles for achieving wealth.	Systems over goals is a way of planning and operating your business that's process-oriented, rather than objective-oriented.
Why is it important?	Because failure isn't something to be afraid of—only failing too big or too often is. What's important is what you do in those moments of failure.	Deep understanding of a niche topic is what's needed to accomplish great things—like heart surgery. It takes a team of specialists, not a single general practitioner.	As Scott Adams points out, the endless pursuit of goals is meaningless if you don't have the proper systems in place to achieve real results.
How to win:	By learning and growing from your failures, rather than letting them discourage you. Often, the greatest successes in life come from a smaller failure that happened first, which gave you new strengths and insights. Every time you fail, use it as motivation to win even bigger next time.	Make sure that not only you, but everyone on your team, is a specialist in their field. If you have excellent systems in place and get niche experts to run them, even the most complex task becomes a relatively simple, routine one.	It's okay to have goals, but focus, first and foremost, on building the right systems to reach those goals. Design every standard operating procedure in a way that produces the maximum possible value for your business (and your customer), and you'll be setting yourself up to achieve success, regardless of what your goals are.

	See Opportunity Everywhere	Suicide Margins
	Journal Entry: Reality Distortion Field	
What is it?	Seeing opportunity everywhere is the ability to look beyond fear, failure, and hardship to find new ways to win, in any environment.	Suicide margins give you enough profit from each sale (at least 10x costs) to make mistakes and have it not matter.
Why is it important?	Because having the agility and innovation to turn problems into solutions, and challenges into opportunities, is what being an entrepreneur is all about. If you can't see the opportunity, you better believe someone else will.	Early on in business, you're bound to make some mistakes. Some of them will be expensive. With suicide margins, you have a cushion to recover. Without them, you're in danger of failing before you even get going.
How to win:	Create your own path, rather than following the one which the world presents you with. Sometimes, we feel like life is giving us no choice, even if there's always a choice. But if all you do is react to circumstances as they happen to you, you'll never be able to take control of a situation and turn it to your advantage. Even when things seem insurmountable, focus on solutions, and invent your own way of getting there.	Find a product or service that you can deliver on a mass scale with very low production costs, and a way of distributing it easily and cheaply. If you're looking into a business model that doesn't have 10x profit margins, look for one that does. Or keep some pretty large reserves handy to cover any emergency expenses.

	Sell the Sizzle, Not the Steak	Building Partnerships
Journal Entry: Reality Distortion Field		
What is it?	Sizzle over Steak means you should focus on building the buzz and excitement around your product, more than on perfecting the product itself.	Building partnerships is finding people who can benefit you on your journey and establishing lasting relationships with them.
Why is it important?	Because the feelings and ideas that are associated with a product are what attract customers to you for the first time. It doesn't matter how good your steak tastes—if they don't smell it cooking when they walk down the street, they'll never even know it exists.	Anyone can tell you that a good network is at the heart of all success—in life and in business. The more partnerships you have, the more opportunities there are to make more money (and more partnerships, and so on and so forth).
How to win:	By generating a huge amount of word-of-mouth or viral interest in your product. How? By playing to people's senses, desires, and existing associations. Link your product to something they know and love, and then design all aspects of your marketing and packaging to reinforce that association (and grab their attention). Worry about what's inside the package last.	Having a great network isn't just about being friendly or outgoing, it's about being able to intuit what's important to the person on the other side of the table and deliver on providing them value. Show your worth, and you'll earn a loyal partner that can consistently bring you business opportunities for years to come.

Journal Entry: Reality Distortion Field		
	Pre-suasion	The Flow
What is it?	Pre-suasion is essentially Cialdini's version of the Sizzle—a way of grabbing your customer's attention and having them sold before they even come to you.	The flow is the state you enter when you're achieving your highest productivity and success, and because of that you keep attracting even more opportunities for success.
Why is it important?	Because effectively pre-suading customers to buy your product means they will seek *you* out, rather than you having to go to them.	You have to be able to recognize when you're in the flow (or not), so you can take full advantage of the opportunities gravitating toward you.
How to win:	Get people to want to buy your product before they've ever laid eyes on it. You do this by architecting their interest prior to them seeing the sales proposition. Do it by creating a buzz—like using social proof or media attention to spark interest amongst new customers. Once they've heard about you from their friends, FOMO kicks in and they rush to buy (all without ever seeing an ad).	If you're not in the flow, focus on how you can get there. Make it a priority because it is in that state that success will find you. Find the source of what last put you in a flow state and try to duplicate that.The book *Flow* by Csikszentmihalyi is a great place to find ideas.

Journal Entry: Reality Distortion Field		
	Don't Let Fear Conquer You	No Deal > Bad Deal
What is it?	Conquering fear is having the courage to face terrifying odds, or seemingly crippling self doubt, and find a way to win in any environment.	"No deal is better than a bad deal" is one of Chris Voss' key principles of a successful negotiation.
Why is it important?	Fear stops you from being able to act in your own best interest and gives the upper hand to your opponent.	Negotiation is crucial for almost all kinds of success. If you're not a good negotiator (e.g. you give in to what the other party wants, to your own disadvantage), you're not going get very far in pursuing your own goals.
How to win:	Say nothing and stand your ground. By keeping control of your fear you maintain a strong position. Portraying confidence and certainty disarms your opponent. If you are having trouble not showing your fear, fake it till you make it.	Know what you want before going into the talk, how you plan on getting it, and where your limit is. Never be pressured into doing what the other party wants. It's okay to walk away, rather than accept a deal you're not happy with. Take the time to revisit it later, and you can always reopen negotiations at a later date. Then you'll be even better prepared, and ready to secure even better terms.

Journal Entry: Reality Distortion Field		
	Explore Your Options	Waiting
What is it?	We know the more choices we have the better decisions we can make. Exploring your options is always assessing every opportunity from all angles, rather than dismissing the seemingly-uninteresting ones offhand.	Waiting is what gives you the time to explore your options and decide on the best course of action.
Why is it important?	Wealth is a result partly of access to options. If you reject opportunities without taking the time to fully consider the possibilities they present, you could be missing out on new paths to success (or deals, or revenues).	Just like "no deal is better than a bad deal," sometimes "a deal later is better than a deal now." So it's important to wait for the right opportunities, rather than blindly seize whichever ones present themselves to you.
How to win:	By having as many options as possible to choose from. By always questioning everything, including your own assumptions about people and situations. Ask yourself: How could this be useful to me? What benefits would this bring? What are the risks? If you're unsure, find out. Don't let your ignorance stop you from spotting a potential opportunity. Seek counsel.	Knowing when to act and when to wait is the key. You need to act and not overthink, especially when it comes to starting your business. The ability to take decisive action is the mark of a successful leader, but so too is knowing when to sit and wait. By judging the playing field, and not jumping to hasty decisions, you can set yourself up for a win in the long-term.

Journal Entry: Reality Distortion Field		
	Currency is Energy	Trust & Loyalty
What is it?	The idea that money is just a form of energy is one of Stuart Wilde's core teachings.	Trust and loyalty are the foundations of every successful team.
Why is it important?	Because seeing money as a vehicle, rather than as an end in and of itself, is part of being in the flow and attracting increasingly better opportunities to you. You have to detach from the monetary value of currency, and instead see it as a means to achieving greater and greater success.	You have to be able to share your "secret sauce" with your team, without fear of them selling it to the competition. But, more importantly, you have to trust the people around you to consistently deliver amazing work if you want to be sure your business will run smoothly. Team building is one of the tasks that should never be delegated or abdicated by a leader according to my friend Marx.
How to win:	In Stuart's words, "Create your life, your energy, your excellence, and the world will beat a way to you." Don't chase having money—chase having the energy that having money brings. That energy will magnetically attract money (and people) to you, anyways.	Cultivate trust first by hiring experts who you can rely on to do their jobs well, and then by having full transparency (and a system of checks and balances) within your organization to keep everyone honest. Cultivate loyalty by being generous (but not too generous), fair, and giving people autonomy. Remember as a boss it is your sole responsibility to build the team and inspire them to win for you.

Journal Entry: Reality Distortion Field		
	Self-Belief	Destroying Self-Doubt
What is it?	Knowing and believing in who you are and what your mission is, regardless of what others may think or say of you.	Ignoring others' opinions is owning your weirdness and staying true to yourself and your path. It is the foundation of any decent Reality Distortion Field.
Why is it important?	Because facing problems head-on and with absolute belief and courage is what gives you the grit and experience to continuously succeed, in any environment, even if that belief may seem unwarranted to someone on the outside. When the going gets tough is when real growth happens.	Especially when you're gaining success and gathering enemies, people are going to try to tear you down. But ignoring those opinions is crucial to staying on track for your own success.
How to win:	By standing your ground. Every successful person in the world has, at least once, been faced with a seemingly insurmountable problem. Or been scared or uncertain about their own path. But they only got to where they are now by conquering those obstacles, not running from them. This becomes much easier when you have what Richard Koch calls an "Unreasonable Self-Belief".	Stay in your own reality distortion field. Stay strong in your beliefs. Be like the palm tree whose deep roots allow it to shake with the wind but not fall. Remember the line between business and personal. Your competitors (and other jealous people) may not like your company coming in and stealing their profits, but you shouldn't take that personally. Never let others' opinions make you second-guess yourself. Create your own reality distortion field and make it so.

Journal Entry: Reality Distortion Field		
	Get Some Enemies	Control the Narrative
What is it?	Getting enemies isn't a bad thing—it's a sign that you must be doing something right; not just because you're pissing someone off but because you have struck enough of an emotional cord to elicit a feeling. This is true influence at work.	Like in the martial arts. Use your enemies momentum to win the battle. Controlling the narrative is using the media's (or the public's, or even your competitors') voice to your own advantage. It's inducting them into your reality distortion field.
Why is it important?	Generally, the more enemies you have, the more successful you are. And the louder they complain about you, the more disruptive your business likely is to your industry.	Because, you don't want to let a perfectly good enemy go to waste. You can use their momentum to propel you to a win.
How to win:	Make it your goal to misbehave regardless of what people think of you. This is what it means to be a true disrupter. No, seriously. "Well-behaved (people) rarely make history." So go out there and step on some toes, in the same way that Airbnb stepped on the hotels' toes, and now they'd all love to stab them in the back. Find a way to disrupt and do something new that people did not expect. When enemies show up and have a strong reaction to it, that's a pretty good sign that you know you're on to a winner.	First, ask yourself how any seemingly confrontational situation can be used to your advantage. Seek the advice of those who know more than you. Mentors often tell you what you *need* to hear, rather than what you *want* to hear. Don't let your need to be right get in the way of seeing their advice for what it is: an intelligent perspective from a trusted source that should be mined for all possible insight. Ideally, find many mentors. The more perspectives, the better.

	Humans are Flawed	Keeping Control & Perspective
What is it?	That all people are flawed is just a fact of life, and one we all need to accept, not just in the pursuit of success.	Sometimes things seem out of your control. That is when you need a new perspective, and to gain control by either taking or not taking some action.
Why is it important?	When it comes to mentors, this helps you sort and choose the information they give you. With other people, it helps you manage your expectations of what they can do for you.	Because our minds seek certainty and we operate best when we have that feeling of certainty. Few people can operate optimally with uncertainty. The good news is you can reach this optimal state simply by changing your perspective.
How to win:	By managing your expectations to avoid disappointment, and being able to separate the valuable from the invaluable when it comes to accepting advice. If you know an imperfect person, they can still give you golden insights into certain things, so don't discredit someone just because they don't fit your idea of perfection.	When things seem out of control, seek perspective. This may be talking to one or more people who can show you an angle you don't see yourself. Then take an action, or make a decision to take no action. This will give you control (or at least the feeling of it) so you can be back in the flow.

Journal Entry: Reality Distortion Field

Journal Entry: Reality Distortion Field		
	Control vs. Perspective (Part II)	Pick Your Battles
What is it?	In every situation, you either have to be in control, or change your perception of the situation.	Picking your battles is being a clever general.
Why is it important?	Because you can't always be in control of every outcome, but you can control how you view the situation.	You need to decide when to fight and when to back down if you want to reach your goals with as little resistance as possible. Action and non-action can be equally valuable when undertaking intelligently.
How to win:	By always looking for opportunities to turn a negative into a positive, and considering perspectives other than your own. What you perceive as your greatest failure may actually be a huge success in the eyes of some, so just by changing your perspective, you can often find a way to regain control of a problem that once seemed like something you were powerless to solve. You gain perspective by having the conversation that leads you to it.	Conserve your energy for the fights that really count, and be okay with walking away from the ones that don't. Sacrificing your pride is better than risking too much on a battle that isn't worth the effort. At the same time, avoid making unnecessary and powerful enemies if you can avoid it (although you still want to have some). A war can only be fought successfully on so many fronts at once.

Made in United States
Troutdale, OR
02/27/2024

18008288R00195